"A" FORCE

"A" FORCE

THE ORIGINS OF BRITISH DECEPTION DURING THE SECOND WORLD WAR

WHITNEY T. BENDECK

NAVAL INSTITUTE PRESS
Annapolis, Maryland

Naval Institute Press
291 Wood Road
Annapolis, MD 21402

Library of Congress Cataloging-in-Publication Data
Bendeck, Whitney T.
  "A" force : the origins of British deception during the Second World War /
Whitney T. Bendeck.
     pages cm
  Includes bibliographical references and index.
  ISBN 978-1-61251-233-4 (hardcover : alk. paper) — ISBN 978-1-61251-234-1
(ebook) 1. World War, 1939–1945—Deception—Great Britain. 2. World War,
1939–1945—Secret service—Great Britain. 3. Clarke, Dudley, 1899–1974. 4. World
War, 1939–1945—Egypt. 5. World War, 1939–1945—Middle East. 6. World War,
1939–1945—Africa, Eastern. 7. Intelligence officers—Great Britain—Biography. 8.
Deception (Military science)—History—20th century. I. Title. II. Title: Origins of
British deception during the Second World War.
  U167.5.D37B44 2013
  940.54'8641—dc23
                                                        2013021114

Maps created by Charles Grear.

21 20 19 18 17 16 15 14 13   9 8 7 6 5 4 3 2 1
First printing

CONTENTS

MAPS

TERMS AND ABBREVIATIONS

AA	antiaircraft
Abwehr	German military intelligence organization
"A" Force	British deception organization in the Middle East under the leadership of Dudley Clarke
ATk	antitank
B1A	double-cross subsection of MI5
AEF	Allied Expeditionary Force
BEF	British Expeditionary Force
BGS	Brigadier General Staff
CBME	Combined Bureau Middle East
CIGS	chief of the Imperial General Staff
DAF	Desert Air Force
Deuxième Bureau	French intelligence organization
DSO	defense security officer
Enigma	German cipher machine
FUSAG	First U.S. Army Group (notional)
GAF	German Air Force
GC&CS	Government Code and Cipher School
G(CAM)	camouflage organization attached to GHQ in the Middle East
GHQ	general headquarters
GSI(d)	General Staff Intelligence (deception)
GSI(N)	escape and evasion division of "A" Force (MI9)

GSOI	general staff officer (grade 1)
HQ	headquarters
I	intelligence
ISSB	Inter-Services Security Board
JIC	Joint Intelligence Committee
JPS	Joint Planning Staff
LCS	London Controlling Section
L of C	lines of communication
Luftwaffe	German Air Force (GAF)
MEIC	Middle East Intelligence Centre
MI5	British Security Service
MI6	Secret Intelligence Service (foreign), also known as SIS
MI9	Escape and Evasion
MT	motor transport
Ops	operations
Ops B	deception organization at SHAEF
PAIC	Persia and Iraq command
POW	prisoner of war
PWE	Political Warfare Executive
RAF	Royal Air Force
RTR	Royal Tank Regiment
SAS	Special Air Service
SHAEF	Supreme Headquarters Allied Expeditionary Force
sigint	signals intelligence
SIM	Servizio de Informazione Militare (Italian military intelligence)
SIME	Security Intelligence Middle East
SOE	Special Operations Executive
SS	Schutzstaffel
Ultra	code name for signals intelligence
USAAF	U.S. Army Air Force
W/T	wireless telegraphy
XX	Twenty Committee

Introduction

Warfare is the art (tao) of deceit. Therefore, when able, seem to be unable; when ready, seem unready; when nearby, seem far away; and when far away, seem near. If the enemy seeks some advantage, entice him with it.

—Sun-Tzu, *The Art of Warfare*

In battle, the desire to deceive and achieve surprise is ever present. The records of "A" Force, Britain's chief deception organization of the Second World War, state, "To gain surprise over the enemy is an aim that every Commander, down to the smallest unit, should try to achieve. To contrive to deceive the enemy as to the intention of the Commander will invariably be necessary to gain surprise."[1] The ability to deceive requires great skill, cunning, and resources. During the Second World War, the British mastered the art of deception. They practiced deception on a scale never before seen in history and, largely owing to the changing nature of warfare, not replicated since.

Examples of deception abound from ancient times until the present. The Greeks deceived their Trojan foes with the infamous Trojan horse in the twelfth century BC; Sun-Tzu, a Chinese military expert who lived from 544 to 496 BC and wrote the classic military treatise *The Art of Warfare*, endorsed deception as a fundamental aspect of war.[2] Clearly the concept of deception is not new, but what the British did with deception in the Second World War was most certainly novel.

Credit for Britain's deceptive exploits in the Second World War falls to two men: General Archibald P. Wavell and Dudley Wrangel Clarke. Wavell, acting as the commander in chief of the Middle East theater, recognized the need for deception in the first months of the war and was the first British commander to skillfully and successfully execute deception on the battlefield in that war. After his first triumphant attempt at deceiving the enemy, Wavell concluded that deception had the potential to make a tremendous contribution to Britain's war effort and could be employed on a much grander scale. Thus, he needed an organization solely responsible for the conduct of deceptive activities, commanded by an officer of exceptional ability and creativity. The officer he chose was Dudley Clarke, a man whom he had worked with in Palestine before the war and whom he judged to be suitably unconventional in his approach to warfare.

Clarke arrived in Egypt in December 1940; by the end of March 1941 he had established the "A" Force organization, which was dedicated almost exclusively to deception. Under Clarke's leadership, "A" Force grew into a highly sophisticated and functional agency capable of deceiving the enemy on multiple levels. The deceptionists employed classic ruses, such as spreading rumors and misinformation, feigning attack or withdrawal, and using camouflage, but they also developed new tactics—sonic deception, wireless and radio deception, and the formation of a completely notional order of battle, for example. Clarke and his team of experts perfected their techniques, creating the blueprint for all future deceptions, just in time for the pivotal Battle of El Alamein. The most well-known deception of the war, Operation Bodyguard (the cover plan for Operation Overlord), was in fact founded on the model provided by Clarke, based on his many years of experience in the deserts of Africa.

Numerous aspects of British deception in the Second World War separate it from earlier deceptive operations. First and foremost was the scale on which it was practiced. British efforts in the 1940s doubtless represented the most elaborate use of deception in warfare to that point. The British recognized early on in the war the benefits of using deception, namely, its potential to help achieve victories and minimize loss of life. Because deception was seen as an asset, the British eventually created multiple organizations in London, the Middle East, and India for the singular purpose of facilitating the implementation of deception. Moreover, the use of deception was not confined to the military alone but was also practiced by Britain's industrial sector, film industry, civilian and diplomatic channels, intelligence networks, and administrative sectors. As deception proved its worth on the battlefield, "A" Force was accorded the same degree of respect as any other military organization, and its tactics were accepted by most as an essential part of military planning. The deception organizations did not work alone but operated in close conjunction with the military throughout the war in an unceasing effort to mislead the enemy. At no other time in history has deception been so highly systematized in the military, government, and civilian sectors alike.

British deception in the Second World War further differed from previous deceptive efforts in its use of modern technology, including simulated wireless traffic, bogus radio messages, sonic cars, and the employment of dummy guns, vehicles, tanks, planes, and landing craft. By the Second World War, the means of deception had become highly developed and increasingly scientific, largely owing to extensive advances in technology. The "A" Force tactical deception file states that the "application of modern means, such as action in the air, wireless telegraphy and mechanical movement, provides much scope for novelty, which is often the essence of successful surprise."[3]

At the same time, modern advancements in the weaponry and machinery of war made deception all the more necessary and difficult. For example, by the Second World War, aerial reconnaissance had become more sophisticated and was conducted continually by both the Allied and Axis air forces. Thus, armies could not hide their presence from the enemy as easily as they had before.

As a result of the innovations in aerial technology, camouflage activities became a staple of most deception plans. Tremendous demands were placed on the creative imaginations of the camouflage artists as they learned how to create or conceal the signs of military activity from the land and to hide armies from the enemy's eyes. In other words, camouflage artists had the daunting task of drawing the enemy's attention to what they wished him to see and of hiding, or disguising, what they did not want him to see.

Perhaps the most significant advancement of the period was wireless technology. Without doubt one of the greatest contributions to the war effort was the ability to decode the enemy's secret wireless transmissions. One cannot begin to overestimate the value of the decryptions to the deception planners. Because British cryptographers at Bletchley Park were able to crack the German codes, the British gained inside knowledge of what Hitler and his high command were thinking and planning. As a result, the deception planners could formulate plans based directly on the Germans' preexisting notions and assumptions, which made their deceptions considerably more plausible to the enemy.[4] Moreover, the decryptions enabled the British to monitor the enemy's reaction to information he received from British-controlled channels and to determine the enemy's assessments of double agents. The ability to read the enemy's transmissions allowed the deceptionists to take huge risks that they otherwise may not have taken. Knowing that the enemy was just as eager to read British wireless traffic, the deception planners filled the lines with misleading information.

The great effort undertaken by the British to control the enemy's intelligence channels underscores the vital connection between deception and intelligence. As the war progressed and its scope broadened, the British deceptionists became increasingly dependent on intelligence to achieve success in deception. As John Robert Ferris notes, it was not until the British established sound control over their communications and intelligence that they finally began to achieve notable success against Erwin Rommel in North Africa.[5] This observation applies to both the military and deception efforts equally.[6]

Whereas the idea of deception readily captures the imagination, the practice of deception was complicated and much less glamorous than one might expect. In fact, often the work was tedious and time consuming, but there was no alternative. In one instance, Clarke created an expansive false order of battle in a deception code-named Cascade. On top of initially convincing the enemy that the notional units were genuine, Clarke and his officers at "A" Force had to maintain the existence of the phantom units through painstaking administrative measures backed by an extensive trail of paperwork and double-agent reports for the remainder of the war. If they had not done so, they would have run the risk of the enemy discovering the ruse.

Deception could not be sloppy or attempted halfheartedly. Attention to detail was essential at all times. If the deceptionists let their guard down, even momentarily, the entire effort could be exposed. Deception was, therefore, an incredibly delicate endeavor. It was also an art, and as artists, the deceptionists had to achieve the highest degree of realism possible. If they fed the enemy too much information too quickly, he would naturally suspect a trick. The key was to let the enemy piece the deception story together himself. Clarke explains,

"The complete picture must never be presented through any one source: the enemy must be left to build up a jig-saw puzzle himself: the pieces, consisting of rumours, leakages and visual evidence, must be supplied to him through varying sources, all in their turn supplied by a central controlling authority. . . . All lies, however big, must themselves form pieces in one grand jig-saw puzzle."[7] Charles Cruickshank similarly writes, "The perfect deception plan is like a jig-saw puzzle. Pieces of information are allowed to reach the enemy in such a way as to convince him that he has discovered them by accident. If he puts them together himself he is far more likely to believe that the intended picture is a true one."[8] Thus, there was a fine line between deceiving the enemy and arousing his suspicions. Fortunately for the British, Clarke had a natural talent for knowing the limitations of his methods.

The means of deceiving the enemy were countless. Some forms of deception, such as the clever use of camouflage, the employment of dummy vehicles, and the well-known use of double agents, have captured the public imagination more so than others; yet these familiar methods were only a few of the techniques used on a regular basis. The deceptionists spread rumors, orchestrated leakages, fed false information to the press, arranged for diplomatic indiscretions, employed sonic deception, simulated radio traffic, sent bogus wireless messages over compromised signals, planted fake documents, spread propaganda, organized the distribution of misleading maps or currency, cultivated relationships with enemy agents in neutral countries, carefully calculated activities that would naturally draw the enemy's attention to the deception story, and as mentioned previously, created phantom formations.

In addition to devising and implementing deceptive measures, Clarke secured the military's cooperation in propagating the deceptions. Accordingly, the Royal Air Force (RAF) flew reconnaissance missions or conducted bombing raids over cover targets. The Royal Navy assisted in a similar manner. The army, most closely involved with "A" Force's efforts, moved its forces to cover locations, conducted misleading exercises, built roads, constructed dumps, granted or suspended leave, and generally did whatever it took to support the deception plan.

Clarke nurtured many forms of deception to maturity between 1941 and 1943 in the deserts of Africa. Because the military situation in the Middle East was so precarious for the British for the first two years of the war, the type of deception they first practiced was, by necessity, defensive. The aim of defensive deception, according to the "A" Force records, was to prevent or delay an enemy attack on a British weak spot. The key to preventing or delaying an attack was to demonstrate greater strength than was truly available. Clarke masterfully accomplished this through the creation of bogus orders of battle, which led the Germans to overestimate the size of British forces by 30 percent or more.[9]

By the fall of 1942, as the British military was preparing for the Battle of El Alamein, the Allies' situation had improved enough to allow the deceptionists to employ offensive deception. The goal of offensive deception was to "create a threat to a weak point in the enemy's dispositions in order to force him to maintain or divert his reserves in the wrong direction."[10] Offensive deception also aimed to mislead the enemy as to the exact timing of an attack and typically involved extensive visual support. Oddly enough, by the time of the D day cover activities, German airpower had been crippled to the point that visual deception was of little use. Operation Bodyguard was instead conducted largely through intelligence, specifically through double-agent reports.

Genuine offensive operations should always be accompanied by a plausible cover plan that causes the enemy to make false assumptions regarding visible troop activity. For the Battle of El Alamein, for example, the deceptionists did everything in their power to make the Germans believe that the attack was aimed at their southern flank. Therefore, genuine preparations in the north were carefully concealed, while those in the south were made visible.

Offensive and defensive deception can be strategic or tactical in nature. Strategic deception targeted the enemy high command and was typically carried out through intelligence measures. Tactical deception was designed to mislead the enemy leadership in the field and was thus executed mostly through physical means of deception. Although strategic and tactical deception had different objectives and methods of implementation, the line between the two was often ambiguous.[11] It was therefore important that control of strategic and tactical deception remained under a single unit of command. In the Middle East theater of operations, that single authority was Clarke.

British deception in the Second World War was possible only because it was approved at the highest level. Had the wartime leadership rejected deception as frivolous, unnecessary, or too costly, the requests to create deceptive bodies, increase personnel, and allocate resources to execute the deception plans would have been denied, and deception would have never developed into the weapon it became.

Deception prospered specifically because Prime Minister Winston Churchill was a major advocate of the strategy. He had experienced firsthand the carnage of the First World War. He was familiar with the devastation that resulted from launching frontal assaults on defended positions, such as at Gallipoli in 1915, when he was the First Lord of the Admiralty. The horrific trench battles on the western front provided further evidence of the folly of unprotected direct attacks. The prime minister was therefore committed to using deception to prevent the unnecessary bloodshed that he had witnessed in the previous war. Anthony Cave Brown confirms that deception "was a theory born of Churchill's own experience in another war with a military operation that had ended in disaster—Gallipoli."[12] Martin Young and Robbie Stamp further explain, "The determination to use clever deception methods arose out of Britain's vulnerability in the early part of the war and was strengthened by memories of the carnage of the First World War where military strategy dug itself into a muddy impasse in the trenches. The men who experienced the heartless lack of imagination that caused such destruction—and Winston Churchill was among them—resolved that there must be better ways of organising military strategy."[13]

Churchill took a personal interest in his country's deceptive operations, and he often met with the deception planners to review and discuss their plans.[14] Moreover, he frequently expounded upon the benefits of using deceptive techniques in his speeches and personal conversations. On November 11, 1942, for instance, while speaking in the House of Commons, the prime minister declared, "It is perfectly justifiable to deceive the enemy."[15] Then, in December 1943, while meeting with the Soviet leader, Josef Stalin, to discuss Operation Overlord, Churchill said, "In wartime, truth is so precious that she should always be attended by a bodyguard of lies."[16]

The history of wartime deception has generated tremendous popular interest. Because Britain practiced deception on an unprecedented scale in the Second World War, it is understandable that the vast majority of deception studies focus on British deception in particular. Scholarship on this topic, however, has developed sporadically since the war's end, largely because the official documentation remained sealed. The British government closely guarded its wartime secrets under the Official Secrets Act.

Historians' pursuit of Britain's deceptive past has at times been a frustrating enterprise. Scholars knew that Britain was heavily involved in deception during the war but did not have access to the official records necessary to build an argument. When researching any topic, historians consult the records of the key figures of the event in question. However, the memoirs of Churchill and Bernard Law Montgomery, for example, reveal excruciatingly little. Montgomery briefly mentions the use of deception but provides few details. Churchill does not even mention the topic, even though he was one of its greatest advocates.

In the case of the chief deceptionists themselves, such as Wavell, Clarke, and Charles Richardson, the man who devised and implemented Bertram—the tactical deception plan used in preparation for the Battle of El Alamein—the historical pursuit becomes even more discouraging. Although Clarke's personal papers are now available at the Imperial War Museum, a review of his wartime correspondence and diaries fails to shed light on his deceptive activities. He, of course, recognized the absolute importance of security and, thus, did not write on the topic. Furthermore, although many of the deceptionists did publish books and articles after the war, their works explored topics other than deception.

This does not mean that the deceptionists did not write memoirs, however. Immediately after the war, Clarke wrote a five-volume history of "A" Force that is now open for public use at the National Archives in Kew. When he tried in 1953 to write and publish the history of his eighth wartime assignment—when he was head of "A" Force—permission was denied. Like Clarke, J. C. Masterman, the head of London's Twenty Committee (XX), who was responsible for all double-cross activity in Great Britain, recorded the activities of the double-agent organization immediately after the war's end. His work was not published until 1972—in the United States and without the approval of the British government. Until that time, the use of double agents, or "special means" deceptions, had remained a closely guarded secret. Although the stories of some more isolated deceptions, including Ewen Montagu's *The Man Who Never Was* (1953),[17] were cleared for publication in the first decade or two after the war, the real story of

Britain's wartime trickery did not truly come to the forefront until the release of Masterman's forbidden tale. After that, the flood gates were opened.

In 1974 F. W. Winterbotham exposed another of Britain's secret weapons, which incidentally had greatly facilitated the development of deception. In *The Ultra Secret*, he revealed British cryptographers' highly successful efforts to crack the German Enigma at Bletchley Park.[18] After Winterbotham's tale became available, numerous histories of Britain's wartime intelligence operations began to appear. Most notable, of course, was the official work—*British Intelligence in the Second World War*—a five-volume series published by the British government.[19] The first installment appeared in 1979.

Once Britain's clandestine enterprises were finally revealed, the practitioners of deception (in many cases the actual double agents) began to write their stories. Likewise, secondary works detailing wartime deception and intelligence coups started to appear on bookshelves. Some of the more notable secondary publications include Anthony Cave Brown's *Bodyguard of Lies* (1975) and Charles Cruickshank's *Deception in World War II* (1981).[20] Although these works did a respectable job of unveiling the extent of British deception, the authors' access to official documents was greatly limited. Of the two, Cruickshank's work has best stood the test of time. A later work also worth mention is *Trojan Horses* by Martin Young and Robbie Stamp (1989).[21]

The official history of strategic deception by Michael Howard (volume 5 in the *British Intelligence in the Second World War* series) was completed by 1980 yet not cleared for publication until a decade later.[22] Although Howard was granted full access to the government records, most were not available for use by the general public at the time of his writing, and there was much that he was not permitted to discuss.

Most of the original deception studies tended to focus on the London-based deceptions, specifically the work of the double agents and the more well-known Operation Bodyguard. Knowledge of the work of "A" Force and of its creator, Dudley Clarke, was sparse. To his credit, Cruickshank provided an early glimpse into the deception effort in the Middle East.

One of the deceptionists who worked with Clarke, David Mure, made it his mission to shed light on the deception practiced in the Middle East. Mure became an "A" Force suboperator in 1943 and thus had personal knowledge of the organization. His first work, *Practise to Deceive* (1977), is an autobiographical account of his deceptive duties beginning in 1943.[23] His second book, *Master of Deception* (1980), is in essence a biography of Dudley Clarke.[24] Mure's purpose in writing *Master of Deception* was to counter those works that emphasized the London-based deception efforts without acknowledging the origins of deception in the Middle East. More specifically, Mure set out to demonstrate that Clarke had provided the foundation for all deception in the war. Thus, Mure's focus is similar to my own, yet we approach the subject from different angles. Mure clearly respected and admired Clarke, though his narrative is colored by his personal memories and close connection to his subject. Moreover, he lacks objectivity on numerous points and includes information that has yet to be confirmed by other sources.

After *Master of Deception* was released, the public did not hear again of Clarke and "A" Force until Howard's book was finally published in 1990. Howard's study is not confined to activities in the Middle East, but he does identify it as the home of British deception in the war. Although he discusses the larger and better known "A" Force deceptions, his account of the organization is far from complete. Similarly, Howard's emphasis is on strategic deception, so discussion of tactical deception is for the most part excluded.

In 1991 all five volumes of the "A" Force Narrative War Diary became available at the National Archives in Kew. By 1997 H. O. Dovey had published two articles based directly on the information contained within the war dairies.[25] These articles provided the first detailed secondary account of "A" Force activities throughout the war. The only real flaw of the articles is that they generally retell stories from the war diaries rather than provide a broader analysis of British deception. Nevertheless, they did give a first glimpse into what the diaries contained.

In 2004 Thaddeus Holt published *The Deceivers*, the most comprehensive history of deception in the Second World War to date.[26] Holt's work details both British and American deceptive efforts and evaluates the practice of deception in every theater of war. Even though his work extends far beyond the realm of Clarke and "A" Force, Holt certainly emphasizes Clarke's leading role in Britain's deceptive exploits. Like Mure, he recognizes Clarke as the "master of deception." Holt also underscores the importance of "A" Force in laying the foundation for all future deceptions.

Following *The Deceivers*, two additional works have been released. In 2008 Terry Crowdy's *Deceiving Hitler: Double Cross and Deception in World War II* was published.[27] Although heavily focused on Britain's double-cross activity, Crowdy's work provides a condensed, but accurate, description of Clarke and "A" Force. Also published in 2008, Nicolas Rankin's *Churchill's Wizards* gives us a thorough account of British deception in both the First and Second World Wars.[28] Rankin identifies Clarke as one of two chief practitioners of deception in the Second World War.

Since the release of the war diaries, most deception studies acknowledge the primary role of Clarke and "A" Force in developing deception in the Middle East. None of the authors of the aforementioned deception studies, however, appear to have consulted the complete "A" Force history. In the spring of 2008 I had the opportunity to visit the National Archives and review the extensive collection of more than eighty files. My work, to the best of my knowledge, is the first to be based on the expansive "A" Force collection in its entirety.

Supported by the official "A" Force documents and Clarke's personal papers, this work traces the origins of deception in Africa (the Middle East theater) and clearly demonstrates that the deception blueprint used for future campaigns, including the D day deception operation, was developed in Africa. Thus, this book, with the exception of the conclusion, is confined to the deception effort in Africa. My work differs from those already discussed in a number of ways.

The majority of the deception studies, excluding the more recent publications, have focused on the London-based deceptions. In fact, many descriptive histories of D day and Operation Bodyguard, replete with intriguing tales of trickery, have been written. Certainly, the idea of an entirely fake army, the First U.S. Army Group (FUSAG), notionally commanded by the illustrious Gen. George S. Patton, is captivating. However, the many stories of D day and the elaborate deception plans that secured its success have created the impression, presumably unintentionally, that British deception originated in London.

In reality, deception had its origins not in London at all, but in the deserts of North and East Africa. There Clarke developed his unique idea of deception, learned how to effectively mislead the enemy through painstaking trial and error, and created an elaborate deception machine. Moreover, this all occurred before London had a need for tactical deception and even before it had an organization in place to coordinate global deception at the strategic level. Thus, both strategic and tactical deception were developed by Clarke, without precedent, in Africa. Incidentally, the use of double agents arose concurrently, albeit independently, in London and the Middle East.

My first goal, then, is to build on my predecessors' works and demonstrate beyond question that the deception operations of the Second World War began in the deserts of North and East Africa, not in London. Whereas the authors of the most recent studies all acknowledge that deception began in the Middle East theater under Wavell and Clarke, I take the subject beyond a discussion of the role of the chief deceptionists in masterminding wartime deception policies; instead, I look at the origins, development, and maturation of "A" Force as an organization in detail, as well as at the activities of deceptive bodies outside of the realm of "A" Force that contributed to the growth of deception as a viable weapon of war.

A unique aspect of the "A" Force organization was that it lacked a parent organization to use as a model. Thus, "A" Force operated with little guidance from London until June 1942, when the London Controlling Section (LCS) was created to provide centralized control of strategic deception. Furthermore, LCS was formed only after repeated urgings by Wavell and Clarke, who saw the need—and urgency as the war widened—for a central coordinating body to determine worldwide deception policy and strategy.

The second aim of this work is to explain why the British resorted to deception in the first place. It might be assumed that the British had the means and opportunity, were already practiced at organized deception, or perhaps were simply inclined toward the use of roundabout methods. The truth is that the British turned to deception, not because the opportunity presented itself or because they were particularly experienced at deception, but because the situation was so desperate that they would try anything to avoid losing Egypt and their vast interests in the Middle East. In other words, the British used deception as a weapon of war because it was one of the few weapons they actually possessed.

To truly grasp why the British were so quick to embrace deception during the Second World War, one must understand both the legacy of the First World War and Britain's interwar policies regarding future warfare. The appalling bloodshed of the First World War led to a universal and absolute revulsion toward war in Britain. The population abhorred even the idea of fighting another major conflict.

When the British found themselves at war yet again, the idea of deception became appealing because it had the potential to limit wartime casualties.

Britain's experience in the First World War played a significant role in determining its interwar policies. During the interwar period, the British completely rejected the possibility of another large land war in their near future, drastically cut their defense expenditure, and let their defense industries decay. Thus, the British found themselves utterly unprepared to fight a major war when the Second World War erupted in 1939. Britain's defeat in France and subsequent evacuation from Dunkirk completely stripped the military of its already meager stores of equipment and supplies, leaving the British Isles exposed and unprotected. To confound the problems, British forces in Egypt were situated uncomfortably close to massive Italian armies in both Libya and East Africa.

When the Italians declared war on the British in June 1940, the British were dangerously outnumbered and facing possible defeat in the Mediterranean and Middle East theaters. Wavell, therefore, turned to deception out of desperation. He was willing to try anything that might give his men an advantage, even if that advantage had to be manufactured through deceit. Had Britain entered the war with a large, well-trained, powerful, and abundantly equipped military, the commanders likely would not have seen an immediate need for deception. Deception, then, was born out of absolute necessity, not opportunity, experience, or the desire to fight a creative war.

The third goal of this work is to synthesize military and deception histories into one cohesive narrative. The vast majority of military histories provide painstakingly detailed accounts of battles and leadership, but more often than not, these histories neglect to even mention the accompanying deception campaigns. Works on deception tend to discuss elaborate ruses and tricks played on the enemy but all too often fall short of providing an understanding of the military situation sufficient to place the deceptions in their proper context. The reader, therefore, is rarely informed as to exactly why the British needed to use deception. The story might be amusing, but it is also devoid of historical context and analysis of the true military significance of the deceptions.

The ultimate goal of deception is to serve the interests of the military. Its role, as Michael Handel points out, is supportive, not independent. Handel describes the supportive role of deception as follows: "Deception can provide the military commander with excellent, almost always effective support in any operation: it facilitates the achievement of surprise in terms of the timing or direction; acts as a force multiplier by enabling the numerically weaker side to achieve superiority at the point of engagement through diversion of the enemy forces; is one of the very few ways for the attacker to compensate for the inherent superiority of the defense; and allows the achievement of more decisive results at a lower cost."[29] Thus, the intention here is to provide a more thorough understanding of British deception by interweaving military and deception studies into one cohesive unit.

That being said, this is not a traditional military history and does not attempt to provide an all-encompassing analysis of the military campaigns in the Middle East. That task has already been accomplished by many highly qualified military scholars. The official history of the Middle East and Mediterranean by Major General I. S. O. Playfair provides perhaps the most comprehensive military account of the war in those theaters.[30] Nor is this an exhaustive history of Clarke or "A" Force, although they are the main focus of this work. I have omitted numerous "A" Force deceptions that I thought were unessential to this narrative or that fell outside the region of focus. Likewise, I have included deceptions by organizations independent of "A" Force.

This study begins with a brief look at Britain in the interwar period. In chapter 1, I show how its reactionary antiwar policies and mind-set left it unprepared for the Second World War. In chapter 2, I examine the military struggles Britain faced once war became a reality and discuss Wavell's first use of deception. Chapter 3 picks up with Clarke's arrival in Cairo and the beginning of organized deception in East Africa. Chapters 4 to 6 analyze the ever-changing military situation in the region and the growing pains experienced by "A" Force as it learned how to deceive. In these chapters, I discuss "A" Force's organizational development and its maturation into a highly efficient deception organization, capable of carrying out successful tactical and strategic deception campaigns. In chapter 7, the deception blueprint is developed as Clarke and his team at "A" Force master the art of deception in preparation for the Battle of El Alamein. Finally, the conclusion goes beyond the borders of Africa and into Europe to show how the foundation laid in Africa was then applied to later deception efforts accompanying the military campaigns in Sicily, Italy, and France.

On a personal and somewhat comical note, I must admit that more than a half century later, Dudley Clarke is still deceiving. This time I found myself as the unlucky victim. I based part of my analysis of Sentinel, one of Clarke's many deception plans, on a document I found in the "A" Force file titled "Western Desert Plans for 1942." After a few days had passed, I became somewhat suspicious and went back to double-check the facts. At that point I discovered that the document I had used was a fake that Clarke had intended to plant on the Germans. Feeling duped but admittedly amused, I dutifully deleted many paragraphs and started over.

On a similar note, my husband generously agreed to travel with me to London to serve as my assistant and digital photographer while I conducted the research for this project. After weeks of reading "A" Force files describing elaborate hoaxes, the creation of dummy units, and movement of phantom armies all over the Middle East, my husband looked at me with amusement and asked, "Did World War II actually happen?" I can only imagine that Clarke would be proud of his handiwork.

All joking aside, the reality of the Second World War was anything but amusing. No one can claim that deception won the war—that credit goes to the men who fought and died. What Clarke did was create the conditions that helped facilitate victory, while minimizing British, and later Allied, casualties. In effect, his task was to create his own war—a war of the imagination, paint and canvas, fake equipment, phantom armies, scripted conversations, bogus wireless transmissions, and simulated radio chat—all cleverly conceived by the master deceiver. Albeit contrived, it was a war that the enemy believed to be real, and that was the key to its success.

When all is said and done, it must be acknowledged that Clarke used an unconventional weapon—deceit and trickery—to help the British achieve victory in the speediest manner and at the least possible cost to the troops in the field. By using his ingenuity to generate phony threats, thereby misleading the Germans as to British intentions, he managed to divert the enemy's attention away from Britain's primary objectives. His greatest achievement came when he tied down approximately 600,000 German troops in a wasted effort to defend the Balkans plus ten additional divisions in southern France at the exact time that the Allies were landing in Normandy. How the war might have played out had Clarke's bluff failed may never be known with certainty, but Clarke's contribution to the ultimate Allied victory simply cannot be denied.

–1–

The "Mighty" British Empire during the Interwar Years

In the wake of the First World War, the British Empire emerged intact and victorious. As victors, the British readily partook of the spoils of war. In fact, their empire greatly expanded under the terms stipulated during the Paris Peace Conference in 1919. They gained the Middle Eastern mandates of Iraq, Palestine, and Transjordan. In addition, they took possession of various German colonies—these either came under direct British rule or were administered by their dominions, which included Australia, Canada, South Africa, and New Zealand. These acquisitions contributed to an already vast colonial empire spanning multiple continents.

The First World War signaled a turning point for British global economic dominance and naval supremacy. The empire might have grown as a result of the war, but the British were struggling to maintain their holdings and readily recognized that they could not protect their enlarged empire if called upon to do so. Moreover, the devastation of the First World War had a profound psychological impact on the British. Although they won the war, and seemingly benefited from its spoils, it was nonetheless a Pyrrhic victory that left their nation weaker as opposed to stronger.

It can be argued that British weakness during the interwar period stemmed, in part, from the British revulsion to the devastation of the First World War. British losses during the Great War were shocking: approximately 745,000 killed, or 9 percent of the male population under forty-five, and 1.6 million injured.[1]

The numbers were especially staggering for a population unaccustomed to fighting major land wars.[2] Equally distressing was the financial toll of the war. Naval expenditure reached £160 million, and army expenditure totaled £405 million.[3] The result of this massive spending, and inevitable borrowing, was that Britain emerged from the war facing a sobering debt of £7,435 million.[4] In other words, Britain's economy, along with its status as the world's most powerful nation, was faltering.[5] Britain's economic troubles were only exacerbated by the global depression of the 1930s.

Once the war ended, Britain began to repay its war debt, but the interest on that debt alone amounted to 40 percent of its total budget.[6] Because Britain had assumed its traditional role as the banker of the alliance during the war, it had had to take out considerable loans. After the war ended, the United States was eager for the British to begin repaying their loans, yet Britain was unable to secure adequate repayment from its own debtors.[7] At the same time, exports fell, industries stagnated, and unemployment rose. Facing an economic crisis of this magnitude, the British had little choice but to eliminate unnecessary spending. Given the pervasiveness of war revulsion, the Treasury opted to cut the nation's defense expenditure. The government felt secure in cutting arms production and defense spending because it believed that Britain was unlikely to face another war for at least ten years. According to David French, the Ten-Year Rule, promulgated in 1919, not only presumed that the British armed forces would not have to fight for another ten years but also had the unintended consequence of ensuring that they would be unable to if the need arose.[8] In 1919–20 total defense expenditure totaled £766 million; by 1932 that number was reduced to £102 million.[9]

With military spending severely limited, arms production decreased, and the defense portion of the industrial sector declined.[10] The cuts to military spending affected the army the most. The army had the task of garrisoning the empire and providing small expeditionary forces for colonial wars. After the First World War, army planners had hoped to expand the size of the army, but the financial crisis and widespread aversion to the prospect of another land war (which was passionately shared by the politicians and population alike) prevented such an expansion.[11] Instead, Britain cut the army's expenditure more than that of any other branch of the armed services. As a result, according to Williamson Murray, from "1920 until early 1939 the British Army existed in an antimilitary milieu, one in which *all* the democratic parties rejected the experience of World War I."[12] David Dilks adds that the "events of the First World War, instead of being used to demonstrate how vital it was for Britain not to allow her strength on land to fall hopelessly out of line with the tasks she might have to perform, seem on the contrary to have deepened the ingrained and ruinous British distaste for an adequate army."[13] In addition, Britain's primary goal in the postwar period was the protection and preservation of its empire, and that responsibility fell predominantly to the navy, not the army—which was viewed by many as nothing more than a "colonial police force."[14]

Equally unfortunate for the army was the way in which warfare was changing. The use of aircraft during the First World War signaled a change in how wars of the future were to be fought. British defense planners acknowledged that aircraft would be the new defense and strike weapon. Thus, the British officially formed the RAF in 1918 to "provide a *deterrent* against any conceivable attack on the United Kingdom, by possessing the capacity to inflict unacceptable and unavoidable punishment against the homeland of any aggressor."[15]

To prepare for war, the British knew they needed to develop an air force able to strike the enemy and defend the home islands. They would also need to build a formidable antiaircraft defense system.[16] For the army, and to a lesser degree the Royal Navy, this was a disconcerting development. The limited defense expenditure that was approved during the interwar period was allocated to the RAF in far greater proportions than to the army or navy. Whereas the army was not seen as paramount for the defense of Great Britain, the navy, although losing ground to the RAF, was still viewed by the defense planners as instrumental in the security of Britain and its empire.

The navy was, indeed, vital for the protection of the empire. Without the navy, Britain would be unable to safeguard the British Isles, its trading routes, its lines of communication (L of C), or its global interests. It was essential that the British maintain a strong naval presence in their home waters, the Mediterranean, and the Far East, given the growing strength of the Japanese navy. The British planned to build a "great fortress" at Singapore to command the "Indian Ocean and at least the western Pacific, provide an earnest of Britain's determination to protect her interests east of Suez, enable supply lines and communications to be maintained and, in the last resort, battleships to be matched against

Japan."[17] Construction began in 1923, but political differences halted the project until the 1930s. By that time, Japan presented a serious threat to British interests in the Far East.

In the face of Britain's economic weakness, defense cuts, and emphasis on expanding its air program and home defense systems, the Royal Navy could no longer maintain its position as lord of the seas. It also faced two major competitors: the United States and Japan. The navy's loss of power was solidified during the Washington Conference (1921–22). At the conference, Britain agreed that the British and American navies could maintain 525,000 tons of capital shipping, Japan could maintain 315,000 tons, and France and Italy were both allowed 175,000 tons. The significance of this treaty was that the Royal Navy no longer commanded dominance of the seas but instead settled for equality with the United States. Although the agreement did ensure that the British would avoid a naval arms race with the United States, it nevertheless demonstrated their loss of naval supremacy.[18]

Owing to the cuts in defense expenditure and the weakness of the armed services, the British Empire was increasingly vulnerable and facing a situation of "fundamental but concealed insecurity."[19] The British were counting on lasting peace and the ability of the League of Nations to settle any international disputes and thus prevent future wars. The 1930s proved this to be naive thinking.[20] In 1931 the Japanese army invaded Manchuria. By March 1932 the Japanese controlled Manchuria, renamed Manchukuo, and had established a puppet government under the last Chinese emperor, Puyi. This was the first international challenge the league faced. According to the Covenant of the League of Nations, the member nations had a responsibility to defend the integrity of Manchuria.[21] The league refused to acknowledge the new Japanese state, which prompted Japan to withdraw from the league in 1933, but that was the extent of the league's response. This first challenge to the league proved the organization's utter ineffectiveness as a force of deterrence.

For Britain, the Japanese move posed a potential threat to the security of its empire. In 1932 the Defence Requirements Committee of the Committee of Imperial Defence (CID) was given the task of determining how to strengthen Britain's imperial defense system. Its report on the state of Britain's armed forces was jarring:

The picture was steadily built up of an alarming lack of military force to defend what was still the largest conglomeration of political and economic interests and commitments in the world. There was not one adequately defended base throughout the Empire. An out-of-date navy was not strong enough to take on the Japanese fleet, let alone preserve its maritime dominance in European waters at the same time. A rundown army could not possibly play its traditional role of preserving the European equilibrium. Britain's anti-aircraft defences were virtually nonexistent. The RAF itself possessed neither the bombers to deter aggression, nor the fighters to keep the homeland safe.[22]

If the British did confront the Japanese with military force, their interests in the Mediterranean, Persian Gulf, and Indian Ocean would be left exposed. This crisis led to the demise of the Ten-Year Rule and underscored the need to resume work on the Singapore base.[23] As a direct result of the increasing Japanese threat, the Far East became Britain's highest priority and the chief focus of the Admiralty throughout the 1930s.

The threat in the Far East could not have come at a worse time for Britain, particularly because Adolf Hitler became chancellor of Germany in 1933. With Hitler's rise to power and the "illegal but poorly concealed" rearmament of Germany under way, Britain potentially faced a dual threat and readily realized that British involvement in one theater would leave the empire exposed to attack in the other.[24]

Likewise, the armed forces were so inadequate from the shortage of funding during the interwar years that there was little they could do if war erupted. The Chiefs of Staff observed, "Should war break out in Europe, far from our having the means to intervene, we should be able to do little more than hold the frontier and outposts of the Empire during the first few months of the war."[25] The escalating crisis encouraged the British to reevaluate their defense plans. They abandoned the Ten-Year Rule in 1931, and the Treasury decided to allocate additional funds to the armed services in 1935, although plans to rebuild the military remained limited.

The situation worsened in 1935, when Benito Mussolini sent his army into Ethiopia.[26] The Italian invasion posed a third threat to British security, this time to its African interests, specifically the Sudan and Egypt. Should the tensions escalate into war, the Sudanese would have a hostile neighbor to their east.[27] At the same time, the Italians began fortifying their garrison in Libya, further threatening the security of Egypt.[28] The potential threat to British interests forced Britain to maintain its naval fleet in the Mediterranean, which meant that it could not send any naval forces to the Far East if the need arose. Because the British had taken for granted that Italy was a friend, they were unprepared to deal with the new threat.

The League of Nations met to discuss its response to Italy's aggression. On October 11 fifty of the fifty-four member nations condemned Italy as an aggressor under article 16 of the covenant.[29] On November 18 sanctions were agreed upon. Again, however, the weakness of the league became apparent. Winston Churchill records that the league,

> charged with devising sanctions, kept clear of any that would provoke war. A large number of commodities, some of which were war materials, were prohibited from entering Italy. . . . But oil, without which the campaign in Abyssinia [Ethiopia] could not have been maintained, continued to enter freely, because it was understood that to stop it meant war. . . . Thus the measures pressed with so great a parade were not real sanctions to paralyse the aggressor, but merely such halfhearted sanctions as the aggressor would tolerate. . . . The League of Nations therefore proceeded to the rescue of Abyssinia on the basis that nothing be done to hamper the invading Italian armies.[30]

Although some members of the British government wanted harsher sanctions, the reality was that Britain had to tread carefully—it was militarily weak and facing three potential enemies. Although the British were confident that they could defeat the Italians, they simply could not afford to make a move given the delicate nature of the international situation.

Furthermore, as the British assessed Italy's weaknesses, they had no choice but to recognize their own.[31] The Italians were building up their naval forces in the eastern Mediterranean and reinforcing their airpower in Libya; yet, Britain's Mediterranean fleet was poorly defended, specifically lacking antiaircraft guns, and therefore unable to protect itself. In addition, if the British went to war with Italy, they would no longer be able to protect their holdings in the Far East, which were under the greatest immediate threat, given increasing Japanese aggression in the region. Admiral Sir Ernle Chatfield, the chairman of the British Chiefs of Staff Committee, advised Britain not to become involved in a war with Italy, "not because the Royal Navy doubted its ability to defeat the Italian navy, but because in the process of doing so it might incur losses which would make it all the more difficult to get an effective fleet to Singapore if a crisis developed in the Far East."[32]

It must also be remembered that the British were increasingly wary of Hitler by the mid-1930s, and they had to tread carefully with Mussolini so as to not push him into Germany's corner. Moreover, while Mussolini was emboldened by the rise of Hitler, the German chancellor most certainly took advantage of the Ethiopian crisis to assert his power in Europe. In March 1935 he reintroduced conscription and planned for an army that would equal the size of France's (roughly thirty-six divisions, or 500,000 troops).[33] In 1936, when the British were preoccupied with events in Ethiopia, Hitler sent his forces into the Rhineland.[34] France was not in a political, economic, or military position to respond and most certainly would not risk war without a guarantee of British support.[35] German forces, therefore, reoccupied the Rhineland without incident. With Hitler on the move and his intentions unclear, it proved most prudent to appease Mussolini by simply going along with the token sanctions, as opposed to demanding harsher sanctions or threatening war. In the end, the British recognized Italy's conquest of Ethiopia and suspended all sanctions in July 1936.[36]

By the mid-1930s the British had to acknowledge that their worst fears might come true—they could be facing another continental war, and potentially another world war. Given these dire circumstances, the Defence Requirements Committee recommended rearmament. In 1936 the British government accepted the recommendation, and limited rearmament began. However, the British were prevented from pursuing full rearmament because the country was facing bankruptcy. The idea of forming an expeditionary force was proposed but outright rejected owing to the public's aversion to another continental land war.[37]

Most of the funding that was approved for defense went to the RAF because it was seen as a deterrent, the army was still not considered a priority, and a massive naval buildup could potentially antagonize the Japanese.[38] Yet the navy was not completely ignored; it received renewed interest and financial allocations because the Chiefs of Staff recognized that Britain's entire trade and shipping routes, not to mention its L of C, were endangered if war came.

The year 1938 saw further escalation in European tensions, as Germany annexed Austria and Hitler set his sights on Czechoslovakia. In September 1938 British prime minister Neville Chamberlain traveled to Munich to meet with Hitler. In an effort to avoid war, the British, French, and Italians recognized Hitler's claims to the Sudetenland. The British were simply unwilling to go to war for an Eastern European country in which they had little or no interest. Chamberlain returned home confident that Britain had avoided war with Germany. In his defense, had he been dealing with any leader other than Hitler, that very well may have been the case.[39] But peace was not to be.

In March 1939 Hitler reneged on his agreement to limit his expansion to the Sudetenland and overtook the whole of Czechoslovakia.[40] This latest attack succeeded in convincing the British public that Britain would have to use force to prevent further German aggression and compelling the British government to take a firm stand against Germany, in direct opposition to appeasement. On March 30 Chamberlain issued a guarantee of British support to Poland in the event of a German invasion. Appeasement of Italy ended in April 1939, after it invaded Albania. The British still hoped to avoid war with Italy but realized that war was a real possibility. As far as Japan was concerned, by 1939 the British were less concerned about a Japanese threat, as the Japanese army had become bogged down in China. Equally important, British intelligence reports, received in the first months of 1939, suggested that the Japanese were unwilling to sign an alliance with Germany and Italy that was targeted at Great Britain or the United States because they feared that any such agreement would result in the loss of essential imported supplies.[41] That intelligence freed the British to focus exclusively on the European threat.

With the crisis mounting in 1939, Britain began preparing for war. In February the government began making plans for the formation of a continental army. By April Britain had sent guarantees to Greece, Poland, Romania, and Turkey; had committed itself to the defense of France and the Low Countries; and had alerted the Germans and Italians that any further aggression would lead to war.[42] Limited conscription began for the first time in British history during peacetime, and the armed services were finally ordered to begin full-scale rearmament.[43] The problem was that the order came too late. At the outbreak of war, Britain had a navy that was largely obsolete. The RAF had a total of 1,660 planes, but the aircraft were not up to modern standards.[44] Similarly, although British air production roughly matched Germany's by the outbreak of war, the Germans nevertheless held the advantage. Adam Tooze explains that "due to the rapid pace of expansion since 1933, the German air force still enjoyed a clear margin of superiority both in terms of the number of combat-worthy aircraft and in terms of overall war readiness."[45] Furthermore, because Britain's war industries had generally sat dormant since 1919, they were in no shape to begin war production. According to Paul M. Kennedy, "When the decision for rearmament was made in the more threatening circumstances of the 1930s, industry itself could not adequately respond. The long lean years of virtually no construction, the lack of incentive for technological innovation, the unwillingness to invest capital in fields regarded as unprofitable, and in general the steady decay of the country's industrial sinews during the depression, produced their own results."[46]

As early as April 1939, the British began to formulate their strategy for the impending war. With the Japanese threat minimized, at least temporarily, the British planned for an all-European war. Although they were not yet at war with Italy, they knew that it was only a matter of time before Mussolini formally joined forces with Hitler. The British, therefore, devised a strategy to deal with both adversaries. Because the greatest immediate threat would be to France, the first goal was to hold the line against the German onslaught aimed at France and the Low Countries. Then, with Germany contained, the British intended to focus on Italy, as they assumed they could easily defeat Italy by capturing its possessions in North and East Africa. Finally, with Italy eliminated, the British planned to turn their complete attention on Germany.[47] The British assumed that they would ultimately have the advantage if fighting a long war against Germany. Major General I. S. O. Playfair explains, "The warlike preparations of Germany and Italy were well advanced, but these countries could not hope to add appreciably to their resources in the course of a war, and would therefore be likely to stake their chances on a knock-out blow. Great Britain and France, on the other hand, though less well prepared, were in a position to increase their war potential steadily, provided they could protect their war industries and sea communications from air and submarine attack."[48]

Tooze points out that the Germans were painfully aware of Britain and France's combined "overwhelming material advantage," which would only grow if they were aided by the United States. He argues that the German leadership assumed the Western Allies would try to "draw Germany into a long war of attrition."[49] As a result, Hitler decided to act quickly while Germany still enjoyed the advantage; waiting would only allow the British and French additional time to rearm.[50]

Germany invaded Poland on September 1, 1939, and the Chamberlain government made good on its promise by declaring war on Germany on September 3. Britain, however, was ill-prepared for war. It had a strategy but lacked the military might to see it to fruition. Whereas Germany had devoted considerable effort to rearming since the ascendancy of Hitler, the British began full-scale rearmament only in the spring of 1939, and even then they had still hoped to avoid war and therefore did not dedicate themselves to rebuilding the armed forces with the determination deemed necessary in hindsight. The British also faced tremendous financial challenges and were only two years away from bankruptcy when the war erupted—which further hampered the rearmament process. Finally, although the British had made considerable strides toward preparing their home defenses, the RAF was in no position to act as a strike force or a deterrent.[51]

Because the British had pledged to support France in a war against Germany, they began preparing for a continental land war, in direct opposition to interwar policy. Although the British Expeditionary Force (BEF) existed on paper prior to 1939, it was nothing more than a skeleton force. With the outbreak of war, Britain planned to increase its continental force to thirty-two divisions. This was, however, at the expense of the territorial forces (reserves).[52] According to Churchill, the BEF began its move to France "immediately upon the outbreak of war."[53] By October the BEF had four divisions stationed in France. By March 1940 it had increased to ten divisions, five regular divisions and five territorial divisions, totaling approximately 237,000 troops.[54] Three additional territorial divisions arrived in April, but they lacked any heavy equipment. In fact, the BEF in general was poorly armed and supplied. By May Field Marshal Lord Gort commanded a total of thirteen inadequately equipped divisions.[55] One obvious weakness was that the BEF lacked armored divisions. This was because the construction of tanks was not a priority during the interwar period.[56] The British hurried to put together an armored division, the 1st Armoured Division, but it never totaled an entire division in strength.[57] Furthermore, to Gort's dismay, there was an appalling shortage of cruiser tanks, and the heavier Mark I infantry tanks were equipped only with machine guns, which proved completely ineffective against the German panzers.[58]

The British did send sixteen air squadrons to France, but they lacked dive-bombers. On May 16 the British approved the transfer of ten additional squadrons to France, but that left Great Britain with only twenty-five squadrons to protect the entire United Kingdom. Thus, Britain could not send any further aerial reinforcements.[59]

Despite the efforts of the French and British, the Germans quickly out-maneuvered and overpowered the Allied forces. The Allied forces were swiftly beaten back by the powerful German offensive until they reached the beaches of Dunkirk, where the British organized a large-scale evacuation over the English Channel (Operation Dynamo). By June 4 French and British troops numbering 338,000 had been rescued. Despite the evacuation, 100,000 British soldiers continued the fight south of the Somme River, and an additional 60,000 troops arrived in France just days after Operation Dynamo officially ended.[60]

Although the evacuation was a triumph of heroism and determination, it was hardly a victory for the British army—the army had no choice but to leave the majority of its equipment behind: 88 percent of its artillery and 93 percent of its vehicles.[61] Churchill remarked, "We had lost the whole equipment of the Army to which the first fruits of our factories had hitherto been given. Many months must elapse . . . before this loss could be repaired." He added, "Our armies at home were known to be almost unarmed except for rifles. Months must pass before our factories could make good even the munitions lost at Dunkirk."[62] For the British, who had only recently begun the process of rearming, the loss of equipment proved to be a major setback.

With France on the brink of collapse, the question of Italy still hung in the balance. Most British leaders expected Italy to join efforts with Hitler, but they still hoped to dissuade Mussolini from any such commitment. Churchill, who became prime minister on May 10, 1940, tried to persuade Mussolini to reconsider. In a letter to Mussolini dated May 16, Churchill wrote, "Is it too late to stop a river of blood from flowing between the British and Italian peoples? We can no doubt inflict grievous injuries upon one another and maul each other cruelly, and darken the Mediterranean with our strife. If you so decree, it must be so; but I declare that I have never been the enemy of Italian greatness, nor ever at heart the foe of the Italian lawgiver."[63] It was all to no avail. On June 10, 1940, Italy declared war on Great Britain.

On June 22 France surrendered to the Germans. That left the British standing alone. Not only were they alone, but they lacked even an army for home defense. The singular goal became the protection of the British Isles. Britain was vulnerable and poorly defended, with the German army, and more threatening, the Luftwaffe, positioned just across the English Channel. If ever the situation for Britain was desperate, it was at that moment.

On the one hand, the British were confident that the Royal Navy was strong enough to prevent a cross-channel German invasion. On the other hand, the British knew that they would come under heavy attack from the Luftwaffe and that they could expect extensive damage, especially to the air industry. In the meantime, the goal was to focus on rebuilding the armed forces. Britain would not be content living on the defensive—it needed to arm quickly in order to take the offensive.[64] Unfortunately for the British, their interwar policy left them terribly unprepared to face the challenges of the 1930s and thus unable to prevent the Second World War. It took a few years of war, and a tremendous amount of creativity, for the British to gain the upper hand against the Axis powers.[65]

If the British were ill-prepared to fight a conventional war, then they were equally unprepared to fight a deceptive one. For one, intelligence organizations, such as the British Security Service (MI5), saw their numbers reduced to an absolute minimum during the interwar period. Moreover, their focus was generally on the Communist threat emanating out of Soviet Russia, not on Nazi Germany.[66] As for deception, no deception organizations existed at that time; thus there were no formal attempts to organize deception or prepare for future deceptive campaigns. As Britain lacked an organizational apparatus for deception, interwar developments in deception were limited to the imagination of individuals.

In the arena of deception then, the British were truly at a disadvantage. They lacked not only an organizational structure but also experience. The First World War was not particularly known for deception. To the contrary, it stood out most specifically for its suicidal frontal charges and staggering loss of life.

It was a war in which creativity was generally lacking. However, a few notable exceptions deserve mention—especially as they had a profound impact on some prominent individuals later responsible for directing Britain's war effort in the Second World War.

The first exception came from the British evacuation from Gallipoli. The Gallipoli campaign itself was disastrous on a grand scale. As one source states, the campaign "was one of the most spectacular failures in military history. Almost everything that could go wrong in an amphibious operation did, and the campaign was one of the most remarkably mismanaged in a war that saw numerous examples of incompetent generalship."[67] In April 1915 British and French forces attempted a two-pronged landing in Gallipoli without the benefit of cover or surprise. Not surprisingly, the results were catastrophic. By December 1915 the campaign was recognized as a loss, and plans were accordingly made to withdraw Allied troops. This time, however, the British realized that they must conceal their movements or the evacuation would be just as unsuccessful as the invasion had been.

On December 10 the British began to evacuate the northern beachhead. To make it seem like business as usual, reinforcements and supplies were brought in by day. At night, under the cover of darkness, troops and matériel were removed from the peninsula. As the troop numbers thinned, those remaining worked to compensate for the loss. They moved from position to position, sniping at the enemy just as they had at full strength. As a result, the Turkish defenders of Gallipoli did not realize that Allied troops were being significantly reduced. On December 20 the last soldiers were evacuated. To keep the Turks unaware, "the last men to leave the trenches activated various simple mechanisms that maintained the incessant sniping, devices such as water-filled counterweights which slowly dripped away their contents until they activated a rifle's trigger."[68] The ruse was a success. The same strategy was used to evacuate Cape Hellas, the southernmost tip of the peninsula. By January 9, 1916, the Allies had completely withdrawn from Gallipoli, this time with minimal losses.[69]

Gallipoli provided a powerful lesson regarding the use of deception. Leaders such as Winston Churchill realized that amphibious landings should never be attempted without surprise and adequate cover.[70] This lesson was consistently applied to amphibious operations of the Second World War. Moreover, the successful evacuation demonstrated just how far a little creativity could go and how many lives could be spared.

Another notable example of deception, and one that was to have a profound impact on the conduct of deception in the Second World War, was carried out under the leadership of General Sir Edmund Allenby, the commander of British forces in Palestine. Allenby came to command Britain's forces in 1917 after Britain failed twice to take Gaza. He had the unenviable task of trying to take Gaza for a third time. But instead of using the same failed method as his predecessors—that is, a frontal assault—Allenby opted to go around Gaza and capture it from the rear. This maneuver required the British to take Turkish-held Beersheba.

To accomplish the task, Allenby needed to coax the Turks and their German advisers into believing that the British were about to launch another head-on attack, all the while hiding preparations for the offensive against Beersheba. Because it would be virtually impossible to conceal all the preparations, a crafty cover story was devised. According to the story, the British were conducting a reconnaissance mission near Beersheba to divert Turkish attention away from the preparations for the third Gaza offensive. Moreover, the cover story held that the offensive could not begin until after November 4 because General Allenby would be away from the region on leave from October 29 to November 4, 1917.[71]

The crux of the deception plan was formulated by a rather unconventional British officer named Richard Meinertzhagen. Meinertzhagen proposed that a haversack filled with crucial plans for the upcoming operation should be "lost" during the reconnaissance of Beersheba. He was to carry out the ruse himself.

On October 10 Meinertzhagen's plan went into effect. He rode out on horseback near Beersheba, supposedly on reconnaissance duty. In the process, he found himself too close to the Turkish front line, came under fire, and had to withdraw. As planned, he dropped his khaki haversack and other items in the open field as he made his escape. Nicholas Rankin, intertwining excerpts from Meinertzhagen's diary, records the contents of the haversack as follows: "A British staff officer's notebook, Army Book 155, was filled with 'all sorts of nonsense about our plans and difficulties.' The supposed agenda for a staff conference would have told the Turks and Germans the main attack was coming at Gaza, preceded by a mere feint at Beersheba, the opposite [of] the truth. There was also an ardent letter from a wife announcing the birth of a son called Richard. . . .

There were also notes on a cipher which would enable the enemy 'to decipher any camouflage messages we might send later on.'"[72] To support the deceptive scheme, Meinertzhagen was reprimanded for his carelessness, an order was issued to officers regarding the handling of sensitive documents, a patrol was sent out to "search" for the missing sack, and British artillery bombarded Gaza.[73]

The deception was a success. The Turks fortified Gaza, but not Beersheba. On October 31, 1917, the British began their offensive with a feint toward Gaza and then launched a concerted attack on Beersheba. The Turks, completely caught off guard, fell back. By the end of December, Allenby's forces had captured not only Beersheba but also Gaza and Jerusalem.[74]

Allenby was encouraged by his success, enough to attempt another daring deception. This time the objective was Damascus. The problem for Allenby was the narrowness of the front, which stretched from the Mediterranean to the point where the Jordan River meets the Dead Sea. The front was approximately sixty-five miles wide, eliminating the option of a flanking maneuver. Not to be deterred, Allenby opted to draw the enemy's attention to the eastern sector of the line, while the main thrust of the attack focused on the western point along the Mediterranean coast. To draw the enemy's attention to the east,

> engineers and camouflage experts constructed a series of dummy camps, complete with tents, artillery parks, horse lines, and ammunition dumps, suggesting the presence of several divisions. Meanwhile, at the other end of the front, equally elaborate measures were taken to conceal the fact that 35,000 infantrymen (four divisions) and nearly 12,000 cavalrymen (three divisions) with 400 guns were crammed into a space only about ten miles on a side just north of Jaffa. To make sure that the enemy saw only what he was supposed to, the Royal Air Force managed to keep the skies clear of enemy aircraft, save for a few that slipped through the eastern side of the front.[75]

This was another incredibly successful effort. The German general in charge, General Otto Liman von Sanders, was completely fooled by the ruse. As a result, the offensive, which began on September 19, 1918, not only achieved the intended breakthrough but also led to the disintegration of the Turkish forces. On October 30, 1918, an armistice was agreed upon, and the campaign ended.[76]

Although Allenby's exploits stand out for their ingenuity and success, and have since served as a model for successful deception, the reality is that deceptive campaigns were few and far between in the First World War. Such campaigns were the product of creativity on the part of individual commanders, not of any formalized attempts at organized deception. Britain's adoption of organized deception was still decades off. Nonetheless, Allenby's efforts had the profound effect of inspiring a future generation of military leadership. Most notable of these leaders was Archibald P. Wavell—Britain's future commander in chief of the Middle East theater of operations during the Second World War.

Wavell served under Allenby in Palestine during the First World War. He witnessed Allenby's ingenuity and the success of his unconventional approach to warfare.[77] Wavell's receptiveness toward using deception as a military strategy may have also stemmed from his experience on the western front. In 1915 Wavell was injured when his brigade launched a frontal assault upon the German line along the Ypres Salient. He was struck by an object—either a bullet or a piece of shrapnel—and, as a result, lost his left eye. From then on, Wavell wore a glass eye in his left socket.

In his discussion of Wavell's experience on the western front, Rankin remarks that the "stupidity of orthodox military tactics in WWI impressed on Wavell the need for new ways of waging war, including deceptive stratagems, to avoid mass slaughter."[78] It should not be surprising, then, that Wavell was so quick to embrace deception when he found himself commanding Britain's forces against insurmountable odds in 1940.

Although other men in the ranks of Britain's military, like Wavell, saw the value of using deception in warfare, they were not in any position to implement their ideas during the interwar years. Nor were such ideas readily embraced by all. To the contrary, the interwar period saw a sharp reaction against creativity by the conventional leadership. Indirect tactics, such as intelligence—and by default deception—were viewed as deviating from the "gentlemanly" culture of the British services.[79] Thus, because the creative approach was looked down upon and because the British rejected the mere idea of fighting another war, there was no opportunity for people such as Wavell, Dudley Clarke, and Noël Wild, who later played a vital role in British deception, to come together and officially formulate strategy regarding the future use of deception in warfare.

The irony was that the British did find themselves at war, were utterly unprepared to fight that war, and had little choice but to use deception simply to stay in the fight. Unfortunately, though, Britain did not have a deception organization, a manual to read or blueprint to follow, or the necessary experience in the use of military deception; thus, the men charged with implementing deception in the Second World War would have to start from scratch and learn by an arduous process of trial and error as they went along. Considering the stakes, the learning curve was steep.

—2—

Italy Joins the Game

On June 10, 1940, Italy declared war on Great Britain. From the British perspective, the declaration was not unexpected. British intelligence had received numerous reliable reports of Italian preparations and intentions to enter the war.[1] Albeit anticipated, the declaration "added one more disaster to a situation that was already catastrophic."[2] It undoubtedly had far-reaching consequences for Britain. For years the British had carefully courted Italian favor and gone to great extents to appease Benito Mussolini. In the end, however, no amount of appeasement would deter the Italian leader.

The fate of the British forces in the Mediterranean and Middle East fell to three men:[3] Admiral Andrew Cunningham, commander in chief of the navy, Mediterranean Station; General Archibald Wavell, commander in chief of the army, Middle East; and Air Chief Marshal William Mitchell, commander in chief of the air force, Middle East. The three commanders in chief would have to work closely together to devise a strategy to defeat the Italians, all while facing extreme shortages of troops and matériel. They also lacked guidance from London. At their first meeting on August 18, 1939, all three men noted that they had yet to receive clear direction regarding Britain's strategic plans for the Middle East in the event of war; likewise, their only orders were to hold the front for the first few months until they had a better handle on Italy's intentions in the region.[4]

Many scholars criticize Britain's decision to fight in the Mediterranean and Middle East. Yet, as the official British historian for the Mediterranean and

Middle East theaters points out, for nearly two years these were the only fronts on which Britain fought a land war against the Germans.[5] Nevertheless, some see the campaigns there as a sideshow, others see them as having limited strategic value, and still others view the entire venture as a classic example of the British tendency to choose the indirect approach.[6] Neither Adolf Hitler nor President Franklin D. Roosevelt saw the wisdom in fighting for control of the Mediterranean or the Middle East. George Marshall, the American chief of staff, called it a "'prestige' strategy that was 'fundamentally unsound.'"[7] But for Italy and Britain the region was of tremendous strategic value. Mussolini fancied a vast Italian empire that included control of the Mediterranean and the possession of African colonies. For Britain, the Mediterranean served as a lifeline to its empire. Although the British could navigate their ships around the Cape of Good Hope if necessary, this route added considerable time, danger, and expense to voyages. In contrast, the Mediterranean, with its direct access to the Red Sea and Indian Ocean via the Suez Canal, provided the British with the most expedient means to reach India and their interests in the Far East. Thus, it is not at all surprising that the Italians and British would first clash in the deserts of Africa and seas of the Mediterranean.

For the British, the Middle East and Mediterranean campaign served another strategic purpose: it allowed them to pursue their initial three-phase strategy as laid out in 1939. In the first phase, the British intended to hold the Germans and maintain as much control of Allied territory as possible. The second phase called for the defeat of Italy, and the third phase envisioned the final defeat of Germany.[8] Wavell realized that British control of the Mediterranean "will speedily bring Italy to heel . . . and will enable us eventually to make a counter offensive against Germany."[9] In fact, the deserts and mountains of North and East Africa provided the ideal setting for the destruction of the Italian army. Likewise, the campaign bought the British time to rebuild the strength of their armed forces and proved an excellent training ground on which to test their equipment, the quality and training of the troops, the overall capability of their leadership, and the effectiveness of their battlefield tactics and techniques. Moreover, the wisdom of fighting an offensive war in Africa was that a loss there would not have meant the end of British sovereignty.[10] A victory, however, could "sustain morale, undermine Italy, encourage American aid, overextend Axis forces, protect Middle Eastern oil fields, draw the French back into the war, keep Spain on the sidelines, and contain the Arab penchant for creative anarchy."[11] In other words, the British had more to gain from a war in the Mediterranean and Middle East than to lose—particularly if that effort proved successful.

Wavell, for his part, clearly recognized the strategic value of the Middle East. In a memo to the Brigadier General Staff (BGS), he insisted that the "last war was won in the West. . . . The next war, as I see it, will be won or lost in the Mediterranean." Although he overestimated the Middle East's overall importance in the war, he realized early on that Germany would more than likely join the Italians in Africa. He also saw that war there would allow Britain to pursue its original three-phase strategy. Wavell concluded his memo with the following: "The task of the Staff of the Middle East Command is therefore to plan, in conjunction with the other services, not merely the defence of Egypt and our other interests in the Middle East, but such measures of offence as will enable us and our Allies to dominate the Mediterranean at the earliest possible moment; and thereafter to take the counter offensive against Germany in Eastern and SE Europe."[12]

The Middle East presented one last crucial benefit for the British, albeit unintended. The African battlegrounds provided the British with the opportunity to develop the weapon that would become so vital in the overall war effort—deception. The British first attempted tactical deception in the Second World War in the deserts of Africa, and there they perfected its use as both a tactical and strategic weapon. Deception would not only aid in the victory of many African campaigns but also help to ensure the success of the Allied invasion of France in 1944. Its contribution to the war effort ought not be ignored, and its origins in Africa cannot be denied.

Anglo-Italian relations from 1935 until the outbreak of war in 1940 were tumultuous. The quest for peace was a constant "one step forward, two steps back" endeavor. Only three days after the League of Nations abandoned sanctions against Italy in 1936, the Spanish Civil War erupted. Italy soon joined the conflict under the guise of fighting communism, but the British suspected the Italians of maneuvering to gain possession of the Balearic Islands.[13] Regardless of Italy's intentions, its involvement in Spanish affairs certainly did nothing to bring stability to the Mediterranean. The situation continued to deteriorate when, in

November, Mussolini and Hitler signed the Rome-Berlin Axis, drawing the fascist countries closer together.

Undeterred, the British continued to court Mussolini's favor, but with little success. In November 1937 Italy signed the Anti-Comintern Pact with Germany. Italy withdrew from the League of Nations at the end of the year.[14]

By 1939 officials in London realized that diplomatic efforts were failing and war with Italy was only a matter of time. In April the Italians invaded Albania in violation of the Anglo-Italian Joint Declaration and thereby prompted the British to issue guarantees to Greece and Romania. According to Count Galeazzo Ciano, Mussolini's foreign minister, Britain's guarantees to Greece and Romania and its negotiations with Turkey led Mussolini to surmise that the British were trying to encircle him. In May Mussolini signed the Pact of Steel with Germany. Whereas the Italian public was openly anti-German and hostile to the possibility of war, Mussolini continued to draw closer to Hitler and direct his country on a seemingly irreversible course toward conflict.[15]

The precise timing of Mussolini's declaration of war on Britain can be seen as highly opportunistic. Mussolini had oscillated between neutrality and war since the war's initial outbreak in September 1939. At that time, however, Italy was in no position to enter combat. On August 24, 1939, Ciano logged in his diary that Mussolini had opted for neutrality because his military was weak and unprepared. Ciano further wrote, "We are in absolutely no condition to wage war. The army is in a 'pitiful' state. The military review and the maneuvers have fully revealed the sad state of unpreparedness of all our great units. Even the defense of our borders is insufficient. . . . The officers of the Italian army are not qualified for the job, and our equipment is old and obsolete."[16] The duce realized Italy could not afford to join the war in 1939, but he never stopped envisioning his grand entry onto the battlefield.

When Germany invaded the Low Countries and France in May 1940, Mussolini watched carefully. Once he saw that the German army was on the brink of defeating the French and British forces, he prepared to enter the conflict. Historian Douglas Porch explains, "When Mussolini declared war on 10 June 1940, little did he appear to anticipate the risk he was running. All he wanted was a tiny war, or better still, no war at all. He calculated that the conflict in Europe had entered its concluding phase. France was whipped and Britain was on the ropes. His goal was to secure a chair at the peace table, to reap high political gains from minimal military investment, not to superintend the nativity of a major battleground. He had no strategic plan and refused to coordinate one with Berlin."[17] In other words, Mussolini would declare war only if it was obvious that the Germans were going to win, allowing his compatriots to revel in a victory won not by Italy, but by Germany.[18]

When Italy finally declared war on June 10, the British saw their worst fears realized. Not only were they at war with both Germany and Italy, but they had simultaneously lost their French ally. Back in May 1939, the British and French had organized staff talks to devise a joint strategy in the event of war. They agreed to the three-stage strategy that called for a long war and focused on defeating Italy first. The French promised to attack the Italian position at Tripoli from French Tunisia and to come to Britain's defense if the Italians invaded Egypt. The two powers pledged to do everything they could to keep the entrances to the Mediterranean open, with the French controlling the west and the British controlling the east. They also intended to use their air forces to defend Egypt and harass Italian communications. Lastly, France and Britain agreed to bombard Italian ports and harbors in North Africa, Sicily, and Italy immediately upon the outbreak of war.[19] Because of these prewar preparations, British strategy in the Mediterranean and Middle East depended heavily on French military assistance. Little thought was given to the possibility that Britain might very well be fighting alone.

In June 1940 the British found themselves, indeed, standing alone with the unenviable task of defending the entire Mediterranean with a navy that was stretched thin and poorly defended, protecting Egypt with an army that was greatly outnumbered, and maintaining their East African possessions with an army that was ill-equipped for war, poorly trained, and greatly outnumbered. One bright spot was that Hitler had failed to negotiate for French North Africa as part of France's surrender terms because he "did not envisage that the North African coastline would become strategically significant." Similarly, Mussolini had failed to "grasp the importance of Tunis when the armistice was negotiated."[20] Libya did not have a port large enough to support a major influx of war shipping; for that the Italians would need the port at Tunis.[21] Fortunately for the British, this meant that the Italians would encounter great difficulty trying to adequately supply their forces in the Western Desert, that is, the area of the North African desert stretching from Tripoli to Alexandria.

Owing to interwar financial stringency and defense policies reflecting an aversion to war, Britain's army and air force in the Middle East were in no position to defend British interests. Both services desperately needed reinforcements of troops and matériel. The Mediterranean fleet also needed to be strengthened and suffered from an appalling shortage of antiaircraft guns to provide protection from aerial attack. The entire region lacked sufficient protection from an attack in general; in particular, there were hardly any antiaircraft and antitank guns or ammunition in the region.[22] British forces in East Africa were in an even worse state, and plans were accordingly made to reinforce them. The problem was that the need was greater than the Treasury could afford; therefore, many promises were made, but few were carried out to fruition.

Events outside of the immediate region also played a role in determining Britain's ability to resupply its beleaguered forces. For example, during the Arab Revolt of 1936–39, the British transferred ground and air forces from Egypt to Palestine, thus significantly weakening Egypt's defenses. When Germany invaded France in May 1940, the British made every effort to reinforce its continental forces in Europe. With the focus increasingly on Western Europe, it became impossible to resupply the Middle East. As early as October 1939, the government in London advised the Middle East air command not to expect reinforcements.[23]

Wavell, who became the commander in chief of the Middle East theater in the summer of 1939, fully expected the region to be a decisive theater of the war.[24] Greater efforts had been made to bring the British forces in Egypt up to strength as early as 1938, but the efforts were hindered by Britain's nonprovocation policy. Frustrated, Wavell commented that prewar preparations "were considerably hampered by the instructions of the Home Government that nothing whatever was to be done that might impair our relations with ITALY."[25] The British desperately needed to mobilize for war, but any such mobilization might antagonize Mussolini. The British found themselves facing a dreadful predicament. They knew full well that war with Italy was extremely likely, and they were aware that the Italians were busy strengthening their forces in Libya, but they themselves could not make serious preparations for "fear of precipitating a 'mad dog' act of war."[26] On April 23, 1940, the British government reaffirmed the nonprovocation policy.[27] This decision came less than two months before Italy's declaration of war. Britain's hands were completely tied in the Middle East.

When Britain declared war on Germany in September 1939, the Middle East forces consisted of the following: the 7th Armoured Division, the 4th Indian Division, a royal artillery group, and eight infantry battalions in Egypt; the 8th Division, two cavalry regiments, and four British battalions in Palestine; three British battalions and the Sudan Defence Force, consisting of twenty companies, in the Sudan; one company British battalion in Cyprus; and three companies of Camel Corps in British Somaliland. According to Wavell, not one of these formations was complete.[28] From September 1939 to June 1940, Wavell received some reinforcements from the dominions. Although Wavell considered them to be "magnificent material," they were poorly equipped and lacked adequate training.[29]

At the time of Italy's declaration of war in June, Wavell estimated that the Italians had "over 215,000 Italians troops in Libya and over 200,000 in Italian East Africa." To counter the Italians, British forces totaled 36,000 troops in Egypt, 9,000 in the Sudan, 8,500 in Kenya, 1,475 in British Somaliland, 27,500 in Palestine (most of whom were to remain in Palestine to ensure order in the wake of the Arab Revolt), 2,500 in Aden, and 800 in Cyprus. Wavell added that "little equipment had been sent to the Middle East and no single unit of formation was fully equipped. There was a dangerous lack of A.A. [antiaircraft] guns, A.Tk [antitank] guns and other artillery."[30]

As for the air force, Air Chief Marshal Arthur Longmore, who had replaced Mitchell as commander in chief in the Middle East in May 1940, had the daunting task of protecting 4.5 million square miles of land. To cover this vast area, he had only twenty-nine squadrons, totaling 205 aircraft—not one of which was a modern fighter or a long-range bomber. Even worse, most of his planes were obsolete, and all were short on equipment and spare parts. In stark contrast to the British, the Italians had 313 planes in Libya and the Dodecanese and 325 in East Africa.[31] The Italians, therefore, enjoyed numerical superiority not only on land, but in the skies as well. Alan Moorehead, a British war correspondent, soberly observed, "In every department of modern warfare, especially in such equipment as tanks and guns, we were pitifully, hopelessly, weak."[32]

Because Italy's entry into the war came on the heels of French defeat, the British could spare no reserves to send to the Middle East. Major General I. S. O. Playfair explains, "During the first eight months of the war the army's main effort had been devoted to building up the expeditionary force in France.

This was why units in the Middle East remained short of much of their equipment and why their war reserves were so low. Then came the evacuation from Dunkirk, involving the loss of practically the whole of the equipment of the British Expeditionary Force. The bulk of the current armament production had to be allotted to the forces required for the defence of the United Kingdom."[33] Furthermore, the Battle of Britain, which began in July 1940, rendered the RAF unable to send any air reinforcements to the Middle East theater.

The situation could hardly have been worse for the British. If there could be any source of encouragement, it was that the British government recognized the need to defend its strategic interests in Africa. As Churchill related, "With the disappearance of France as a combatant and with Britain set on her struggle for life at home, Mussolini might well feel that his dream of dominating the Mediterranean and rebuilding the former Roman Empire would come true. Relieved from any need to guard against the French in Tunis, he could still further reinforce the numerous army he had gathered for the invasion of Egypt. Nevertheless the War Cabinet were determined to defend Egypt against all comers with whatever resources could be spared from the decisive struggle at home."[34]

Churchill, by then prime minister, saw the theater as vital to Britain's interests and survival. He declared that the "loss of Egypt and the Middle East would be a disaster of first magnitude to Great Britain, second only to a successful invasion and final conquest [of the United Kingdom]."[35] Terry Crowdy further illuminates the strategic importance of Egypt: "The region as a whole was vital to the British for two major reasons: firstly, speedy communication with India through the Suez Canal and, secondly, oil. If Egypt was lost and the Canal Zone occupied, the British Empire would in effect be cut in half. Shipping would be forced to make the long voyage round the Cape, lengthening supply lines and making shipping more prone to attack from German U-boats and raiders. Of equal importance, if the oil reserves of the Middle East fell into German hands, the result did not bear thinking about."[36] The problem for the British was that the desire to defend Egypt and the Middle East did not mean that Britain had the military or industrial ability to do so at that time.[37]

Despite the enormous numerical disadvantage facing Wavell's forces, the commander in chief felt certain that the British troops could hold a defensive front against the Italians. He was also confident that the British were better trained, were better led, and enjoyed higher morale than the Italian troops. Because they were so outnumbered, however, the best they could do at the time was maintain a defensive posture. In the meantime, Wavell began improvising and turned to deception as a force multiplier.

If the situation was bad in Egypt, it was far worse in East Africa. British forces faced the first Italian offensives in East Africa. British troops were greatly outnumbered there, as they were in Egypt. Worse still, the meager British forces were responsible for protecting vast amounts of territory. In the Sudan, for example, the British had a total of 9,000 troops to defend a front 1,200 miles long. Similarly, in Kenya there were only 8,500 troops to defend an 850-mile front. The troops were also dangerously short on ammunition, fuel, spares, and antitank and antiaircraft weapons; they essentially lacked the basic supplies and equipment needed for war.[38] Whereas Wavell assumed the forces in Egypt were strong enough to hold up against an Italian offensive, he extended no such confidence to the Sudan and East Africa. In regard to the Sudan, Wavell commented, "It was obviously impossible with the very small forces available, to cover the long and vulnerable frontier, but I directed that small mobile forces should occupy the principal places on the frontier until attacked by superior forces. Although these small forces could obviously not resist any attack which the greatly superior Italian forces could make, I considered it desirable that they should fight a delaying action against the enemy rather than abandon the frontier posts without any fighting at all."[39] Wavell implemented the same policy in Kenya.

By July Italian forces began moving against the British frontier positions. Within the first two weeks of that month, the British lost Gallabat, Karora, Kassala, and Kurmuk on the Sudanese frontier and a couple of waterholes near Moyale in Kenya.[40] By the end of July, therefore, the Italians clearly had momentum on their side; they had won their first skirmishes against the British forces and enjoyed a tremendous numerical advantage. By August the Italians had more than 92,000 Italian troops, along with more than 250,000 colonial troops, in East Africa. To add to that, they had 24 medium tanks, 39 light tanks, 126 armored cars, and 323 planes, 286 of which were bombers. British numbers paled in comparison. The British had only 40,000 troops and approximately 100 planes in East Africa.[41] They did try to "enlarge" their forces in Italy's estimations. Playfair writes that Major General William Platt, the "Kaid," or commander in chief of the Sudan, adopted "every form of ruse to give the impression of greater strength than he really possessed."[42]

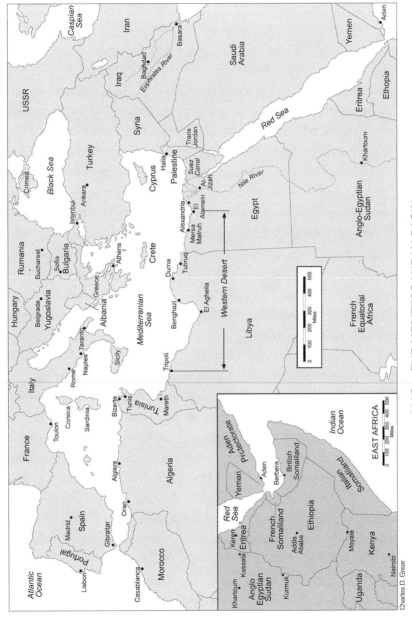

MAP 1. THE MEDITERRANEAN BASIN

Charles D. Grear

Despite all its efforts, Britain's position in East Africa only deteriorated as the war progressed. On August 3, 1940, an Italian force of 40,000 crossed over into British Somaliland, which was defended by only 3,000 troops. The Italians easily overran the British position and captured the protectorate. This was, as it turned out, the first British possession conquered in a hundred years.[43] It was also the first British possession taken during the war.

The implications of the loss were many. For the British, it was a tremendous blow to their morale and prestige. In the opening months of the war, the British were on the losing side of every campaign. Moreover, Italy now controlled an extensive stretch of the East African coastline from the Red Sea to the Gulf of Aden. The situation was a potential disaster for the Royal Navy. Because it considered the Mediterranean to be unsafe, the navy sent most supplies to North and East Africa around the Cape of Good Hope and up from there through the Red Sea to Suez. If the Italians managed to cut off that supply route, they could feasibly prevent Britain from being able to adequately resupply its forces in Egypt and East Africa. In addition to this, British sea communications could easily be cut.

On Wavell's order, Platt began planning an offensive to recapture Gallabat and take Metemma. Before the offensive, the British brought in tanks and artillery under complete secrecy. They moved their equipment by night and kept it camouflaged during the day. They also started calling the 5th Indian Division the "Five Indian Divisions" so that it would appear that they had significantly larger forces at their disposal than they in fact did.[44] The offensive, which was Britain's first real offensive of the war, began on November 6. Unfortunately for the British, secrecy failed, and the Italians expected the advance. Thus, from the outset, the British lost the element of surprise. The Italians pulled back to Metemma and organized a counteroffensive. Although the British initially captured Gallabat, the efforts quickly spiraled out of control. The tanks' tracks were broken by "glass-sharp, ice-hard volcanic trachyte rocks."[45] Anthony Mockler writes that the "Matilda tanks had been torn to shreds in a matter of minutes by a few rocks."[46] Only one tank survived the battle. In the air, the Italian air force shot down six British fighters and launched a concentrated bombing effort on the British position.

Under heavy attack, the British troops panicked and retreated. Wavell attributed Italy's success to Britain's extreme shortage of antiaircraft guns. He points out that the 10th Brigade did not have single antiaircraft gun, so once the Italians routed Britain's fighters, the troops had no way to protect themselves from aerial attack. Of the 184 troops killed, most died as a result of the bombings.[47] By the evening of November 7, the British called off the offensive and accepted defeat.[48] The offensive began as an attempt to turn the tide of the war and raise British morale; it ended in yet another humiliating defeat.

Despite their efforts, the British could do little to strengthen their position in East Africa in the early stages of the war. From the beginning, the plan was to liberate Ethiopia; yet this plan became increasingly complicated once the French fell and the British could no longer count on their support in East Africa. The original plan called for an offensive to be launched from French Somaliland and relied upon full use of the French port at Jibuti.[49] Without French support, the plan was no longer feasible. Along with the early British losses in East Africa, the plan to liberate Ethiopia became ever more difficult.

Because of their dire situation, the British resorted to more creative means to maximize their efforts—they turned to Ethiopian rebels for help. According to Lieutenant Colonel J. E. B. Barton, the Italians had had every opportunity to befriend the Ethiopians since Ethiopia's occupation in 1936, but they had instead regarded them as "people who could be cowed into subservience by brutality." Instead of subduing the Ethiopians, Barton noted, the persecutions led to a rise in rebel activity, "revived the national spirit and tended to unite the whole country against the oppressors." When the British began actively preparing for war with Italy in 1939, Platt suggested that any British offensive into Ethiopia be carried out only if Britain had the support of the local Ethiopian chieftains. In response to this suggestion, British intelligence officers compiled a list with the names of rebels they considered suitable to assist with an internal rebellion in Ethiopia.[50]

After his appointment as commander in chief, Wavell appointed Lieutenant Colonel D. A. Sandford, a man with great knowledge of Ethiopia, to a special section of the Middle East Intelligence Centre (MEIC). Sandford's job was to organize intelligence and make operational plans to support the rebellion. He decided to narrow down the list of rebels and isolate a select number who were considered "sufficiently reliable" to assist the British when war came to the region. Out of more than a hundred chiefs considered, Major R. E. Cheeseman, head of the Intelligence Bureau in Khartoum, selected eleven to be contacted. On May 28, 1940, the Survey Department secretly printed the following message in Amharic to be distributed to the chiefs upon the outbreak of the war: "Peace be unto you. ENGLAND and ITALY are now at war. We have decided to help you in every way possible to destroy the common enemy. If you are in need of rifles, ammunition, food or clothing, send as many men and animals as you can spare to the place which our messenger will tell you. We can help you with your requirements. Also it would be a good plan for you to send your personal representative to consult with us and to arrange the best means of attacking the common enemy."[51]

Like Wavell, Sandford was greatly limited in his prewar preparations. Because of the nonprovocation policy, he could not risk any action that might anger Mussolini. As a result, contact with the rebels had to wait until after war was declared. On June 11, the day after Mussolini declared war on Great Britain, the first six messengers were dispatched with letters for local chiefs.

Upon the outbreak of war, Sandford officially became the head of Mission 101. Mission 101 was a small military mission with the job of supplying the patriots, fostering rebellion against the Italians in Ethiopia, and ultimately facilitating Emperor Haile Selassie's triumphant return to Ethiopia.[52] According to Cheeseman, however, the initial goal was for the rebels to "use the arms we supplied them to harass the Italian forces and keep them confined to their garrisons and in a continual state of nerves, and prevent them from carrying out any plans they might have had for invading the Sudan during the rainy season."[53]

Although the Italians succeeded in taking multiple British frontier positions in Kenya and the Sudan during July, Barton indicated that the moral superiority and initiative lay with the British; this, he claimed, was attributable to the success of the rebel activities. He wrote that the Italians, who clearly remembered the cruelty and disdain with which they had treated the Ethiopians, now greatly feared reprisals. They also began to question the loyalty of their own colonial battalions and native bands.[54] Apparently, the plan to create insecurity and shake the Italians' nerves, as Cheeseman noted, was working.

The rebel activity, or patriot movement, was important because it represented the only offensive action in East Africa at that time. Although it underscored the desperate position Britain found itself in, it nevertheless also highlighted Britain's ability to make the most out of its scant resources. Moreover, it demonstrated the creativity and ingenuity that served the British so well in the Second World War. Although the patriots' role was limited in the first months of the war, they became crucial later, when the British went on the offensive to retake Ethiopia in 1941.

In Egypt, Wavell faced a daunting situation. With war openly declared and the nonprovocation policy no longer in effect, all three commanders in chief hoped to receive sizable reinforcements to strengthen their forces. However, because of Dunkirk and the German aerial attacks on Great Britain, the Middle East theater would have to wait. Although Wavell initially expressed confidence that the British forces could hold a defensive front against the Italians, by July 1940 he conveyed serious concern regarding his position. He noted that it "became obvious that unless reinforcements in men and material were sent to the Middle East forthwith, there was grave danger of our being unable to withstand the enemy's attacks."[55] Moreover, Wavell's original defensive plan for Egypt was based on France's agreement to put pressure on the Italian forces in Libya from West Africa. With France out of the war, Wavell faced an Italian army that was in a position to direct its entire land and air forces based in Libya against Egypt without fear of a French attack.[56]

Immediately upon the outbreak of war, Wavell planned to go on the offensive—in a limited sense. He instructed his troops to do everything they could to harass the Italians by launching raids on Italy's front lines. The commander in chief also hoped to create the illusion of greater strength on the Libyan border. Moorehead called Wavell's strategy a "game of bluff." He wrote,

> It was vitally necessary, the general saw, to convince the enemy that we were much stronger than we actually were. This was not easy in so open a place as the desert. . . . The painfully thin British forces were scattered for hundreds of miles across the desert facing the Libyan frontier. They had one all-important standing order: make one man appear to be a dozen, make one tank look like a squadron, make a raid look like an advance. And so this little Robin Hood force, being unable to withstand any sort of a determined advance by the half-dozen Italian divisions across the border, did the unpredicted, unexpected thing—it attacked.[57]

On the night of June 12, the British captured 220 Italian prisoners. On June 16 they captured an additional 160 prisoners, along with considerable equipment. Throughout June and July, the British repeated this strategy of small-scale raids on a regular basis, inflicting heavy casualties on the Italian forces. By harassing the Italians in this way, the British hoped to gain the momentum and undermine Italian morale.[58]

In July the Italians had two divisions stationed on Libya's border with Egypt. Yet during August they added another two divisions to their frontier posts. With this influx of enemy troops, the harassing raids became increasingly dangerous, and the fear of a large Italian offensive intensified. Because the meager British forces could not launch as many raids into enemy territory, they tried instead to convince the Italians that the British positions were stronger and better defended than they actually were. Wavell reported that a "skillful use was made of dummy tanks to deceive the enemy."[59] The air force made a similar attempt to inflate its numbers and make optimal use of what little it had by flying a single aircraft long distances to attack widespread targets. This, according to Playfair, led the Italians to disperse their airpower and greatly overestimate British air strength.[60]

Although the British may have led the Italians to overestimate their overall strength, the reality was that Wavell's forces were too few, overstretched, and exhausted. The vehicles were experiencing heavy wear and tear, and no replacements were available. Then, in September, the Italian offensive began. As the Italian Tenth Army moved forward in preparation for the offensive, Wavell had no choice but to order his troops to withdraw. On September 13, 1940, five divisions of the Italian army, led by Marshal Rodolfo Graziani, marched into Egypt. By the sixteenth the Italians had reached Sidi Barrani, fifty-four miles inside the Egyptian border, where they stalled. In the meantime, the British forces withdrew to Mersa Matruh, a position they had every intention of defending if the Italian advance continued.

There is no doubt that the offensive could have been worse. Wavell wrote that Graziani's "advance was slow and unenterprising. He made little attempt to use his immensely superior numbers or his mobility to outflank and overwhelm our small force."[61] For his part, Graziani, convinced that the Italians were not ready, was opposed to the offensive. His sentiments were shared by many Italian officers. Ciano recorded that never "has a military operation been launched with such opposition from the commanders."[62] Mussolini, however, wanted a major victory and pushed for the offensive to begin. After the capture of Sidi Barrani, Ciano recorded in his diary that Mussolini was elated that Italy had achieved "a success in Egypt which gives her the glory she has sought in vain for three centuries."[63] Although the Italians technically won the battle, it was far from a British defeat.

After waiting one month for the Italians to resume the campaign, Wavell decided to plan his own offensive—Operation Compass. In October Anthony Eden, the secretary of state for war, visited Wavell in Cairo. After learning of Wavell's intentions, Eden promised to send reinforcements, equipment, and supplies. When Churchill first heard of the plan, he "purred like six cats" and pledged "immediate sanction and all possible support to this splendid enterprise."[64]

Wavell intended to launch the offensive at the end of November, but it had to be pushed back into December. The delay stemmed largely from Italy's invasion of Greece in late October. Wavell reported that the War Cabinet instructed him to send support from the Middle East to Greece at that time. Britain's guarantee to Greece obligated the British to provide the Greeks with military assistance. As a result, Wavell had to part with troops, antiaircraft guns, transport vehicles, and engineers. The RAF sent a few squadrons as well. The reinforcement of Greece significantly weakened Wavell's strength, but by December Wavell was once again ready to launch Compass.[65]

Wavell planned his offensive in complete secrecy. Only approximately twelve men were aware of the plans, and hardly anything was committed to paper.[66] The troops who were to carry out the offensive were not informed of their mission until two days before it began. They had participated in multiple training exercises but were unaware that the exercises were in fact rehearsals for the attack.

Wavell's decision to go on the offensive both provided the ideal opportunity to use deception and underscored the necessity of deception. Michael Howard argues that in the environment of the Middle East, deception was "from the very outset urgent and continuous."[67] It was impossible to hide advancing forces in the desert. Inevitably, the Italians would learn of British movement. Because the Italians could easily overwhelm the British by sheer numbers alone, the British had to do everything in their power to prevent the Italians from suspecting the offensive in the first place; if the deception worked, the Italians would be caught unprepared and vulnerable. Surprise, therefore, would be Britain's greatest asset.

To cover the training exercises and administrative planning, the British spread rumors that they were strengthening their defenses in anticipation of the next Italian offensive. This was imperative, they claimed, because the British forces in Egypt would be significantly weakened after they sent an "expeditionary" force

to Greece. They hoped that the training exercises and preparations would thus
not alarm the Italians.[68] The task of spreading rumors fell on Britain's Security
Intelligence Middle East (SIME), headed by Lieutenant Colonel Raymund
Maunsell. As the former defense security officer in Cairo, Maunsell had significant experience serving in the Middle East. He was well aware that there were
many Axis sympathizers living in Cairo who would gladly pass along any information of British preparations to the Germans, so he single-handedly arranged
for false rumors to reach known Axis informants.[69]

In their effort to further mislead the Italians, the British readily embraced
deception to give them the advantage on the battlefield. Because the British army
was so short on troops and equipment, deception provided an additional weapon
with which to fight the war. As David French puts it, deception was a "force
multiplier" for the British.[70] An article titled "How and Why Italy Lost Ethiopia"
from *Il Tempo* newspaper in Rome describes the early British techniques used in
the Western Desert:

> In such a dramatic situation, not to say desperate one, the British High
> Command did not lose its usual coolness and resorted to a very risky but
> fully successful stratagem which gave them the necessary delay for reorga-
> nising their African Forces. Their propaganda was continually announc-
> ing the arrival of new reinforcements; their counter-espionage succeeded
> in passing to the Italian and German agents faked reports on strength and
> military plans; they also made small Units continually change their posi-
> tion and appear in and disappear from the most extraordinary places in
> the Desert. By all these means the British High Command succeeded in
> making their enemy believe that they had secretly piled up in EGYPT a
> large army capable, not only of resisting any attack, but also of carrying
> the war into enemy territory. That was the scarecrow which paralysed the
> Italian High Command.[71]

Howard specifically credits Wavell with the initial use of deception in the
Middle East, calling it his "brainchild." He contends that behind "an inarticulate
and ruggedly orthodox exterior, Wavell concealed one of the most fertile minds
ever possessed by a British senior officer. No one understood better than he the
role that deception and its child, surprise, should play in all military operations—

especially operations conducted by numerically inferior forces far from home."[72] Wavell himself wrote that every "commander of any grade should constantly be considering methods of misleading his opponent, of playing on his fears and of disturbing his mental balance."[73]

For Operation Compass, Wavell attempted numerous forms of deception. According to the "A" Force Narrative War Diary, deception was "effected by means of administrative measures, dummy wireless traffic, rumours and false information planted on a Japanese source in EGYPT, and did much to gain surprise for the first offensive at SIDI BARRANI in early December."[74] Wavell also used dummy tanks and artillery as decoys to attract the Italian air force's attention away from the main area of concentration.[75] The British made the dummies realistic by creating "noisy flashes of fire emanating from the length of metal piping attached to each dummy gun."[76] David Mure, who later helped carry out deception in the Middle East, added that double agents spoke for weeks before the offensive of "hundreds of tanks and massive build up of forces." These reports were confirmed by the Italian air force, which spotted the "tanks" in the desert. Mure further explained that locals used rakes to stir up the sand and create dust to support the existence of large forces.[77]

The first phase of Operation Compass, otherwise known as the Battle for Sidi Barrani, began December 9, 1940. Under the field command of General Richard O'Connor, Wavell launched one British infantry division and one armored division against seven divisions of the Italian Tenth Army.[78] Yet from the outset, Wavell enjoyed the advantage of surprise.

Before the offensive, the RAF bombarded Italian airstrips to ensure British dominance of the skies and, therefore, to prevent the Italians from observing the extent of the forward movement of O'Connor's Western Desert Force. On the morning of the attack, the British created a diversion by firing into the Italian camp at Nibeiwa from the east, leading the Italians to believe that an attack was coming from that direction. Just over two hours later, the offensive began in the northwestern section of the camp, catching the Italians by surprise. Owing to the success of the various deception techniques, the Italians were completely caught off guard. They were also surprised at the appearance of British Matilda I tanks. Italy's intelligence sources, which generally outperformed the British at this stage in the war, had failed to discover the arrival of the Matildas.[79]

By December 12 the British had largely forced the Italians out of Egypt, reclaimed Sidi Barrani, and penetrated the Libyan border. The only areas that remained under Italian control were Bardia, Siwa, and Jarabub. The British captured 38,000 prisoners, 400 guns, 50 tanks, and more than 1,000 vehicles. In contrast, the British suffered only 133 killed, 387 wounded, and 8 missing.[80]

Operation Compass was a resounding success and greatly boosted British morale. It was, after all, Britain's first major victory of the war. As one historian puts it, "For the first time in more than a year of war the British were not retreating, as they had from France, Norway, and British Somaliland, but driving forward."[81] General Erwin Rommel, soon to head the German Afrika Korps in Libya, claimed that the British succeeded because their forces were better equipped, their air force was more modern, and they had longer-range artillery and better, faster tanks. He concluded, "What was most important, its striking columns were fully mechanized."[82] Playfair observes that the victory was also a coup for British deception. He points out that Italy's intelligence community was aware of the British movements but, thanks to the deceptive efforts, misinterpreted their true purpose. Wavell's attempt to cover the troop movements and lead the Italians to an erroneous assessment of the activity worked. Playfair similarly credits the British with achieving tactical surprise. He writes that the "assault came at an unexpected moment from an unexpected direction, and was led by a type of tank whose presence was entirely unsuspected."[83]

Operation Compass represented Britain's first concerted attempt at tactical deception in the Second World War, and it was a success. Wavell realized even before this experience that deception was a valuable weapon, one that he could use to his full advantage. Given their numerical disadvantage and the acute shortage of supplies and equipment, the British could use anything that might tip the balance in their favor. Deception proved to be Britain's secret weapon, and Wavell had the keen foresight to recognize it—yet he also realized that he could not manage a war and coordinate deception himself. According to Howard, Compass "convinced Wavell that it was necessary to have a special section on his staff to initiate and to orchestrate deception measures by all the multiple means that were now available; and if possible to develop more."[84] Wavell needed someone of a like mind who could make it his sole duty to deceive Britain's enemies. For that job, he chose Lieutenant Colonel Dudley Wrangel Clarke. Wavell had worked with Clarke in Palestine during the Arab Revolt and considered him to have an "original, unorthodox outlook on soldiering." Wavell further recalled, "I can only say that I have always believed in doing everything possible in war to mystify and mislead one's opponent, and that I was right in judging that this was work for which Dudley Clarke's originality, ingenuity and somewhat impish sense of humour qualified him admirably."[85]

On November 13, 1940, Wavell sent a telegraph to the War Cabinet requesting Clarke's appointment to the Middle East: "Wish to form special section of intelligence for deception of enemy by spreading false information and other means for which there is special scope in Middle East due to conditions in Egypt and elsewhere. We are already working on these lines but possibilities are so important that I want additional G.S.O.1 [general staff officer (grade 1)] to concern himself solely with this work. Require uncommon type of officer and can think of no one better suited than Dudley Clarke. Could he be spared?"[86] Three days later the War Office wrote that Clarke was being sent. Clarke arrived in Cairo on December 18; he began work the next morning. He would come to head "A" Force, an organization that was specifically designed to carry out deception. Through trial and error, Clarke perfected the use of deception. He was truly instrumental to Britain's war effort, although few people ever knew what he did.

The British survived 1940, but 1941 would bring many new challenges. The first German forces began arriving in Libya in February, and this presented a grave danger to Egypt. Moreover, it greatly increased the burden placed on the exhausted British forces. Although the British had ended 1940 with a decisive military victory against the Italians in North Africa, the Germans were a much more formidable enemy. While the British used the Italians' lack of readiness for war, ineffective military leadership, and poor morale to their advantage, this strategy would not work against the Germans. Clarke thus had a major task on his hands. Deception would play a crucial role in British war planning in 1941, but at the same time, Clarke and his men had much to learn. Clarke's first learning experience took place during the British conquest of Italian East Africa in the first half of 1941. The experience taught Clarke and his men invaluable lessons that helped to shape the strategy and policy of deception used for the remainder of the war.

-3-

Clarke's Grand Debut:
East Africa

When Dudley Clarke accepted his assignment to coordinate deception in the Middle East theater, he took on an enormous responsibility. At its most basic level, his job was to mislead the enemy into making decisions detrimental to the enemy's war effort. That in and of itself was much easier said than done. In addition, he tackled the task of artificially strengthening the British forces, thereby compensating for Britain's extreme deficiencies in troops, equipment, and supplies. But no one was better suited for the post. Clarke was a man of great intelligence, creativity, and ingenuity who possessed a certain mischievousness that made him the ideal candidate for the job.

Clarke was born on April 27, 1899, in Johannesburg, South Africa, during the Boer War (1899–1902). After the war, the Clarke family returned to London. Clarke had three siblings but was always closest with his sister Dorothy, better known as Dollie. The Clarke children were all known for their intelligence, but Dudley Clarke stood out as unique. He was not only intelligent but uncommonly perceptive. He was keenly aware of subtleties that went unobserved by the average person. He was rather ordinary in appearance and not particularly talkative, but he was unquestionably distinctive and decisive in his thinking. Not surprisingly, he was often perceived as rather mysterious.

By the time of his appointment to the Middle East at the end of 1940, the forty-one-year-old Clarke had spent the majority of his adult life in the military and thus was not unaccustomed to conflict. At only seventeen years of age, Clarke had joined the Royal Military Academy. Because he was too young to fight with the Royal Artillery in France during the First World War, he transferred to the Royal Flying Corps so that he could actively participate in the conflict. He served as a pilot in Egypt for the remainder of the war and then returned to the Royal Artillery in 1919. During the 1920s and 1930s Clarke's military duties took him to Mesopotamia, Constantinople, Transjordan, Italy, Germany, Aden, and finally, Palestine during the Arab Revolt. There he met Archibald Wavell for the first time. Clarke clearly made a favorable and lasting impression upon Wavell. By the outbreak of the Second World War, however, Clarke had returned to London.[1]

Before joining Wavell in Cairo, Clarke carried out seven wartime assignments ranging from reconnaissance work in Africa to assisting Britain's forces in Norway. Perhaps his most well-known exploit was the creation, and naming, of the British Commandos. After the British evacuation from Dunkirk, Clarke suggested forming the Commandos as a way to gain offensive momentum. The Commandos were designed to hit the Germans hard and fast in guerrilla fashion, just like the Boers of South Africa. Clarke personally organized the missions and participated in the first Commando raid.[2]

Clarke was an enigma in the British military. Although he was an officer trained in the conventions of the day, his outlook on warfare was anything but conventional. Moreover, his thought process in general was uncommon, if not perplexing, to those who made his acquaintance. David Mure, who served as a deception officer under Clarke but knew him only by his code name, Galveston, described him as "'artful', baffling, devious. When you met him he was none of these things. He was however inscrutable. Superficially he looked rather like somebody's butler. . . . Beneath his bland rather old world exterior it was impossible to guess what he was thinking, and what he said nearly always came as a surprise. He was certainly the most unusual Intelligence officer of his time, very likely of all time. His mind worked quite differently from anyone else's and far quicker; he looked out on the world through the eyes of his opponents."[3] As Mure pointed out, Clarke had the unique ability to evaluate a situation and innately grasp how the enemy high command would perceive it. Clarke's capacity to understand the enemy's mind-set, reasoning, and predisposition allowed him to excel at deception.

Before the British and German armies met on the battlefield in the Second World War, Clarke was thinking about the possibilities of deceiving the Germans.

On October 5, 1939, Clarke recorded in his diary, "Therein, in my mind, lies the one way of winning the war against Germany without the mass slaughter of 1914–18. And I feel more and more convinced each day that it *can* be won by subterranean methods so much better than by formal military ones, which must at least take a long time and a crippling number of lives [emphasis in original]."[4] While this diary entry demonstrates Clarke's predisposition toward deception, it also reveals his motivation for favoring such an unconventional approach. Clarke offered additional insight in the foreword he wrote for *The Secret War*, his unpublished account of his last assignment to the Middle East—his eighth overall assignment—as head of "A" Force: "For the secret war was waged rather to conserve than to destroy: the stakes were the lives of front-line troops, and the organisation which fought it was able to count its gains from the number of casualties it could avert."[5] Clarke, as this passage suggests, viewed deception as a special means by which to minimize the loss of life. After the appalling bloodshed of the First World War, it is not surprising that the British willingly embraced deception in an effort to avoid a repeat of the previous war's carnage.

Early in the war Clarke contrived a number of deception schemes, although none of his ideas were accepted by the war planners. His fortune changed when Wavell recognized the need for coordinated deception in the Middle East and remembered Clarke from their earlier service together. Wavell specifically recalled Clarke's "unorthodox" approach to military matters and that alone qualified him for this "less orthodox employment" in the Middle East.[6] In November Clarke received his summons to the Middle East, thus beginning his eighth assignment, which he called the "longest and infinitely the most gratifying assignment of them all."[7]

On December 18, 1940, Clarke arrived in Cairo. He was met by Tony Simonds, a British military intelligence officer who later came to work for Clarke at "A" Force as the head of the MI9 (Escape and Evasion) division. Clarke apparently made quite the impression when he arrived in full flare, dressed "like a golfer from Chicago, wearing loud black and white plus-fours, a check cap and dark glasses, claiming to be an American journalist called Wrangel."[8] Clarke, as it turns out, tended to travel incognito and was known to don disguises when on deception missions in foreign lands. In October 1941, for example, he was arrested in Madrid dressed as a female wearing a "floral patterned dress, with opera gloves, what appears to be a fashionable cloche hat, necklace, high heels, stockings, and a clutch bag."[9] The Spanish reported that they had "arrested 'Wrangel Craker,' correspondent of *The Times*, in drag."[10] The incident led British officials in London to question whether or not Clarke was of sound mind. One scholar defends Clarke, writing that there was "nothing to suggest that the life-long bachelor Clarke was fulfilling a personal need or fetish by acting this way, but in the conservative world of the British establishment in the 1940s this sort of behaviour led to questions being asked of his sanity."[11] Guy Liddell, director of MI5's counterespionage division, commented in his diary, "Dudley Clarke is now on his way home. . . . Before he is allowed to go back to the Middle East he will have to give a satisfactory account of himself. It may be that he is just the type who imagines himself as the super secret service agent."[12] Before Clarke returned to the Middle East, he was thoroughly interviewed by Lord Gort, who ultimately concluded, "He seems in all other respects to be mentally stable. I also feel that we can reasonably expect that this escapade and its consequences will have given him a sufficient shock to make him more prudent in the immediate future."[13] This was, apparently, the last time that Clarke played the undercover agent.

Clarke presented himself to General Wavell on the morning of December 19 and was given the title of personal intelligence officer (special duties) to the commander in chief.[14] Clarke reported directly to Wavell and received his instructions from the general alone. To conceal the nature of Clarke's duties, Wavell consistently maintained the highest degree of secrecy in dealing with Clarke and administering his orders for deceptive operations.[15] Before "A" Force came into being in March 1941, Clarke's operation was exceedingly small—it was, in effect, a one-man show. His office was a converted bathroom at general headquarters (GHQ) in the Grey Pillars Building in Cairo. His only assistance came by way of Wavell's personal secretary and the personal assistant to Wavell's chief of staff.[16]

Part of Clarke's responsibilities as personal intelligence officer (special duties), and part of his cover, was his assignment as head of the Middle East equivalent of MI9, beginning January 5, 1941. The goal of this organization was to obtain intelligence from British prisoners of war (POWs) and to facilitate their escape. According to the "A" Force Narrative War Diary, "Although this had nothing to do with Deception, it was one of those undefined secret activities which fell to Col. Clarke as personal Intelligence Officer for special duties to the Commander-in-Chief. Later it proved to be a useful cloak for the more essentially secret work of Deception, and afforded a measure of economy in isolated 'Outstations' where one officer was able to combine both roles, sometimes using the one as cover for the other."[17] Clarke's role as head of MI9 occasionally superseded his deception duties.[18] All told, under Clarke's leadership approximately 7,500 Allied personnel, 4,000 of whom were British and American, were rescued.[19]

From the beginning of his assignment, Clarke's efforts relied heavily upon a close working relationship with Britain's intelligence organizations in the Middle East. Conducting intelligence in the Middle East was a complex matter. First of all, it was difficult to coordinate intelligence between London and the Middle East and especially to devise a "logical division of labour between the two theatres," as F. H. Hinsley puts it.[20] Second, each of the three branches of the military had its own intelligence staff in the Mediterranean and Middle East, but they were not unified under common leadership, nor were they predisposed to working together. Finally, security was exceedingly hampered in the Middle East because of Egypt's declaration of neutrality, the antipathy of the Egyptian nationalists toward Britain, colorful court intrigues, and Britain's inability to control who was or was not allowed into Cairo.[21] Consequently, there was a continual influx of hostile agents and enemy informants, whom the British could not always identify or control, into Egypt, and this severely complicated matters for the intelligence agencies. Michael Howard calls the region "an intelligence officer's paradise and a security officer's hell."[22]

Before the outbreak of war, in June 1939, the British formed the MEIC in an effort to centralize intelligence work in the Middle East and to "co-ordinate and furnish intelligence both for GHQ Middle East and for the Joint Intelligence Committee in London."[23] Because MEIC was created before hostilities began, it was greatly restricted in its activities. Consequently, it had to be reorganized after the British declaration of war on Germany in September 1939. Thereafter, the organization was modeled after the Joint Intelligence Committee (JIC) in London, which had wide-ranging responsibilities, including collecting intelligence for all three services.[24]

Upon the outbreak of war, security was catapulted to the utmost of importance in the Middle East. MEIC, however, was ill-suited to meet the security needs of the region. A War Office conference held on November 1, 1939, produced the following analysis: "M.E.I.C. are not authorized by their charter to deal effectively with matters affecting security. M.I.5 are responsible for security within the British Empire. There is at present no co-ordinating authority competent to deal with German penetration in the Middle East. S.I.S. organization provides information, but is not authorized and has not the means to take counter measures."[25] To provide adequate security and avoid bitter fighting between MI5 and the Secret Intelligence Service (MI6, or SIS), SIME was established in December 1939. SIME was given the task of monitoring hostile agents in the Middle East, coordinating efforts against enemy agents, organizing security services throughout the theater, and working with the other intelligence organizations and the armed services.[26] Like MI5 in London, SIME devoted much of its time to running double agents and helping to pass along Allied deceptions to the German and Italian high commands by means of those agents. Brigadier Raymund Maunsell, who had served as MI5's defense security officer (DSO) in Cairo since 1935, became the head of SIME.[27] Maunsell created SIME from the ground up with rather meager resources and fought successfully to maintain its independence.[28]

In his many years in Cairo, Maunsell had developed invaluable contacts and established relationships with influential people and organizations. Among his more useful contacts were Egyptian police, Turkish secret police, and Sephardic Jewish agents. Additionally, he successfully infiltrated the Muslim Brotherhood and Spanish consulate, as well as established his own censorship bureau.[29] All the aforementioned contacts and numerous others greatly facilitated Maunsell's efforts as head of SIME and aided Clarke in influencing the enemy. In fact, Thaddeus Holt argues that an "early order of business for Clarke would have been to get acquainted with Lieutenant-Colonel Raymund Maunsell . . . for SIME was to be the primary agency for passing deceptive information to the enemy in that theater."[30] The passing of deceptive information was accomplished specifically though Maunsell's double-agent network.

All intelligence and deception organizations in the Middle East, and especially the double-agent network, were greatly aided by signals intelligence (sigint). The ability to read the enemy's wireless transmissions was of tremendous value to the war effort. However, the inability to do so proved a fatal handicap to the British in 1941. In the Middle East, all three branches of the military had their own sigint sections before the war. After Italy declared war on the British, Wavell instinctively saw the need to centralize sigint activity within a single organization. By November 1940, at Wavell's request, the British created the Combined Bureau Middle East (CBME). The CBME was to coordinate all cryptanalysis efforts and was staffed with personnel specially trained at the Government Code and Cypher School (GC&CS) at Bletchley Park.[31]

Although there were numerous intelligence agencies in the Middle East, not a single British organization was devoted solely to deceiving the enemy in that theater—or elsewhere, for that matter. Hence, Clarke was given the task to build the first deception organization from the ground up. Unlike the intelligence organizations, "A" Force did not have a counterpart in London. In London, deception was theoretically the responsibility of the Inter-Services Security Board (ISSB), but ISSB was more concerned with security than actual deception. On the occasions when ISSB did attempt deceptive measures, they were defensive—meant to conceal British intentions—rather than offensive—meant to persuade the enemy to act in a way that was harmful to his war effort.[32] As a result, "A" Force did not have a model for organization; instead, "A" Force *was* the model. And, as Michael Howard points out, "A" Force was completely indigenous to the Middle East.[33]

Advanced Headquarters "A" Force officially came into being on March 28, 1941. By that time Clarke had demonstrated that deception could play an instrumental role in aiding the British on and off the battlefield, but it was becoming increasingly obvious that he could not continue his deceptive operations without help. With a formal war establishment granted to "A" Force on April 7, Clarke finally received some assistance by way of two officers and ten other ranks.[34] In early April Clarke's headquarters moved out of the converted bathroom at Grey Pillars and into two flats at No. 6 Sharia Kasr-el-Nil. As it so happened, a brothel occupied the upper floors of the building, and this worked to Clarke's advantage because "visitors of all types could be admitted discreetly and interviewed under conditions of secrecy."[35] According to Mure, Clarke, being "a man of exquisite courtesy, was reluctant to inconvenience the ladies and permitted them to continue their activities in those parts of the house which he did not actually require for his."[36]

As one would expect from Clarke, the name given to "A" Force was anything but random. It was intentionally ambiguous, but with the expectation that the enemy would assume that the *A* in "A" Force stood for "airborne." This assumption fit neatly with one of Clarke's ongoing deception schemes known as Abeam. The goal of Abeam was to "persuade the Italians that 'the 1st Special Air Service

Brigade' [SAS], of one Parachute and two Glider Battalions, had arrived by sea from ENGLAND on 30th Dec. and were now completing their training secretly in the TRANSJORDAN DESERT."[37] The 1st SAS was a notional brigade specifically formed to play on the fears of the Italians. The "A" Force Narrative War Diary explains that it "came into being largely as a result of an entry found in the diary of an Italian Officer captured in the SIDI BARANI battle. This showed that that Italians were apprehensive of parachute landings behind their lines."[38] Clarke christened his organization Advanced Headquarters "A" Force to suggest that it was the forward headquarters for the much-feared 1st SAS.

Throughout 1941 Clarke received minimal instruction from London. At this early stage, the British government had yet to establish a centralized agency to coordinate worldwide deception efforts. Yet centralized control was increasingly and desperately needed as the practice of deception became ever more elaborate, sophisticated, and complex. Clarke and the Middle East commanders in chief were not necessarily aware of plans or actions beyond their own theater of operations, and they needed a single agency to assume the responsibility of organizing all deception so that they could avoid compromising military efforts outside of their immediate focus. Clarke considered this critically important for the future success of deception and correspondingly noted in the War Diary,

> The Deception Organization which had grown up in the MIDDLE EAST, under the name of "A" Force, was still virtually the only one in existence at this time. . . . The time had arrived when the need of a central guiding hand was beginning to be felt, in order to ensure that Deception policy over the whole British war area was related to one main theme. Failing that, there was a grave risk of "A" Force in the MEDITERRANEAN, knowing nothing of plans outside it, innocently compromising the intentions of another command. To avoid this a LONDON controlling organization was clearly needed, which it was thought might also serve a useful purpose in arranging for the machinery established by one Command to help in implementing the deception plans of its neighbours.[39]

When the Chiefs of Staff met with Clarke on October 7, 1941, they too recognized the need to establish centralized control over deception operations. Speaking behind closed doors, Clarke reiterated, "there seemed to be a need for some strategic guidance from London on which deception could be planned. In the absence of such guidance, there was a danger that information which was passed to the enemy through the available channels might conflict with the plans being prepared by London or elsewhere."[40]

Clarke and the others around the table also recognized that it would be useful to have a greater understanding of London's short- and long-term strategic goals so that deception planners could formulate plans and policies in support of the Allied grand strategy. Finally, as suggested in the War Diary, deceptions being passed on to the enemy high command would be significantly reinforced if the enemy received supporting information from channels emanating from more than one region of conflict. During the meeting, Clarke "stressed the desirability of placing the responsibility for all 'deception planning' in the hands of one man who should be in the closest of touch with the Planning Staffs."[41]

A degree of centralized control came later that same month. Wavell and Clarke, who each lobbied for the creation of a more systematic approach, were two of the driving forces behind the effort. Wavell was by that time the commander in chief of India, where he established a deception organization similar to "A" Force under the direction of Major Peter Fleming. At Wavell's urging and Clarke's instruction, the Joint Planning Staff (JPS) at the War Cabinet Office sanctioned the recruitment of a controlling officer of deception, Colonel Oliver Stanley, to "coordinate deception operations across the globe, developing the cover plans for operations and using existing services to help implement them, including the Army, the Security Service, the Political Warfare Executive (PWE) and the camouflage and decoy units."[42] But Stanley had a difficult time with his overwhelming and rather ill-defined task. One major hindrance was that Stanley was expected to organize global deception even though he had limited knowledge of the deception tools and assets at Britain's disposal. J. C. Masterman, who headed London's Twenty Committee, which was responsible for all double-cross activity in Great Britain, recorded that Stanley was never even informed of the existence of the double-agent network in Britain. Masterman concluded, "One of his hands, therefore, was tied behind his back from the start."[43]

Consequently, a true centralized deception unit was not effectively established until the creation of the LCS, an interservice agency under the leadership of Lieutenant Colonel John Henry Bevan, in June 1942.[44] From then on, Bevan's LCS devised strategic deception for all three services and disseminated objectives to the deception operators—or controllers—in each theater.[45] The local controllers, like Clarke, who were charged with creating the actual deception plans, each had direct access to the commanders in chief and the Chiefs of Staff in London. The controllers made their plans known to suboperators who carried out the fieldwork to implement the ruses.[46] Until June 1942, however, "A" Force was largely on its own to devise and carry out strategic and tactical deception, both defensive and offensive, in the Middle East without either guidance or instruction from London.

Clarke's official deception work began the day after he arrived in Cairo. When he met with Wavell on December 19, 1940, he learned that the commander in chief had already begun planning a deception to accompany his offensive against the Duke of Aosta in Italian East Africa.[47]

Despite their best efforts, 1940 had not gone particularly well for the British in East Africa. They had lost control of British Somaliland, and the Italians had taken a number of frontier posts in the Sudan and Kenya. Because of Italy's vast numerical advantage and early successes, the British feared that the Italians in East Africa would try to link up with their counterparts in Libya and thereby isolate Egypt. Such an effort would have had devastating consequences for the British in the Middle East

To reverse their initial losses, the British attempted their first offensive at Gallabat in November, but it ended in an embarrassing failure. From November on, the British were limited to launching small raids on the Italian frontier positions. The raids were accomplished by Gazelle Force, a small mobile force formed in the Sudan whose mission was to "harass incessantly and intimidate the Italians forces, to keep them off balance, and to create the impression that the Italians faced a British force much larger than it actually was."[48] In his effort to "torment the Italians," the commander of Gazelle Force, Colonel Frank Messervy, ordered his troops to "terrify the enemy. Make his life absolute hell."[49] Gazelle Force is a prime example of Britain's ability to maximize its minimal resources.

The only other form of active resistance, and yet another example of British resourcefulness, came by way of Mission 101 under Colonel Sandford. Mission 101 was steadily arming Ethiopian patriots so that they could "tie the Italian forces to their garrisons" and prepare for the eventual triumphant return of Emperor Haile Selassie.[50] Apart from that, the mission could do little to help bring about British victory in East Africa until the military began its offensive. Once the campaign began, Sandford's intention was to have the Ethiopian patriots attack and harass the Italian formations so as to force them to expend their dwindling resources on defending themselves against the guerrilla-style attacks, render them unable to receive reinforcements, and prevent them from countering the British thrust. Mission 101 was also responsible for ensuring Haile Selassie's safe return to his capital, a key British objective.[51]

In August 1940 Sandford secretly crossed the border into Ethiopia with the aim of finding a suitable route for the emperor to travel. He isolated Mount Belaya as the ideal staging ground. According to the Mission 101 report, "Belaiya was obviously the most advantageous site for his first headquarters. . . . Belaiya offered security from surprise, a natural fortress if attacked from the east, and safe L. of C. and retreat westward to the Sudan if necessary."[52] Belaya would serve as Haile Selassie's first headquarters upon his reentry into Ethiopia, and once the Ethiopians learned that their emperor had returned, his presence, it was hoped, would reenergize the patriot movement.[53]

Although the British offensive at Gallabat had ended in failure, it had also helped to invigorate the patriot activities. As a result, Wavell and the Kaid, General William Platt, "felt that the time had now come to take more active steps in arming the Patriots and in preparing the way for the entry of the Emperor."[54] The renewed focus on Mission 101 coincided with Wavell's decision to launch a large-scale offensive against Italian East Africa. On November 20 Major Orde Wingate met with Sandford, informed him of the upcoming offensive, and promised him arms and ammunition. In addition, the home government allotted Wingate £1 million to finance the movement.[55]

In January 1941, in preparation for the upcoming offensive, the patriots stepped up their efforts against the Italians. They inflicted heavy casualties on the enemy and forced him to collect "all available forces to quell the rising." The RAF also increased its attacks on the enemy garrisons, causing significant damage to the Italian positions.[56]

The patriot activity achieved great success and certainly did its part to undermine the Italians' morale. The Mission 101 report records that the situation was "steadily deteriorating from the Italian point of view. Gubba had already been evacuated . . . , other withdrawals were certainly under contemplation, and in Colonel Sandford's opinion the only thing necessary to complete the enemy confusion was the immediate arrival of the Emperor."[57] On January 21, 1941, Haile Selassie stepped foot on Ethiopian soil for the first time in nearly five years. He proceeded onto Belaya to await the offensive that would allow him to return to his capital.

On February 6 Major Wingate was promoted to lieutenant colonel, took over as head of Mission 101, and renamed the mission Gideon Force. From that point forward, its goal was to attack the main roadways leading to the capital and force the Italians to "commit as many troops as possible to the defence of the capital."[58] On February 15 Colonel Sandford was promoted to brigadier and became the military and political adviser to the emperor; Major Edwin Chapman-Andrews served as his political assistant.[59] The patriots were in position to assist Wavell's offensive from within Ethiopia.

With the early success of Operation Compass in the Western Desert and the Italians largely removed from Egypt for the time being, Wavell felt confident that he could turn his attention to the threat posed by the Italians in East Africa. Three days before Clarke's arrival in Cairo, Wavell developed a deception plan to accompany the upcoming offensive. The code name Wavell chose for the deception operation was Camilla. The objective of the offensive was to liberate both Ethiopia and Italian East Africa. Wavell planned to use his forces in the Sudan to strike the Italians in Eritrea, with the main thrust focused on Keren. Once the British took Keren, Asmara, and Massawa in Eritrea, the path into Ethiopia would be clear.[60] British-led forces in Kenya were planning to simultaneously invade Ethiopia and Italian Somaliland from the south. If everything went as planned, the patriots would also attack from the west.

Because concealing the buildup of regular forces for the offensive would be impossible, it was crucial to make the Italians think that the British intended to launch their offensive from a different location altogether. The "A" Force Narrative War Diary records, "It was necessary to keep the Italian 'Eastern Reserve' in the Eastern provinces of ABYSSINIA; and this was the true 'Object' of the Deception Plan."[61] The British also hoped to keep the Italians pinned down in the southern sector of Ethiopia because the main advance was to be concentrated in the north through Eritrea.

British Somaliland was chosen as the target of the ruse because the Italians assumed that the British were still reeling from the loss of their protectorate. Focusing on British Somaliland would also have the desired effect of holding the Italians in the east and thus preventing them from reinforcing the north. Therefore, the goal of Camilla was to persuade the Italians that the British were going to launch an invasion from Aden, across the Gulf of Aden, into British Somaliland. The target landing zones were the coastal towns of Berbera and Zeila, and from there, troops would move toward Harar in Ethiopia.[62] To tie down the Italian forces in the south as well, Wavell hoped to mislead the enemy into believing that another advance was to be launched from East Africa against Moyale on the Kenyan border and Dolo in southern Ethiopia. As the forces pushed west and north into Ethiopia, they were to meet up at the capital, Addis Ababa.[63]

As the plan for Camilla went into action, it became imperative to convince the Italians that the British would be using Indian troops from Egypt and South African troops from Kenya in their effort to retake British Somaliland. Then, because it was likely that the Italians would observe the concentration of the genuine invasion forces in the Sudan and Kenya, Wavell intended to fool them into believing that he was simulating "an offensive both in the SUDAN and in EAST AFRICA in order to draw the Italian forces towards these points," thus rendering British Somaliland and the eastern portion of Ethiopia vulnerable. Wavell further explained, "As part of this plan of deception I am sending two brigades of Indians to the Sudan, hoping that their presence will become known to the enemy and will make them think an offensive in the SUDAN is intended."[64] Wavell knew that if his double bluff failed, the Italians might actually strengthen the areas he intended to strike.

Although Wavell masterminded Camilla, Clarke was responsible for implementing it. Clarke proceeded to organize the operation as if he were truly planning an invasion of British Somaliland.[65] Thus, from the organizational and administrative standpoint, he put everything into practice—albeit notionally— exactly as he would for a genuine operation, with the exception that he would have been considerably more careful to maintain absolute secrecy for an actual offensive. Preparations began in mid-December and continued though the first week of February 1941.

Before initiating the deception, Wavell wrote letters to the commanders of the Sudan, Aden, South Africa, and India to inform them of the ruse and enlist their help. They participated by circulating rumors, sending private telegrams "in clear," and being less than discreet in their public conversations and speeches.[66] On January 13, 1941, for example, the *Egyptian Gazette* published an article titled "General Smuts Foreshadows Offensive against Abyssinia," in which General Jan Christian Smuts, the prime minister of South Africa, declared that the role of South African forces in 1941 "will be to help clear Abyssinia of the enemy, and not only Abyssinia, but British Somaliland which was overwhelmed by vastly superior forces some months ago."[67] By way of such "indiscretions," the foundation of the deception was laid.

The elaborate preparations for Camilla proceeded as follows: During the latter part of December 1940, word spread around the GHQ Middle East that the home government was pressuring Wavell to retake British Somaliland; thus, the staff should be prepared to organize the campaign on short notice. Rumors were disseminated among the soldiers of the 4th Indian Division in Egypt that they were headed to Aden, although their actual destination was the Sudan. To support the hoax, however, they were issued maps of British Somaliland, and their mail was redirected to Aden. Rumors of the offensive were also circulated in Kenya and the Sudan.[68]

Beginning in January, dummy wireless traffic between Cairo and Aden increased significantly. In England, the press began hinting that Wavell should redeem himself and retake British Somaliland. In Egypt, the British High Command commenced the process of determining which beaches would be most suitable for a landing. In Aden, rumors continued to swirl, an Indian infantry brigade began practicing embarkation and disembarkation exercises, a facility was constructed to accommodate the influx of troops, the RAF began aerial reconnaissance of British Somaliland, and maps and combined operations pamphlets arrived for the "invasion forces." In the Sudan, soldiers were given maps of British Somaliland, and cipher traffic increased. These efforts were intended to suggest that the forces in the Sudan were going to be transferred to Aden to participate in the offensive. In Kenya, the South African Brigade received maps and combined operations pamphlets, and rumors spread quickly that South African troops were also slated to head to Aden.[69]

By mid-January the American press began suggesting that the British were preparing to reclaim British Somaliland. In Aden, the RAF increased its activities over British Somaliland and conducted aerial raids from its bases in Aden to soften up the Italian positions.[70] The 4th Indian Division's mail finally arrived in Aden, as opposed to the Sudan, where the division was by then located. Simulated wireless traffic continued on a busier than usual schedule.[71]

By the latter part of January, diplomatic indiscretions in neutral countries had increased. In Egypt, rumors were leaked that the 5th Indian Brigade, currently on the Gallabat front, was preparing to relocate to Aden. During the last days of January, all propaganda focused on British Somaliland suddenly ended, and references in newspapers to the potential campaign vanished. Rumors circulated that further reinforcements were en route to Aden from India, and reservations were made for war correspondents to arrive in Aden in the beginning of February.[72]

Throughout the entire period, dummy wireless messages were sent on a prearranged schedule between Aden, Cairo, Delhi, Khartoum, Nairobi, and Pretoria, all with the intention of furthering the idea that a major operation was being planned. As was common, the British planted information on the Japanese consul in Egypt.[73] All these efforts combined to paint a clear picture of British intentions for the Italians. This picture matched the Italians' expectation that the British would be eager to reclaim British Somaliland, and that gave the deception credibility.

On the one hand, Camilla was unquestionably a success. The Italians bought the deception and accepted as fact the British intension to launch a large-scale assault on British Somaliland. On the other hand, the deception failed to achieve its intended objective because the Italians responded in a manner completely contrary to what the British had hoped—they abandoned British Somaliland altogether and, as Clarke put it, were "freed to swell the forces in the North which were to block our advance at Keren."[74] The problem, according to Clarke and most deception scholars, was with the "object" of the deception. The "object" was targeted at what the British wanted the Italians to think, instead of what they wanted them to do. Clarke later recorded that the "'Object' paragraph should not be framed to say 'To induce the enemy to think we are going to do so and so'. It is possible that the Plan may succeed in making him think exactly what we want but may fail because he reacts in an unexpected way."[75] That, of course, was exactly what happened with Camilla. Clarke provided further explanation:

In order to persuade the Italians to keep their reserves in the Southern part of ABYSSINIA rather than in the North, a plan was worked with the object of persuading them that we were going to attempt the re-capture of BRITISH SOMALILAND. In this the Plan succeeded, but succeeded so well that they withdrew all their troops from BRITISH SOMALILAND and gave up any idea of defending it. As a result, General WAVELL had to reoccupy BRITISH SOMALIALND, which he had no particular wish to do at that time, while the Italian reserves, released of the responsibility of looking after BRITISH SOMALILAND, were moved North. Thus, although the Deception Plan was successful, it failed to achieve the results required of it, the fault being entirely in the fact that the wrong object was chosen.[76]

From that experience, Clarke learned a valuable lesson that would serve him well for the rest of the war. He wrote, "After that it became a creed in 'A' Force to ask a General 'What do you want the enemy to *do*?', and never 'What do you want him to *think*?'" Clarke was surprised that the generals often had trouble answering the question. He recalled, "Later on I used the trick of asking them to imagine I had a direct telephone line to Hitler himself, and that he would do anything I told him to do. And this proved quite successful."[77]

Although Clarke and the scholars of deception blame the "object" for the deception's unforeseen results, the deception failed in yet another regard altogether, which was likely the real reason for its problems. The failure was, quite simply, the result of choosing British Somaliland as the target of the ruse. The Italians did not pull out of British Somaliland because they feared the British offensive but because they did not consider British Somaliland important enough to defend.

The basis of offensive deception is that the target "must be carefully selected: it must be so vulnerable and so important that the enemy must move troops to its defence."[78] This clearly was not the case with British Somaliland. Wavell's intent was to trick the Italians into weakening their forces in Keren, a well-fortified position in Eritrea, by simulating a threat to British Somaliland. Yet the Italians withdrew from British Somaliland without a struggle and, perhaps ironically, reinforced Keren.

The problem, Clarke acknowledged, was that the "point selected was not sufficiently important to the defence: the Italians preferred to abandon it rather than reinforce it."[79] Thus, the Italians were willing to relinquish control of British

Somaliland in order to better position themselves to defend the route to Ethiopia; after all, they had invested considerable time, money, and resources into making Ethiopia a viable colony.[80] Had the Italians viewed British Somaliland with the same degree of importance as they did Ethiopia, they very well may have fought to hold on to the country. If that had been the case, they would have acted in the exact manner that the British had expected. It stands to reason then that Camilla failed not solely because the "object" of deception was flawed but also because the enemy simply did not deem British Somaliland worth fighting for. Unfortunately for the British, that made the conquest of Italian East Africa more difficult.

Much like the deceptive operation, the conquest of Italian East Africa did not go quite as planned. As Wavell put it, the campaign was "an improvisation after the British fashion of war."[81] The original plan was to attack the Italians after the rainy season passed, in March 1941 at the earliest. However, Operation Compass, the British offensive against the Italians in the Western Desert, had met with considerable success and seemed to have an adverse effect on the enemy's morale in East Africa. On January 18 the Italians abandoned Kassala, a frontier post just inside the Sudanese border, without provocation. Playfair remarks that the Italian withdrawal was "an indication that the disaster to Graziani might be having effects beyond the borders of Libya. The experience of the past month had shown a tendency on the part of the Italians to melt away in adversity."[82] It was apparent that the activities of Gazelle Force were also taking their toll on the Italians. The Italian viceroy, the Duke of Aosta, called for the evacuation of the forward most positions because they were vulnerable to attack from small mobile units—units like Gazelle Force.

The duke viewed the defense of the northern sector as crucial to the survival of the Italian army; thus, he preferred to relinquish the more vulnerable posts and reinforce those areas that were better situated for defense. That, as it turned out, was the Italian strategy throughout its colonial empire. The duke, in Playfair's words, intended to "give ground where resistance would be useless and gradually to concentrate his troops and Italian civilians in districts whose inhabitants were loyal."[83] By withdrawing from their weakest and most exposed positions, the Italians could conserve their troops for the defense of the north.

Fortunately for the British, CBME personnel in Cairo and Nairobi were able to read approximately 90 percent of Italy's wireless transmissions.[84] Hinsley writes that in the beginning of 1941, the British were provided with "complete details of virtually every Italian move." Hinsley adds that the "flood of intelligence was not confined to any one sector or level of command, but was general throughout the whole area of operations and throughout the whole of the enemy's chain of command from the Viceroy himself down to the smallest garrison detachment."[85] As a result, the British command was well aware of the duke's defensive policy.

Although Wavell had not intended to go on the offensive in January, he decided to take advantage of the Italian retreat and ordered General Platt to pursue the enemy forces immediately. In Kenya, General Alan Cunningham saw an opportunity to strike from the south and requested Wavell's permission to attack Kismayu in Italian Somaliland. With permission granted, Cunningham began preparations to go on the offensive.

To achieve the element of surprise, Cunningham maintained complete secrecy regarding his intentions and refused to commit anything to paper. He also implemented his own deceptive measures once his forces began the assault. He reported, "In order to lead the enemy to believe that another column was advancing via EL WAK, a high-powered wireless set was established near WAJIR and was kept in constant operation with dummy messages. This ruse in conjunction with the use of agents was completely successful." Cunningham went on to write that information gathered later demonstrated that the Italians believed that they had faced an entire division. The "'division' consisting in fact of two platoons, a few armoured cars, and a number of dummy tanks."[86]

Because of the shortage of supplies and scarcity of water, Cunningham needed to take Kismayu in a matter of ten days. On February 14 the British entered Kismayu unopposed and days ahead of schedule. The Italians left twenty-five ships intact in the harbor, 222,000 gallons of fuel, and roughly 110,000 gallons of aviation spirit.[87] The British forces in northern Kenya experienced a similar scenario on February 22, when they entered Moyale, already abandoned by the Italians. In keeping with the duke's order to retreat if resistance appeared futile, the Italian forces readily withdrew as the British forces approached.[88]

From Kismayu, Cunningham's forces pressed north, crossed the Juba River, and reached Mogadishu on February 25. Again, the Italians had already abandoned the city and in their haste left large quantities of supplies behind. In the capital city, the British discovered 350,000 gallons of fuel and 80,000 gallons of aviation spirit.[89] Cunningham's troops succeeded in taking Italian Somaliland in only two weeks. Churchill's response to the news was to remark, "At present we seem to have swapped Somalilands with the enemy."[90] But that was not to last. On March 16 the British began landing forces at Berbera in British Somaliland and had resettled their protectorate by April.[91]

The forces under General Platt's command faced a very different Italian army in the north. The Italians were steadfast in their determination to hold the north; consequently, the British had to fight against a well-armed, entrenched, and determined enemy. British troops faced the greatest resistance in Eritrea at Keren. After occupying Kassala in the Sudan and taking Agordat and Barentu in Eritrea, British forces headed east toward Keren. Keren was situated on a plateau particularly well-suited for defense, a fact not lost on the Italians. Harold Raugh describes the Italian defenses, explaining that they "dominated the high ground and key terrain of this region of imposing massifs, deep ravines, and trackless mountains."[92]

On February 3, 1941, the seasoned 4th Indian Division, "believing it was opposed to Italian soldiers of the same low quality that it had encountered during the initial phase of 'Compass,'" attacked the entrenched Italian positions.[93] The Italians counterattacked with tenacity, undoing any gains made by the British. The 4th Indian Division quickly realized that it had underestimated the Italians and was beaten back after six days of bitter fighting. General Platt remarked frankly, "It is going to be a bloody battle against both enemy and ground. It will be won by the side which lasts the longest."[94]

For a solid month the British studied the Italian position and prepared for a second offensive. The RAF did its part to neutralize the Italian air force and bombarded the enemy fortifications at Keren in the days preceding the second offensive. On March 15 the 4th Indian Division attacked the Italians, this time reinforced by the 5th Indian Division. During the night of March 26–27, the Italians abandoned Keren, officially bringing the Battle of Keren to a close. The battle had lasted 53 days and was indeed bloody. Although the British emerged victorious, they suffered 536 killed and 3,229 wounded. The Italians counted at least 3,000 dead.[95] The Battle of Keren proved the sheer determination and fighting ability of both sides and, to Britain's surprise, demonstrated that the Italians still had some fight left in them.

After the Battle of Keren, the British steadily pushed forward, taking Asmara on April 1 and Massawa on April 8. With those victories, the British controlled Eritrea. From there, General Platt commanded his forces to proceed south into northern Ethiopia. In the meantime, after Keren fell, General Cunningham began his push toward the Ethiopian capital from the east. On April 3, 1941, the Duke of Aosta fled Addis Ababa fearing an Ethiopian rising. On the fourth, Cunningham's forces entered the city; Cunningham accepted its formal surrender on the sixth. In less than two months, Cunningham's troops took three of the six main capitals in Italian East Africa, and they succeeded in doing so without help from General Platt or the patriots.[96]

In the west Wingate's Gideon Force persistently pressed on toward the capital. Using guerrilla tactics, the patriots attacked the Italian garrisons and prevented them from reinforcing each other. In six weeks they managed to force General Gugliemo Nasi out of Gojjam. Once Platt had taken Keren and Cunningham had negotiated the surrender of Addis Ababa, Gideon Force prepared the way for Haile Selassie to reenter his capital.[97] On May 5, 1941, five years to the day from Italy's capture of the capital, the emperor triumphantly reclaimed his seat of power.[98]

In the meantime, Platt still had to contend with the duke. After the duke fled Addis Ababa, he headed to Amba Alagi in northern Ethiopia. There he met up with Platt's army. Facing sure defeat, the Italian forces laid down their arms on May 19, and the duke formally surrendered the following day. For all practical purposes, Italian East Africa ceased to exist. Two remaining pockets of resistance held out until November, but they too surrendered on November 27, 1941.

The battle for East Africa, which consumed the first half of 1941, has historically been overshadowed by events outside of the region. Historian Michael Glover argues, "In the month that the capitals of Eritrea and Ethiopia were captured by Commonwealth troops, the Germans invaded and took Greece, Rommel made his first advance in the Western Desert and laid siege to Tobruk and, importantly at the time, there was a pro-German *coup d'état* in Iraq which threatened Britain's supply of oil. In the following month, when the main Italian army in Ethiopia surrendered, the newspapers were more interested in the German airborne invasion of Crete."[99] Although the campaign may not represent the decisive action that ultimately guaranteed Allied defeat of the Axis forces in Africa or elsewhere, it was nonetheless an important conquest for the British.

First, it was a victory when the British desperately needed one, and as such, it most certainly boosted British morale. Second, and importantly, it eliminated the most immediate threat to the Sudan and Egypt, which freed up Britain's forces to focus exclusively on the new German threat in Libya. Third, it represented a step toward fulfilling Britain's three-stage strategy of first defeating the Italians so that they could concentrate their efforts exclusively on the defeat of Germany. Finally, it provided Clarke with the opportunity to attempt his first large-scale, coordinated deception plan. The lessons learned from Camilla were invaluable, and the experience gained provided Clarke with a solid foundation for future deceptions. The means by which Clarke implemented Camilla became the trademark of his deceptions. He would consistently employ similar tricks, and over time he built upon, expanded, and improved his techniques.

For the British forces in the Middle East, 1941 started off well with the success of Operation Compass in the Western Desert and the first victories in Italian East Africa. In February, however, Britain's fortune took a sudden downturn when General Erwin Rommel arrived in Libya commanding the Afrika Korps. Although the British had met with astounding success fighting the Italians, the strategy and techniques used against the Italians would simply not work against the Germans.

Given the gravity of the situation, Wavell again turned to deception and called on Clarke to do everything that he feasibly could to give the British the advantage on the battlefield. As in East Africa, the early deceptions in the Western Desert were learning experiences, but the situation in the Western Desert was considerably more complicated. Because of Rommel's sudden arrival in Libya and the unexpected swiftness of his attack, Clarke was forced to throw deceptions together with limited planning and preparation. The situation was clearly not conducive to deception, which typically required immense planning and extensive preparations.

Clarke's deception efforts in the Western Desert were also greatly hampered by the inability of the British intelligence services to completely break the German Army Enigma until the latter part of 1941. Even then, they were not regularly reading or translating the reports until April 1942.[100] At the same time, Britain had many gaps in its own intelligence security that often negated the effectiveness of Clarke's efforts. Clarke, therefore, had to tackle most of his first deceptions handicapped by his limited knowledge of the enemy, while the enemy had excellent intelligence on the British. Nevertheless, it is clear that throughout 1941 Clarke and his team began to truly understand how to best employ deception as a weapon against the enemy, and their efforts became increasingly sophisticated, scientific, and successful with practice.

—4—

The Western Desert from January to July 1941

In 1940 Britain had confronted its worst fears after losing France as an ally and gaining Italy as an enemy. British forces in the Mediterranean and Middle East experienced extreme shortages of troops and equipment, and reinforcement was impossible because of the ongoing Battle of Britain. The British also faced a massive Italian army that could easily overwhelm their meager forces by sheer size alone.[1] Given the circumstances, the situation appeared desperate. To Britain's advantage, however, were its better-trained and better-led troops, whose morale was high and whose mission was clear. The feeble Italian offensive in Egypt in September 1940 proved that the Italians were ill-prepared for war, despite the immense size of their forces. The enemy advance and resulting halt at Sidi Barrani ultimately provided the British with the opportunity to take the offensive, earning Britain its first campaign victory of the war. Thus, 1940 ended with a decisive British victory.

After the Battle of Sidi Barrani concluded successfully in December, Wavell decided to focus on eliminating the Italian threat in East Africa. To that end, the commander in chief transferred the 4th Indian Division from Egypt to the Sudan to take part in the East African campaign. Even though he had significantly weakened the strength of his forces in the Western Desert, Wavell nevertheless planned to continue the forward thrust that began with Operation Compass and to pursue the Italians into Libya.

The British began 1941 with a second offensive in the Western Desert, the second phase of Operation Compass. As the Italians withdrew from Egypt in mid-December, they fell back into Bardia, just inside the Libyan border. Wavell records that the bulk of the Italian army had concentrated behind the fortifications of Bardia and was essentially isolated.[2] Therefore, Wavell targeted Bardia for the second phase of Operation Compass.

At 5:30 in the morning on January 3, 1941, the 6th Australian Division attacked the Italian Tenth Army in Bardia. The tanks of the 7th Armoured Division entered the city on January 4, and the southeastern sector surrendered on January 5. By January 6 Bardia was in British hands, along with 45,000 prisoners of war, 462 guns, 129 tanks, hundreds of vehicles, and numerous important official documents.[3] British intelligence, however, had underestimated the number of Italian troops in Bardia, and thus the Allies had suffered greater casualties than they had expected.[4] The Australian Division alone counted 456 casualties, and the British lost so many invaluable tanks that only six remained after the three-day battle.[5] Nonetheless, in a matter of only one month, the British destroyed eight Italian divisions.

After the fall of Bardia, Wavell set his sights on Tobruk. The commander in chief defended his decision to continue the offensive, stating that the attack was "justified on both operational and administrative grounds."[6] If the British took the port at Tobruk, it would significantly shorten their supply lines and deny the Italians access to an indispensable port. They attacked the port on January 21, and Tobruk fell the following day with a loss of 30,000 Italian POWs, 236 guns, and 87 tanks.[7] British casualties amounted to 400. By January 24 the British had the port at Tobruk ready to receive Allied ships.[8]

Because the Italian army had suffered repeated losses, German leadership became increasingly concerned about the fate of Italy's campaign in North Africa. To help their faltering ally, the Germans sent their air force, the Luftwaffe, to the Mediterranean in January to assist the Italians by attacking British shipping. The presence of the Luftwaffe seriously threatened Britain's ability to supply its forces in the Mediterranean and the Middle East. In fact, the British did not attempt to send reinforcements through the Mediterranean Sea again until April, and then only because the tank shortage was so desperate that the need clearly outweighed the risk. The Germans also laid mines in the Suez Canal, greatly impeding Britain's efforts to send supplies around the cape to Egypt.[9]

Major General I. S. O. Playfair explains that the arrival of the Luftwaffe necessitated the capture of Benghazi, which had air and naval bases that could

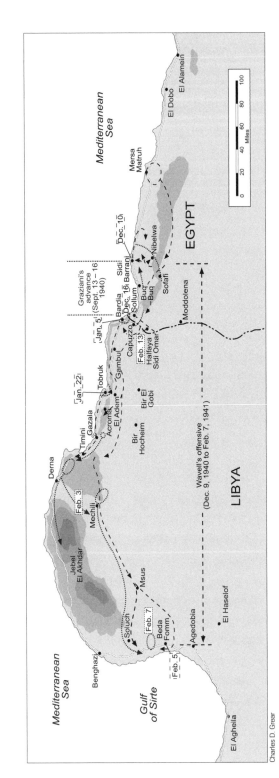

MAP 2. NORTH AFRICA, 1940–41: GRAZIANI'S ADVANCE AND WAVELL'S OFFENSIVE,
SEPTEMBER 13, 1940–FEBRUARY 7, 1941

Charles D. Grear

be of great value to Britain's war effort.[10] Wavell thought that because the Italian forces were dispersed and had yet to receive reinforcements in Cyrenaica, it was an ideal time to push ahead. In addition, Britain's L of C had been shortened following the capture of Tobruk. These conditions provided the impetus and opportunity to continue the advance.[11] Thus, the British decided to press forward, deeper into Libya.

Wavell had initially intended to resume the offensive in mid-February, but intelligence sources revealed that the Italians were retreating. Wavell opted to take advantage of this opportunity and ordered his troops forward on February 4 instead. The British separated into two columns. On the seventh, the northern column took Benghazi, including 25,000 POWs, 100 tanks, and 100 guns. The southern column sped forward to cut off the Italian retreat. The British succeeded in cutting off the Italians at Beda Fomm, and the remainder of the Italian Tenth Army surrendered on February 7. On the eighth the British occupied El Agheila, effectively drawing a line between Cyrenaica and Tripolitania and dividing Libya between east and west.

Immediately following the Italian capitulation, General Richard O'Connor requested permission to press on to Tripoli. The general knew that the Italians could offer little resistance. As for the British forces, O'Connor argued that "despite the battering and unceasing strain put on their equipment, it could be made to function well enough to get them at least to Tripoli, chiefly because the men would not allow its malfunction to stop them."[12] Pointing to the obvious Italian weakness, Rommel made a similar assessment: "If Wavell had now continued his advance into Tripolitania, no resistance worthy of the name could have been mounted against him—so well had his superbly planned offensive succeeded."[13] Although the British had the opportunity to completely force the Italians out of North Africa, Wavell denied O'Connor's request and instructed the general to maintain his position in Cyrenaica. The reason for the halt was the looming German invasion of Greece following the failed Italian effort to take Greece. Churchill had ordered Wavell to send all available reinforcements to assist the Greeks against the forthcoming German assault. Whether in agreement with Churchill or not, Wavell had no other choice but to bring the offensive to a close and again send forces to Greece.

The British advance from December to February had met with remarkable success. Wavell provides a clear picture of his army's achievements: "During the two months from 7th December to 7th February, the Army of the Nile had advanced 500 miles. They had beaten and destroyed an Italian army of four Corps comprising nine divisions and part of a tenth, and had captured 130,000 prisoners, 400 tanks, and 1,290 guns, besides vast quantities of other war material. . . . In these operations we never employed a larger force than two divisions, of which one was armoured. . . . Our casualties were extremely light and amounted to 500 killed, 1,373 wounded, and 55 missing only."[14] Not only had the British expelled the Italians from Egypt, but they had also established themselves well inside of Libya. They were, for the moment at least, the masters of the Western Desert.

Throughout the campaign, the British made use of deception wherever possible. According to Playfair, "Deception and surprise—especially by the choice of the unorthodox course—were sure to be essential ingredients of any plan of General Wavell's, but their use was not confined to the opening phase, where, naturally, there was great scope for it; at Bardia and Tobruk, and on other occasions where an attack was obviously to be expected, the enemy was kept guessing as to the time, the place, and the method."[15] The deceptions were generally basic, largely carried out by the use of makeshift dummy tanks. The "A" Force Narrative War Diary reveals that the British had an independent dummy tank unit known as the 10th Royal Tank Regiment (RTR), which had been formed under the command of a Major Johnston on December 24, 1940. After assisting with the deception efforts for Operation Compass, the 10th RTR continued west with the advancing forces. According to the War Diary, the "unit advanced with the 7th Armoured Division to TOBRUK, and on to BENGHAZI, operating primitive types of wood-and-canvas tanks and lorries carried folded in the unit transport."[16]

An example of the successful use of dummy tanks came at Mechili. As the British forces approached the Italian position on January 26, the Italians decided not to fight and instead abandoned Mechili during the night. They withdrew, as it turned out, because they believed that their armored forces were greatly outnumbered by the British 7th Armoured Division. Ironically, the Italians had a hundred medium tanks and two hundred light tanks, whereas the British had only fifty serviceable tanks by that time. The Italians had greatly overestimated the size of Britain's tank force as a result of its employment of the 10th RTR's decoys.[17] Because of the wear and tear inflicted on the delicate wood and canvas dummies, the 10th RTR was disbanded on February 16, after the British offensive came to a close.[18]

As the British forces pushed their way westward in early 1941, they were accompanied by a man who was to play a key role in deception in North Africa: Colonel Geoffrey Barkas, a prewar film producer who came to head the British camouflage organization in the desert, G(CAM). Barkas arrived in Egypt on December 31, 1940, along with three other members of the camouflage team. He and his colleagues served as Wavell's personal camouflage advisers.[19]

Barkas' purpose in traveling with the army was to observe the desert landscape and evaluate the effects of war on the natural environment. At first it seemed that it would be impossible to employ camouflage in the desert, especially since the land lay largely exposed. The camouflage experts had practiced their art in the United Kingdom, where camouflage was aided by vegetation that provided natural cover. After conducting an aerial reconnaissance of the desert terrain, Barkas reported that "from the air we could see at once that the desert was not by any means so featureless and devoid of opportunities for concealment or misdirection as many people supposed."[20] According to Barkas, the trick was simply to make the enemy see what he wanted him to see, and that was accomplished by replicating the innate features of the land. Barkas explained that it was really quite simple: anything that ran counter to the natural patterns of the land was observable; anything that conformed to those patterns could be hidden.[21]

During the time that Barkas traveled with the army through Libya, he observed how equipment and specific weapons left distinct patterns on the ground. From aerial reconnaissance, Barkas noted that the enemy could see "new dumps, sidings, artillery or armoured units, approach tracks, mine fields, gaps in mine fields, new pipelines, and all the other pointers to what is being prepared."[22] The key to successful camouflage, therefore, was to create or erase those telling markers from the ground. While Barkas accompanied the military, he practiced his techniques, gaining valuable hands-on experience. He would latter assist "A" Force in implementing physical deception in the field.[23]

During the first weeks of January 1941, Dudley Clarke concentrated solely on his deception tasks. He was at once organizing efforts for Camilla in East Africa and trying to artificially increase the size and strength of the forces at Britain's disposal in the Western Desert. On January 11 he began working on a plan he called Abeam. This was Clarke's first attempt at creating an entirely notional force and, as such, constituted his first order-of-battle deception plan. Abeam was also the first deception scheme created by Clarke, as Wavell had been responsible for developing Camilla.

Clarke got the idea for Abeam after he learned that the Italians feared the British would attack their rear lines with parachute units. The British did not then have such airborne units in the Middle East, nor were there any known plans for them to receive parachute forces. That did not stop Clarke—he would simply create them. The War Diary states, "As our forces were always far inferior numerically to those of the enemy, we were constantly seeking means of making him exaggerate our strength. We thought that if we could make him believe we had Airborne troops in reserve it would not only add to our own strength, but would make him dissipate some of his in protecting Lines of Communication, Rear Areas and Airfields against possible airborne attack."[24] Not only would such a deception play right into the enemy's fears, but it would also make the British forces appear larger and more versatile. With the idea formed in his mind, Clarke began to bring the plan to life.

Clarke's goal was to convince the Italians that Britain was training the 1st SAS, containing one parachute battalion (500 strong) and two glider battalions (750 strong), for use in the Western Desert.[25] For the moment, Clarke did not intend to employ the 1st SAS in the field. His immediate aim was to build it up in the enemy's estimations of British strength. To do that, he had to provide proof of the notional brigade's existence. That proof was supplied through the following means:

a) Arm bands of the staff of the "1st Airborne Division" were made to appear in the MIDDLE EAST. Also the new arm-badge of the Parachutist.

b) R.A.F. pilots were warned to look out for towed gliders in flight.

c) Two specially-coached soldiers in the uniform of Parachutists were circulated in EGYPT in the role of convalescents from the S.A.S. Bde.

d) The manufacture of dummy gliders was started.

e) The Arab Legion was employed to cordon a "Prohibited Area" around BAIR WEELS to encourage speculation among the Bedouin tribes near the SYRIAN border.

f)   Photographs of parachutists in training (including an Abyssinian) were published in the CAIRO Illustrated Paper "PARADE".

g)   Documents identifying the Brigade were "planted" in EGYPT and PALESTINE, including one on a Japanese consular official travelling to TURKEY.

h)   The usual rumours and "leakages" of information were arranged. In this the Jewish Agency assisted.[26]

Clarke's efforts were meticulous, and he paid attention to minute detail throughout the planning process. For example, the background information provided for the notional battalions was incredibly detailed. It included the background of the personnel, the location where the units were formed and trained, the troops' level and specific type of training, the kind of weapons they carried with them, and even descriptions of the atmosphere of competition between the units. Clarke's instructions for the two "specially-coached soldiers" who were sent to Cairo were just as thorough. He provided them with a comprehensive summary of their movements during the course of the previous months, which they were to memorize before taking on their assumed roles.[27] Clarke left nothing to chance. He was well aware that any slip, indiscretion, or inconsistency in their story could expose the entire operation.

For months Clarke worked diligently to make the Italians believe in the 1st SAS's existence. In April 1941 a unit known as "K" Detachment came into being under the command of Lieutenant J. M. Robertson, one of the first officers assigned to "A" Force, to operate dummy gliders. Robertson had the help of Jasper Maskelyn, a camouflage expert who, like Barkas, was specially trained in England and sent to the Middle East. Maskelyn was a well-known magician in England, and thus, he was particularly well-suited for camouflage work.[28] Hervie Haufler, a Second World War cryptographer, recorded, "Clarke's visual deception magicians, which included well-known conjuror Jasper Maskelyn, were turning out rows of bogus craft lined up on RAF airfields." These craft were positioned so as to be observable by enemy reconnaissance.[29]

The 1st SAS was finally employed in the field in April. Although initially it was ordered to assist the British effort in Crete, the German offensive in Libya presented the greater threat. Accordingly, new orders arrived: "'K' Dct. was required to display dummy gliders at the disused HELWAN Aerodrome, near

CAIRO, to create an airborne threat to the Desert Lines of Communication of the advancing Germans, and that at the same time a proportion of gliders should be converted to twin-engined bombers and displayed at a forward air-field to increase the apparent strength of our sadly-depleted Desert Air Force."[30] The dummies caught the attention of German reconnaissance, and on the night of June 12 the Germans dropped sixty bombs on the dummy position at Fuka. They continued their bombing raids until mid-July.[31]

By the middle of July the Germans had settled into a defensive posture; hence there was little reason to continue the deception. Abeam was called off. "K" Detachment went on to operate dummy planes and gliders for the entirety of the war. Clarke continued to support the existence of the 1st SAS, and in August an actual 1st SAS came into being, in part to give credence to the early deception efforts.[32]

As is often the case with deception, it is difficult to determine Abeam's exact effect on the enemy. It is not known whether the Italians held forces in their rear areas to protect their lines of communication and supplies as Clarke hoped. Nor is it clear whether the Germans altered their strategy in any way after observing the British "aircraft" on the ground. However, the German handbook on the British army for 1941 included the 1st SAS in its list of British formations. Likewise, captured Italian and German documents from May 1942 both ascribed to the 8th Army one parachute battalion.[33] Thus, Clarke's first deception in the Western Desert ought to be viewed as a success. Clarke gained invaluable experience while planning and executing Abeam, and his success at creating his first notional unit encouraged him to continue with his strategy of artificially inflating Britain's strength in the Middle East. By the end of the war, Clarke had invented eight brigades, thirty-two divisions, ten corps, and three armies, all of which he moved around the Middle East in support of his various deceptions.[34]

On February 1, while Clarke was wrapping up Camilla and working on Abeam, he began his next order-of-battle deception—this time with the goal of supplementing Britain's armored strength. From the outbreak of war, Britain's lack of tanks had been a major concern. By February the few tanks left in the 7th Armoured Division, which had fought for eight months straight, were in a dismal state of disrepair. The division was "mechanically exhausted and needed complete overhaul."[35] The 2nd Armoured Division, which arrived in January, had already sent two regiments to the 7th Armoured. When the call came to support Greece, the 2nd Armoured lost one of its two armored brigade groups. As a result, the entire 2nd Armoured Division in Cyrenaica consisted of only one armored brigade group. To make matters worse, the remaining tanks were in a poor state mechanically, and their tracks were worn.[36] At the time there was no chance of receiving armored reinforcements in the Middle East.

To create the impression of greater armored strength, Clarke began working on the 10th Armoured Division Plan. The opportunity to launch the deception arose with the arrival in Egypt of the 3rd Indian Motor Brigade from India. Clarke's plan was to make the enemy believe that the Indian brigade was part of the newly formed 10th Armoured Division. The War Diary records that the "usual steps were taken, such as rumours and planted documents etc., to establish the presence of the notional Division in EGYPT during February."[37] Clarke put the notional 10th Armoured Division to use to threaten the enemy's L of C in April.[38]

In February 1941 the situation in the Mediterranean and Middle East took a devastating turn. Although Hitler had initially been unconcerned with the war in the Mediterranean and Middle East, the wholesale defeat of the Italian Tenth Army raised grave concerns among the German military leadership. The naval staff argued that the "Italian defeat removed at a stroke the threat to Egypt and hence to Britain's entire position in the Eastern Mediterranean"; Britain, therefore, was now in a position to "send strong forces from Egypt to Greece—in fact the process had already begun."[39]

According to General Erwin Rommel, to address the "highly critical situation with our Italian allies, two German divisions—one light and one panzer— were to be sent to Libya to their help."[40] Rommel was appointed as the commander of the German Afrika Korps; he arrived at Tripoli on February 12. Since Rodolfo Graziani was the commander in chief of the forces in Libya, Rommel was under orders to submit to his command (Graziani left Tripoli on February 11 and officially resigned March 25; thereafter, Rommel reported to his replacement, General Italo Gariboldi). Ironically, his arrival coincided with Churchill's order to Wavell to begin preparations to send "all available forces" to assist Greece.[41] The first troops of the Afrika Korps reached Libya two days behind their commander.

Although the British expected the Germans to come to Italy's aid, the actual presence of Germans in the desert came as a surprise to the British. Intelligence sources learned in January that German forces had arrived in Italy, but their ultimate destination was unknown. The Foreign Office eventually concluded that the Germans were uninterested in Libya. By January the British knew that the Luftwaffe was operating in Libya, but they erroneously assumed that the army was not going to follow. In February new information revealed concentrations of German troops in southern Italy and Sicily, but again, their objective was unclear. Finally, on February 9, intelligence sources learned of convoys going to Tripoli, but it was uncertain whether they were German convoys.[42] Some leaders in London concluded that the convoys were actually there to assist the Italian evacuation from Tripoli.[43] Because the British lacked the planes to conduct thorough reconnaissance of the area and their intelligence was inadequate, they were unable to gather any definite information regarding Germany's intentions in the Mediterranean and Middle East.

In late February reports began trickling in that reconnaissance planes had spotted German vehicles near El Agheila. Evidence continued to flood in, and by the end of February the British believed the Germans had established a headquarters in Libya. On March 8 Wavell correctly guessed that the Germans' commander was Rommel, but the size of his forces remained unknown.[44]

Wavell had assumed that the Germans would eventually join Italy, yet he was surprised to learn that they had already arrived in Africa. He recorded,

Though unconfirmed reports had been received from time to time of the preparation of German troops for dispatch to Libya and their progress via Italy and Sicily, no definite information to justify our expecting the presence of German troops in Africa had been received up to the middle of February. Our intelligence from Italy was meagre in the extreme and usually unreliable; nor were sufficient long range aircraft available for more than a very occasional reconnaissance of shipping in Italian harbors or in Tripoli. From North Africa itself our intelligence reports were practically none, since no service of agents had been established there during the period before Italy came into the war nor was it possible now to establish one. We were thus completely in the dark as to the possibility of German formations being sent to Libya, and on the whole the balance of our information was against any such troops having been sent or being on their way to Libya. Actually, the landing of German Light Armoured Division at Tripoli had begun early in February.[45]

Based on what little information could be gathered on the German buildup and what Wavell knew of the difficulties of supply over such vast areas of desert, the British general guessed that Rommel would not be in a position to launch a strong offensive until May at the earliest. Because British forces were committed to defend Greece, reinforcing the Western Desert force was not an option. Yet, the commander in chief believed that Rommel would be unable to advance until May, so he decided that Cyrenaica could be held with only one weak armored division and one infantry division. The existing forces were untrained and poorly equipped, but Wavell fully intended to send trained reinforcements to Cyrenaica before Rommel struck.[46]

As it so happened, Rommel had a different plan. His intelligence on British strength was highly accurate, so he knew that the British forces in Cyrenaica had been significantly reduced owing to their involvement in the Greek operation. Wavell had, all total, sent the 1st Armoured Brigade, the New Zealand Division, and the 6th Australian Division to Greece, which totaled 50,000 men and 8,000 vehicles.[47] In Churchill's own words, these groups "were all fully equipped at the expense of other formations in the Middle East."[48] As a result, Wavell had only the skeleton 2nd Armoured Division and the 9th Australian Division to defend the whole of Cyrenaica.[49]

Rommel knew that even if the British wanted to, they did not possess the strength to launch an offensive; they would similarly be hard pressed to mount a successful defense. According to Churchill, "We were inferior in the air; and our armour . . . was utterly inadequate, as was the training and equipment of the troops west of Tobruk."[50] Rommel was bold and hoped to take advantage of the weakness of the British before they had the opportunity to strengthen their positions. Contrary to his orders from Berlin, Rommel decided to seize the opportunity and take the offensive as early as possible.[51]

On March 24 Rommel sent his troops forward to take El Agheila. General P. Neame, who had replaced General O'Connor as head of the Cyrenaica Command, had orders from Wavell to retreat if attacked in force. The British could not afford to lose what little fighting power they had left, and there was no prospect of reinforcement until at least May; therefore, it made more sense to withdraw than to fight a useless defensive action that could result in a total loss.[52] When Rommel struck at El Agheila, the British fell back. Capitalizing on the British withdrawal, Rommel sent his troops ahead to Mersa Brega, which they took on March 31. Because of the success of the first two minor operations and intelligence reports revealing that the British had continued the retreat, Rommel decided to stage a large-scale offensive to capture Cyrenaica. Rommel claims that the British decision to retreat was based on Britain's overestimation of the size of his forces, for which he credits his own deception efforts—the use of dummy tanks.[53]

Throughout April Rommel continued his forward momentum. On April 2 the Germans took Agedabia; they captured Benghazi on April 4. Rommel's advance, albeit successful, angered General Gariboldi, who ordered Rommel to discontinue the offensive. Rommel writes that Gariboldi "berated me violently, principally because our operations were in direct contradiction to orders from Rome."[54] In a letter to his wife dated April 3, 1941, Rommel wrote, "We've been attacking since the 31st with dazzling success. There'll be consternation amongst our masters in Tripoli and Rome, perhaps Berlin too. I took the risk against all orders and instructions because the opportunity seemed favourable. No doubt it will all be pronounced good later and they'll all say they'd have done exactly the same in my place. We've already reached our first objective, which we weren't supposed to get to until the end of May. The British are falling over each other to get away."[55] As Rommel predicted, the German High Command was pleased with his success and encouraged him to continue. Despite Italian displeasure, Rommel ordered the Afrika Korps to press on.

The Germans took Derna next and captured Generals Neame and O'Connor on April 7. They reached Bardia and Sollum by the middle of the month and captured Halfaya Pass on April 26. In the meantime, the British repulsed two separate German efforts to take Tobruk, which thus remained in Britain's possession, although completely surrounded. After Rommel's second attempt to take Tobruk failed on May 4, General Friedrich Paulus advised Rommel not to attempt to capture Tobruk again unless the British abandoned the city on their own.[56] Paulus' message, which stated that the exhausted German troops were in a "precarious logistical situation," and should not advance beyond Bardia-Sollum until the 15th Panzer Division arrived, was sent to Berlin by wireless and intercepted by the British.[57]

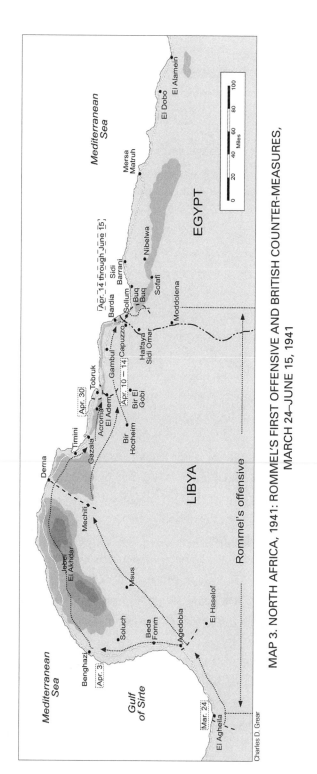

MAP 3. NORTH AFRICA, 1941: ROMMEL'S FIRST OFFENSIVE AND BRITISH COUNTER-MEASURES,
MARCH 24–JUNE 15, 1941

Charles D. Grear

With the situation deteriorating at an alarming rate, the need for deception—for anything that could give the British an advantage—became urgent. On March 30 Wavell had ordered Clarke to develop a deception plan to assist against Rommel. Plan A-R (anti-Rommel) became Clarke's first attempt at strategic deception after Camilla.

Clarke's goal was to convince the Germans that the British were preparing to attack their L of C between Tripoli and El Agheila and that armored reinforcements were en route to Cyrenaica. Clarke's preparations were complete on April 4, and the story was passed over to the enemy intelligence services in "devious form."[58]

The "A" Force Narrative War Diary lists the various stories the British intended to feed the enemy: First, the British were going to stage a landing between Tripoli and Benghazi, using Glen transport ships, aimed at destroying the German and Italian L of C. Second, the (notional) 1st SAS was preparing an airborne assault on the enemy L of C in Libya from a temporary base in Crete. Third, the (notional) 10th Armoured Division was moving into Cyrenaica to attempt a flank attack of the enemy's L of C. Next, Free French troops from French Equatorial Africa were planning to attack the L of C from the south. Finally, to help pass the story, the British intended to provide verifiable information that additional tank reinforcements were arriving from Nigeria. This last bit of information was important because, in all likelihood, the enemy intelligence services would know that tank reinforcements had not arrived via the Mediterranean or around the Cape of Good Hope, so Clarke had to provide a plausible land route for the notional reinforcements to travel.[59] In April, as the Germans approached Mersa Matruh, Wavell added an additional story to Plan A-R—that the British had laid extensive minefields to the south and southwest of Mersa Matruh that could be electronically operated.[60]

Before the British could supply physical evidence to support the ruse, they began feeding the stories to the enemy through established Allied networks. The deception was passed through the following means and channels: "an elaborate rumour campaign in EGYPT, by planted leakages in ATHENS and ISTANBUL, by deliberate indiscretions of officers in PALESTINE and at General DE GAULLE's Headquarters in WEST AFRICA, and by the same agent in touch with the Japanese circles in EGYPT who had helped us with CAMILLA and other plans. LONDON and LISBON were also asked to help with 'leakages', and finally discreet use was made of the Press."[61] In addition, the British issued a report based on the arrival in Egypt of a U.S. tank corps, sent to instruct the British on the latest American armored technology. It included a photograph of a tank transporter, which, as it turned out, was the only one on the entire continent of Africa. The basis of the report was true, but greatly exaggerated, and published with American permission.[62]

As part of the effort to disseminate false information to the enemy, Clarke wrote numerous letters and reports containing deceptive information. For example, he drafted a description, supposedly based on a report by a French staff officer to General Charles de Gaulle, of the new British tanks, specially designed for desert conditions, being transported from Nigeria to Fort Lamy. According to the report, the French officer saw the tanks himself and was particularly impressed because they were fitted with air-conditioning devices that would allow them to function in the extreme heat of the summer. The detailed report was circulated in Lisbon, among General de Gaulle's staff, and to select British officers in Cairo. Clarke used the same technique to indicate the arrival of reinforcements, the movement of armored divisions, and the training of RAF pilots using new American aircraft.[63] In all these efforts, Clarke paid meticulous attention to every aspect of his deception plans, micromanaging the project from beginning to end.

Feeding the enemy the story was only the first challenge of the deception; the second was to provide actual proof. Incidentally, Plan A-R represented Clarke's second attempt to provide physical support to a deception plan.[64] The main physical proof came by way of the movement of Glen ships from Port Said to Suda Bay. Accordingly, Clarke issued the following order: "To give colour to the idea of a sea-borne attack on the LIBYAN coast, move the S.S. Bde. in their GLEN ships to SUDA BAY. The moment they sail an immediate threat is created, as a leak through PORT SAID is practically certain."[65] Clarke correctly surmised that the move would not go unnoticed. The Japanese secretary of the consulate at Port Said happened to travel to Cairo on April 14 and promptly informed his superior that the Glen ships had left the port and sailed into the Mediterranean on April 13.[66]

Additionally, as they had for the Abeam deception, the British placed dummy gliders and twin-engine bombers supposedly belonging to the 1st SAS at airfields where they were considered likely to be spotted by German reconnaissance.

The trick worked, and the Germans dutifully bombed the dummies.[67] The only other visible evidence was in the form of the photographs of the new American tank transporters being used in the desert. Otherwise, little physical support could be provided.

It is doubtful that Plan A-R succeeded in convincing the Germans that the British could mount a serious assault against their L of C. First, the German advance through Cyrenaica was incredibly swift, moving more quickly than the deception team could fabricate the threat. By mid-April Rommel had already reached Sollum and Halfaya, barely giving the deception time to become effective. Second, the Germans had excellent intelligence on British positions and strength, and Rommel tended to ignore any evidence that ran counter to his trusted intelligence reports.[68] In addition, the objectives of the deception plan were limited. By Clarke's own admission, Plan A-R "had no clear-cut strategic object beyond diverting the attention and resources of the Germans from an advance in strength on MERSA MATRUH."[69] According to Clarke, Plan A-R was more a war of nerves plan than a true strategic deception plan. Thus, it was largely intended to lessen the power of the offensive directed at the British, not to prevent it.

It does not appear, therefore, that Plan A-R succeeded in deceiving the Germans or persuading them to alter their strategy in any way.[70] Given the hastiness with which Clarke had to prepare the operation, the swiftness of the German advance, and the superiority of German intelligence, Clarke could not have done much more. Nonetheless, the effort did provide Clarke with another opportunity to experiment with deception and learn from the process.

By early April Clarke was simultaneously, and single-handedly, working on three deception plans for the Western Desert and two focused on Rhodes (Byng Boys Scheme and Plan Dolphin).[71] Although Clarke's early deceptions had not all met with tremendous success, he had still managed to demonstrate that deception could play a vital role in the war effort. Like any other weapon of war, deception could be perfected to achieve the maximum results with the greatest benefit to the British armed forces. As it then stood, however, Clarke had too many responsibilities for one person to efficiently handle alone, especially given that the British troops were being forced to retreat and facing potential destruction at the hands of the Germans in North Africa. If Clarke had access to greater resources and had help in planning and implementing his ruses, deception could play an even greater role in the war—potentially a decisive role. To that end, "A" Force was granted an official war establishment on April 7, 1941, and Clarke was assigned a staff of two officers and ten other ranks.[72] With the official establishment of "A" Force, Clarke was able to expand the scope of his work and increase his efforts to make a greater contribution to the Allied struggle.

In late April Clarke traveled, incognito, to Turkey.[73] His purpose was three-fold. First, he intended to plant evidence of Plan A-R on German intelligence officials in the region. Second, he hoped to establish additional channels through which he could pass deceptive information to the enemy. Clarke attached great significance to his networks and channels in neutral countries. He explains that agents in "neutral countries are extremely useful. . . . The quickest way and surest way of giving information to the enmy [*sic*] is to let it be known in an important neutral centre. What is whispered in LISBON or CONSTANTINOPLE is known in the AXIS Capitals within a few hours."[74] Finally, assuming his role as head of MI9, Clarke worked to set up an organization in Turkey to facilitate the recovery and return of British personnel captured in the Balkans.[75]

The expansion of the deception organization, as well as Clarke's determined efforts to extend "A" Force's influence to neutral lands, came at an ideal time. In the spring of 1941 Wavell faced numerous threats resulting in action on multiple fronts, which required increased military and deception efforts.[76] Clarke wrote, "The spring of 1941 was a bad time for General Wavell's armies, and the work of 'A' Force increased alarmingly. The fall of GREECE and CRETE left thousands of British and Dominion troops to be contacted by the MI.9 organization, while ROMMEL's appearance in strength on the borders of CYRENAICA, with the ominous growth of a threat against CYPRUS, necessitated urgent strategic plans."[77] In the Western Desert, Rommel's forces had taken Cyrenaica and set up defensive positions as far forward as Halfaya, which posed a grave threat to the British in Egypt. In East Africa, British forces, although still engaged in combat against the Italians, were in the final phases of liberating Ethiopia.

In the Balkans, the situation was dire. The Germans invaded Yugoslavia and Greece on April 6. As Playfair notes, for the British the Greek campaign was "from start to finish a withdrawal."[78] The evacuation began during the night of April 24 and continued until May 1.[79] A large portion of evacuated forces was relocated to Crete, so the situation took another unfortunate turn when the Germans attacked Crete on May 20. Churchill recorded that nothing "like it had ever been seen before. It was the first large-scale air-borne attack in the annals of war."[80] Incidentally, owing to a hefty casualty toll amounting to 6,453 paratroopers killed, wounded, and missing, it was also Germany's last airborne attack of the war.[81] By May 31 the British had carried out yet another evacuation. All told, the British evacuated 50,732 troops from Greece and approximately 18,000 from Crete, but suffered more than 29,500 casualties between the two campaigns; as many as 21,600 troops were left behind. In addition, the British lost much of their equipment, including almost every Hurricane sent to Greece.[82]

The situation in the Middle East proper was equally discouraging, although the fighting there ended favorably for Britain. In Iraq, Wavell had to contend with a pro-German coup d'état led by Rashid Ali, who assumed control of Iraq after ousting the British regent. Because Wavell had too few troops to spare, Indian troops, largely provided by General Claude Auchinleck, the commander in chief of India, engaged the pro-German Iraqis from May 2 until May 30.[83] Some British soldiers independently, and successfully, used deception to greatly exaggerate the size of their forces to frighten the opposing Iraqis.[84] Facing defeat, Rashid Ali fled to Persia, ending the menace of a pro-Axis Iraq.[85]

Meanwhile, German involvement in Syria was increasing, as was the presence of the Luftwaffe, posing a significant threat to Britain's position in the Middle East and, ultimately, its control over the Suez Canal.[86] Wavell's forces were already stretched too thin, and thus he was reluctant to provide substantial forces for an operation in Syria. Under direct orders from London, however, he began preparing for a minor offensive.[87] He employed Clarke to help lessen the vigilance of the Vichy troops stationed in Syria so that British troops from Palestine could enter Syria without meeting serious resistance.[88] With the assistance of Free French forces, the British commenced fighting on June 8. The battle lasted until July 12. At the conclusion of the campaign, Syria was transferred to Allied control.[89] Churchill explained the strategic value of the Iraqi and Syrian campaigns as follows: "The successful campaigns in Syria and Iraq greatly improved our strategical position in the Middle East. It closed the door to any further attempt at enemy penetration eastward from the Mediterranean, moved our defence of the Suez Canal northward by 250 miles, and relieved Turkey of anxiety for her southern frontier."[90]

For Wavell, the first half of 1941 brought one daunting challenge after another. The task of simultaneously organizing so many diverse operations presented the greatest difficulty for the commander in chief and most certainly tested his leadership abilities. Unfortunately for Wavell, because he was obligated to defend such a vast theater, he had little choice but to spread his forces dangerously thin. As a result, he was unable to concentrate his forces in strength in any one area and was therefore ill-prepared to meet the most serious threat posed by Rommel in the Western Desert.

Rommel's eastward advance to Egypt had stopped in late April, yet the British did not have the luxury of sitting idle. Wavell had no choice but to strike the Germans, regardless of whether his own forces were ready for combat. In April Wavell learned that the German 15th Panzer Division had arrived in Tripoli. Aware of Paulus' intercepted telegram to Berlin about the enemy's reduced strength, Wavell hoped to hit the Germans while they were still exhausted from the two unsuccessful assaults on Tobruk, and before the 15th Panzer Division could arrive in full force and be readied for action.

On May 15 Wavell launched Operation Brevity. The goal of Brevity was to retake the region of Bardia-Sollum and advance the forward line so that the British would be in a better position to relieve Tobruk when Wavell commenced his large-scale offensive, Battleaxe, in June. Brevity failed in its objective, however. It succeeded only in temporarily retaking the Halfaya Pass, which the Germans regained control of on May 27. As Churchill stated, the "opportunity of defeating Rommel before he could be reinforced has passed."[91]

According to F. H. Hinsley, Brevity failed for many reasons. First, the Germans had better tanks and antitank guns, yet British intelligence had given no indication of the superiority of German equipment. Second, British intelligence was unable to keep up with the pace of the battle. Information was relayed too slowly and was irrelevant by the time that it reached headquarters. Similarly, by the time intelligence had passed from headquarters to the battlefield, it was no longer of any use to the commanders in the field. Third, German intelligence was clearly more efficient. Before the battle, Rommel's intelligence sources intercepted British wireless messages that revealed Britain's intention to go on the offensive; thus, surprise was elusive.[92] Armed with such valuable information, Rommel moved his armored reinforcements to the front, and this maneuver went entirely undetected by British intelligence and aerial reconnaissance.[93] Regardless of its causes, the failure of the campaign was costly. There were 160 casualties and the loss of many tanks—losses the British could hardly afford.[94]

Despite the setback, Wavell continued preparations for Battleaxe. The objective of Battleaxe was the wholesale defeat of the Germans in the Western Desert. This time, however, Wavell was able to employ greater numbers of tanks. When the Germans advanced through Cyrenaica in April, the horrible state of the 7th Armoured Division became impossible to ignore. Churchill decided to take a major risk and send a convoy through the Mediterranean to Alexandria to help rebuild the Western Desert forces. The Tiger convoy, as it was known, carried 295 tanks and 53 Hurricanes. One of the ships was sunk, resulting in the loss of 57 tanks and 10 Hurricanes, yet the remainder of the convoy, totaling 238 tanks and 43 Hurricanes, arrived intact at Alexandria on May 12. The next challenge was to train the tank crews and rebuild the depleted 7th Armoured Division.

Under pressure from Churchill to begin an offensive in the Western Desert, Wavell ordered preparations for Operation Battleaxe to begin on May 28. But because the newly arrived tank crews had to be organized and trained and many of the tanks arrived in poor working order, Wavell was unable to commence the offensive until June 15. This delay clearly upset Churchill, who feared that it would allow the Germans too much time to regroup and reinforce their frontline positions. Harold Raugh comments that the "Prime Minister should have known that with the Battle for Crete in full fury, with Wavell's limited resources being further dispersed in Iraq, and while prodding the General to send a sizeable force to Syria, an offensive in the Western Desert was not possible."[95] In complete disregard for the general's other responsibilities, all of them equally pressing, Churchill instructed Wavell to carry out the offensive and made it fully known that the commander in chief's career in the Middle East depended on the favorable outcome of the campaign.[96]

Wavell himself doubted that the operation would succeed. On the same day that he ordered his forces to begin preparing for Battleaxe, he confided in Sir John Dill, the chief of the Imperial General Staff (CIGS), "I think it is right to inform you that the measure of success which will attend this operation is in my opinion doubtful."[97] Wavell's comment might seem pessimistic given the timely arrival of the needed armored reinforcements, but his doubt becomes clear when considered in light of the previous offensive. Operation Brevity revealed that Britain's tanks were inferior to German armor and helpless against the powerful German antitank guns. The Matilda I tank, which had performed so well against the Italians, proved far too slow against the Germans. Wavell was

understandably afraid that his forces might not fare well in the upcoming campaign. In addition, the persistence of mechanical difficulties meant that not all
the tanks of the Tiger convoy, or the "tiger cubs" as Churchill and Wavell called
them, would be ready for action by June 15.[98]

On the deception end of the planning, little could be done because there
was insufficient time to put together a concerted effort to mislead the enemy.
The only thing Clarke could do was attempt to explain the forward movement
of troops that German aerial reconnaissance was certain to observe. To that end,
Clarke put out the following story: "British Military circles are anxious about the
safety of the WESTERN DESERT while operations are in progress in SYRIA.
They are particularly nervous about their forward dumps in the SIDI BARANI
area, so much so that a reserve tank unit has been sent up there from EGYPT to
guard against possible raids."[99] Although great efforts were made to quickly convey the story to the Germans, German intelligence "appreciated the imminence
of 'BATTLEAXE'" as early as June 11, only three days after the deception story
was released. Clarke justifiably credits the failure of the deception effort to the
"lack of time for implementation." [100]

Operation Battleaxe began on June 15. The British attacked the German
positions at three points: Halfaya, Capuzzo, and Hafid Ridge. While the British
were beaten back at Halfaya and held at Hafid Ridge, they did manage to break
through the German line at Capuzzo. On the sixteenth, the Germans counterattacked at Capuzzo, but the British repulsed the attacks and made it to Sollum.[101]
In a complete reversal of fortunes, the battle momentum shifted in Germany's
favor on the seventeenth. Owing to highly accurate German intelligence reports,
Rommel knew of Britain's plans and supply troubles. Rommel wrote,

> In wireless messages which we intercepted they described their position as
> very serious. The commander of the 7th Armoured Division sent a request
> to the Commander-in-Chief of the desert force to come to his headquar-
> ters. It sounded suspiciously as though the British commander no longer
> felt himself capable of handling the situation. It being now obvious that
> in their present bewildered state the British would not start anything for
> the time being, I decided to pull the net tight by going on to Halfaya. . . .
> The British were seriously in trouble over petrol and ammunition and
> I hoped to be able to force them into a stand-up fight and destroy their
> whole force.[102]

On the morning of the seventeenth, Rommel ordered his forces to attack at 4:30 a.m.—the exact same time he expected the British to attack. The British found themselves in a position where they could easily be cut off, so they began to pull back. With the situation confused and deteriorating quickly, Wavell ordered a complete withdrawal.[103]

As Wavell feared, Battleaxe failed. There were many reasons for the failure of the offensive. For one, it was planned too hastily and launched before the forces were sufficiently trained. Also, there was a complete breakdown of communication once the battle commenced. The British system of communication was generally poor and resulted in chaos on the battlefield. The Germans, in stark contrast, had a highly effective system for maintaining communication on the battlefield. They converted tanks into mobile command posts, each equipped with an ultra-shortwave radio, for the divisional commanders. Closely behind the command post tank was another tank used specifically to maintain contact with headquarters and reconnaissance units.[104] By this method, the Germans avoided the loss of communication in the midst of battle and the subsequent confusion that debilitated the British units.

British intelligence was also inefficient and failed to detect the arrival of German armored reinforcements in the days prior to the offensive. Based on the intelligence at his disposal, for example, Wavell expected to encounter a hundred German tanks; in reality, he faced at least twice that number. At the same time, German intelligence was highly effective and provided Rommel with a detailed picture of the coming offensive, along with enough time to make necessary adjustments.[105]

Probably the greatest reason for Britain's defeat was the weakness of its armored units—namely, the overall inferiority of its armor and the absence of a sound strategy for armored warfare. In his dispatch to London, Wavell explained that the cause of the "failure was undoubtedly the difficulty in combining the action of cruiser 'I' tanks, the cramping effect on manoeuvre of having only two regiments in each armoured brigade and the lack of training in the 7th Armoured Division."[106] Rommel concluded that the quality of Britain's armor was its greatest weakness. He wrote that Wavell "was put at a great disadvantage by the slow speed of his heavy infantry tanks, which prevented him from reacting quickly enough to the moves of our faster vehicles. Hence the slow speed of the bulk of his armour was his soft spot, which we could seek to exploit tactfully."[107]

David French claims that the greatest problem for the British was that they did not understand German armored strategy and failed to develop a combined arms doctrine of their own; therefore, they misused their tanks in battle and completely threw away any advantage they may have had going into the fight. French points out that the British tried to fight tank-to-tank battles, whereas the Germans sought to avoid destructive armored engagements. The Germans held the position that the "best antidote to the tank was not another tank, but an anti-tank gun."[108] To that end, the Germans used their 50 mm and 80 mm antitank guns to steadily pick the British tanks off piecemeal, resulting in great loss to Britain's armored units.

Playfair proposes yet another explanation for Britain's problems. He lays the blame directly on Britain's interwar policy. Playfair contends, "The fundamental cause of the troubles of the British in the armoured field was that between the wars they had allowed research and experiment on their own invention the tank, and also its manufacture, to dwindle almost to nothing. The main reasons for this state of affairs were financial stringency and a policy which for many years assumed that a major war was not to be expected."[109] In stark contrast, the Germans placed considerable emphasis on the tank during the interwar period. They had also developed a sound strategy for effectively employing their tanks in battle and neutralizing the strength of the enemy's armor.[110]

Even though the offensive failed to achieve its objective, Wavell did the best he could with the resources at his disposal. Perhaps ironically, Rommel had high praise for Wavell as a commander. He concluded, "Wavell's strategic planning of this offensive had been excellent. What distinguished him from other British army commanders was his great and well-balanced strategic courage, which permitted him to concentrate his forces regardless of his opponent's possible moves."[111]

Churchill most certainly did not share Rommel's praise for the commander in chief. The prime minister was extremely disappointed with the failure of Battleaxe. Churchill had hoped that the tiger cubs would play a decisive role in the upcoming offensive and that the risk he had taken would help produce a decisive British victory and German defeat. For the prime minister, the failure of Battleaxe was a bitter blow. He wrote, "Success in the Desert would have meant the destruction of Rommel's audacious force. Tobruk would have been relieved, and the enemy's retreat might well have carried him back beyond Benghazi as fast as he had come. It was for this supreme object, as I judged it, that all perils of 'Tiger' had been dared."[112] Churchill was even more disappointed with Wavell's leadership and the way he had conducted the war in the Middle East. Furthermore, he questioned whether Wavell possessed the energy and creativity for the job. He recalled, "At home we had the feeling that Wavell was a tired man. It might well be said that we had ridden the willing horse to a standstill. The extraordinary convergence of five or six different theatres, with their ups and downs, especially downs, upon a single Commander-in-Chief constituted a strain to which few soldiers have been subjected."[113] As a result, Churchill decided to relieve Wavell of his command.

The decision was made that General Claude Auchinleck, nicknamed "The Auk," who had impressed Churchill with his willingness to send forces to help during the crisis in Iraq, would become the new commander in chief of the Middle East. Wavell was, in turn, to assume Auchinleck's position as commander in chief of India. The transition took place on July 5, 1941. Upon his arrival in the Middle East, Auchinleck found the situation to be generally favorable. He concluded, "I found the general position incomparably better than it had been a year earlier on the collapse of France. The improvement was entirely due to the energy of my predecessor, General Sir Archibald Wavell, and to his vigour in seeking out the enemy wherever he was to be found."[114]

Even though Auchinleck was pleased with Wavell's efforts, he also realized that he had an overwhelming challenge on his hands. Germany's occupation of Greece and Crete, and more important, the close proximity of the Luftwaffe, threatened Britain's supply routes and L of C from the north. The German presence also greatly restricted the movement of the British fleet in the Mediterranean. The British faced an additional threat from Libya as a result of Rommel's firm hold on Cyrenaica. Yet Auchinleck acknowledged that Wavell was responsible for reducing the number of threats facing the British and for ultimately keeping the British effort in the Middle East alive. The new commander in chief's appreciation for his predecessor's accomplishments is clearly seen in the following: "General Wavell's campaigns in Libya, Eritrea, Abyssinia, Greece, Crete, Iraq, and Syria had followed each other with such bewildering rapidity and had been undertaken with such inadequate forces and equipment that a considerable degree of disorganisation in the Army as a whole was inevitable." He continued, "In no sense do I wish to infer that I found an unsatisfactory situation on my arrival—far from it. Not only was I greatly impressed by the solid foundations laid by my predecessor, but I was also able to better appreciate the vastness of the problems with which he had been confronted and the greatness of his achievements, in a command in which some 40 different languages are spoken by British and Allied Forces."[115] It must also be remembered that everything Wavell accomplished occurred in just over one year's time.

Wavell's achievements in the Middle East were truly remarkable. With minimal supplies and little chance of receiving reinforcements, he managed to avoid a complete collapse of the British war effort. What is even more astonishing is that he did so while fighting a numerically superior Italian army and a technically superior German army. In just over a year he had won decisive victories against the Italians in East Africa and the Italian Tenth Army in Libya, as well as helped stabilize the potentially threatening state of affairs in Iraq and Syria.

Perhaps one of Wavell's greatest accomplishments was recognizing the necessity and usefulness of deception in warfare. Wavell was the first Allied commander to use deception in the Second World War, and he clearly realized its potential to aid to the overall war effort. It is solely because of Wavell that Clarke came to the Middle East and established "A" Force; therefore, he must share the credit for the tremendous achievements of deception throughout the course of the war. Wavell's deception efforts were not limited to the Middle East either. After he left the Middle East command to assume his post in India, he established a comparable deception agency under the leadership of General Peter Fleming. From beginning to end, Wavell was a commander of great vision, and that alone sets him apart from many of his contemporaries.

While the first half of 1941 presented many challenges for the British army in the Western Desert, it posed similar difficulties for Clarke and his deception team. Clarke's goal was to use deception to induce the enemy to make poor decisions, thus giving Britain the advantage. This task was extremely challenging in the conditions of early 1941. With the British on the defensive and the army crumbling under the weight of the powerful German-led advances, Clarke had little time to plan, prepare, and execute adequate deception plans. He was also, like Wavell, forced to meet threats throughout the entire Middle East and Balkans and was consequently unable to focus exclusively on the German threat in the Western Desert.

Where Clarke met with considerable success was in the development of his first order-of-battle deceptions. The creation of the 1st SAS and the 10th Armoured Division allowed the British to artificially inflate their strength. Captured documents indicated that the enemy believed in the existence of the phantom units; thus, Clarke succeeded. The order-of-battle deception was in its formative phase, but it proved worthwhile, and these initial successes persuaded Clarke that he should continue to work on creating notional units. In fact, order-of-battle deception became the foundation of Clarke's work. Clarke wrote, "I cannot stress the building up of the false Order of Battle. This must be the first task of all Deception staff, and it must go on unceasingly."[116] In 1942, having benefited from the experiences of his first experimental year, Clarke made significant strides toward expanding Britain's bogus order of battle.

For Clarke and the "A" Force organization, the second half of 1941 provided a more favorable environment for deception. The Germans halted their advance and settled down defensively. This halt allowed Clarke and his team time to work on more sophisticated deception plans. In addition, British cryptographers managed to break the German Army Enigma in September 1941. Although the messages were not regularly read until mid-1942, increased access to intelligence greatly facilitated the work of the deception team. Advances in wireless technology also allowed Clarke to fully employ his first and most successful double agent, Cheese. The Cheese network came to play a major role in Clarke's deception efforts during the last half of 1941 and continued throughout the war.

Fortunately for Clarke and his team, General Auchinleck fully supported the work of the deception planners.[117] As a result, by the end of 1941 "A" Force began achieving its first major deception coups. In addition, the "A" Force organization continued to develop into a well-functioning agency, although there would be some organizational bumps along the way. Clarke masterfully nurtured "A" Force and brought in the most qualified and creative men to assist with his plans. As "A" Force expanded, he continued to cultivate excellent relationships with other agencies and deceptive bodies in the Middle East, such as G(CAM), and that was in part the key to his success. The end of 1941 saw a fresh wave of deception coups, so that by 1942 the value of deception could no longer be disputed.

–5–

Cruising Along during the
Last Half of 1941

The summer of 1941 saw significant changes to Britain's position in the Middle East, mostly in its favor. First of all, the pace of the war finally slowed. The Axis forces settled into a defensive position that gave the British time to study German strategy, review and revise their own, and plan for a fall offensive (Crusader).[1] The lull also provided Britain the opportunity to rebuild its battered forces after the failure of Operation Battleaxe. Second, the change of leadership from General Archibald Wavell to General Claude Auchinleck brought a fresh approach to the war in the Middle East and a sense of renewed energy to the battlefield.

Similarly, the elimination of the threats emanating from Iraq, Syria, and East Africa had many positive effects: the British could devote greater attention to the Western Desert, vast quantities of troops and matériel were freed for use, and perhaps of greatest consequence, the way was paved for increased shipping to reach the desert from Britain, the Dominions, and at long last, the United States. After the British defeated the Italians in East Africa and the Red Sea was no longer classified as a combat zone, the Americans began sending large quantities of equipment and supplies to the British forces in Africa. The influx of provisions, especially from the United States, finally reversed Britain's desperate supply situation and allowed its forces to build a reserve.

As for deception, "A" Force took advantage of the temporary lull in fighting and experienced its own changes during the summer of 1941. First, Dudley

Clarke and his team benefited tremendously from the calm. The enemy halt and greater access to resources gave Clarke the time and supplies he needed to devise more elaborate deceptions. Second, "A" Force began to work with its first double agent, known as Cheese. The Cheese network, officially run by SIME, came to play a pivotal role in Clarke's deception campaign to cover the upcoming Crusader offensive. Finally, "A" Force saw some modifications to its organizational structure during the summer, although the restructuring proved to be temporary.

For the most part, the changes brought tremendous relief to the British in the Middle East. For the first time since the war began, the flow of supplies was steady and the outlook generally optimistic. In addition, for the first time since the Germans joined the fight in Africa, the British enjoyed some breathing room without having to fear that a powerful enemy offensive loomed on the horizon. Therefore, British morale was high, and the military grew stronger.

When General Auchinleck assumed command of the Middle East theater, Winston Churchill expressed confidence in the new leadership, but he was soon disappointed. He wrote, "I started my relations with our new Commander-in-Chief in high hopes, but an exchange of telegrams soon made it clear that there were serious divergences of views and values between us."[2] As a result of their disagreements, Churchill had immediate misgivings about his selection for leadership in the Middle East.

Churchill had specifically hoped that Auchinleck would act quickly and decisively against the German and Italian forces in Libya. Although Operation Battleaxe had failed in its objectives to remove the enemy from Cyrenaica and to relieve the siege of Tobruk, the offensive had nonetheless taken its toll on the enemy. The British were well aware that Rommel's forces were exhausted and in need of reinforcements.[3] Given the weakened state of the German and Italian armies, Churchill wanted Auchinleck to apply constant pressure on the enemy.[4] Much to the prime minister's chagrin, the new commander in chief disagreed with that strategy and refused to employ his troops until he thought that they were ready and capable of mounting a successful large-scale offensive.[5] Thus, Auchinleck proved much like his predecessor in his desire to wait until his forces were well-prepared, properly trained, sufficiently acclimated to desert warfare, and well-supplied with a sizable reserve in the rear.

Churchill also clashed with Auchinleck over the deployment of the 50th British Division to Cyprus. The prime minister intended to send the 50th

Division to Egypt, in part to provide needed reinforcements, but also to counter the negative perception that the British sent only non-British troops into battle.[6] Auchinleck, however, ordered the all-British 50th Division to Cyprus instead. Churchill was clearly unhappy with the decision, and he was not the only one to question Auchinleck's move. As Churchill recalled, the Chiefs of Staff were "astonished on military grounds that so strange a use should be made of this magnificent body of men."[7] What Churchill and the Chiefs of Staff must not have realized was that the move was not merely intended to contribute to the strategic defense of the island but also to add life to one of Clarke's ongoing deceptions— the Cyprus Defence Plan.

After Greece and Crete fell to the Germans, in April and May 1941, respectively, Wavell worried that the Germans would set their sights on Cyprus next. Although information now reveals that the Germans never intended to attack Cyprus, there was no way for Wavell to know this at the time. To counter the perceived threat, Wavell ordered Clarke to create the impression that substantial British defensive forces were on the island.[8] At that time, in early June, Cyprus was defended by only 4,000 troops, yet Clarke set out to make it appear as if an entire British division, totaling approximately 20,000 troops, was present on the island. He began on June 8 by sending wireless messages over a signal that was known to be compromised, spreading rumors, and orchestrating leakages of information. Then, Brigadier R. M. Rodwell, who was already stationed on the island, assumed the rank of major general and took over command of the fictitious 7th Division.[9] The British constructed a headquarters building, erected signs around the island, and issued bogus orders pertaining to the notional unit. Furthermore, on June 24 Major Victor Jones' dummy 39th Battalion RTR was transferred to Cyprus to represent the 7th Division's armored component.[10] Finally, the British planted a bogus defense plan for Cyprus in Cairo, complete with a map and fake order of battle.[11]

At the end of July the 50th British Division arrived to help strengthen the defensive forces on the island. The reinforcements increased the total strength to two divisions—one genuine and one notional. Although Churchill disagreed with the orders, the arrival of the 50th Division provided legitimate protection in case of an attack, which at the time was considered to be probable. It also freed Jones' dummy tank unit to return to the Western Desert so that it could participate in deceptive maneuvers in preparation for Operation Crusader.

In July intelligence sources uncovered information to suggest that the Cyprus Defence Plan had worked. Captured documents showed that the enemy, presumably the Germans, estimated Britain's defensive strength at more than 20,000, just as Clarke had intended. In addition, the notional 7th Division was incorporated into the enemy's overall estimation of British strength. The "A" Force Narrative War Diary records that both the Germans and Italians included the imaginary division in the British order of battle until 1944. Similarly, the British discovered copies of both the map displaying nonexistent defenses and the bogus order of battle in December 1941, when they captured an Italian corps headquarters. The Italians had inflated the number of defenses on Cyprus and listed Britain's strength at 30,000. The War Diary states that the "satisfaction given to 'Adv. HQ "A" Force' . . . by the sight of this lucky seizure can well be imagined."[12]

Throughout the summer and fall of 1941, the staff at "A" Force focused on cultivating the art of deception. That period can now be recognized as one of remarkable progress and innovation, but it was possible only because "A" Force employed the most creative minds. Although the men of "A" Force were military men, they were not conventional soldiers. Clarke recalled that on two occasions traditional officers of the regular army came to work at "A" Force. Although these men could be taught the art of war, they lacked the creativity to grasp the art of deception. Clarke wrote, "What they lacked was just the sheer ability to create, to make something out of nothing, to conceive their own original notion and then to clothe it with realities until eventually it would appear as a living fact. And, since that is precisely what the Deception Staff must do all the time, it follows that the art of creation is an essential attribute in all who are charged with such work."[13] Thus, what made the deception machine function so well was that it was manned by imaginative and resourceful men. Interestingly, many of those who participated in the deceptive activities during the war were not employed by the military during peacetime; instead, they held civilian posts that catered to their creative inclinations. They were professors, novelists, journalists, film-makers, and artists—there was even a master magician in the group. Because of the ingenuity of its inspired staff, "A" Force propelled deception forward to levels never before conceived of.

One of the most notable areas of advancement was in the use of dummy equipment and vehicles. "A" Force placed considerable emphasis on the innovation and development of its dummy units, but especially on its dummy tanks.

The use of dummy tanks, in consequence, became more frequent and increasingly sophisticated.

Most often, the dummies were used to simulate strength in an effort to compensate for British weakness. One such instance occurred immediately after Operation Battleaxe came to an end. After the battle, the 38th RTR, one of three static dummy tank units, moved up to Sofafi to relieve the 7th Armoured Division. In secrecy, the dummies replaced the battered division, allowing it to refit and reorganize after the grueling battle.[14] The employment of dummies helped the British to maintain the facade of strength while providing needed relief to the exhausted 7th Armoured Division.

At times, however, the imitation tanks were used to display weakness for strategic purposes. For example, the British occasionally erected dummies where they could be observed by the enemy. They would then allow the enemy to "discover" that the tanks were merely fakes to induce him to draw the erroneous conclusion that the British were weak in that area. After the enemy had discovered Britain's feigned attempt to conceal its supposed weakness, the British replaced the dummies with real tanks.[15]

The ways in which the dummies were most often used were as follows: to artificially augment a genuine armored unit; to convince the enemy that a new formation had arrived in the region; to replace a genuine tank formation (as was the case at Sofafi after Battleaxe); to represent a reserve when reserves were limited or nonexistent; to cover the movement of an armored unit by drawing the enemy's attention to the decoy force; and to create the impression that the enemy had inflicted greater casualties than he in fact had, causing him to underestimate the size of Britain's remaining armored forces.[16]

As one might imagine, there were many advantages to using the dummy tanks. The most obvious benefit was the ability to give the impression of strength, especially in the early part of the war when the British suffered a desperate shortage of tanks. Because the original static tanks were simple in design—constructed of canvas and piping rendering them lightweight and easy to assemble—they could be employed on short notice with minimal effort.[17] As the war progressed and more sophisticated, mobile dummies—constructed by mounting a tank superstructure on top of a truck—were developed, the use of dummies allowed the British to prepare for battle while drawing the enemy's attention away from the concentration of genuine forces and toward the decoys. Dummies, moreover, enabled the British to manipulate the enemy into acting as they wanted him to act. Thus, they were invaluable to the war effort.

Yet there were challenges to using the dummies as well. The static variety could be used for only short periods before the enemy would notice that they never moved; because it would be highly unusual for a genuine tank to remain stationary for days at a time, the enemy would naturally deduce that static dummies were fakes. The mobile dummies, on the other hand, had greater maintenance requirements and were more difficult and costly to construct.

The deception team faced other problems when trying to ensure the security of the dummies. It was essential that no one other than the deception planners and those who operated the dummies knew of their existence or the details of their employment. In other words, the use of dummies could work only if "no whisper of the scheme" ever reached the enemy.[18] At times, however, it proved arduous to conceal the dummies. The War Diary provides an amusing tale of the difficulties encountered in Palestine while transporting tanks of the 37th RTR by train in July 1941: "First the Palestinian engine-driver expressed voluble surprise at the weight of his trainload of tanks when the engine started to pull out of the siding! And later a faulty lashing caused one 'tank' to blow off its truck en route. The result was a distressing struggle for Sense of Security over Sense of Humour."[19] An additional problem for security was that although the dummies appeared real from the air, they would not deceive the enemy if he was allowed a close inspection.

A further challenge came from the need to provide proof of the tanks' existence for the benefit of aerial reconnaissance. If the enemy spotted a formation of tanks from the air but saw no visible evidence of their movement over the landscape, the deception would be exposed. The "A" Force records explain that it was "essential that when movements are made by dummy tanks, track marks should be left behind, skid marks made apparent, and considerable dust raised."[20] One way to create realistic patterns on the landscape was for the dummies to travel with actual armored units. Another option was to artificially manufacture track marks. In the summer of 1941 "A" Force devised track simulators to create tank tracks in the sand—which allowed them to provide visible proof of the tanks' movements.[21] The invention of track makers, track eliminators, and sun shields (canvas coverings that made tanks look like trucks) is just another example of how resourceful and imaginative the men at "A" Force truly were.[22] These inventions also demonstrate how incredibly thorough they were; the deception team paid attention to every aspect of the deception so that the illusion would always appear absolutely genuine.

On August 14 the organization and control of "A" Force's dummy tank units became more centralized after a war establishment for an "A" Force Depot was approved. The depot was to control and administer all dummy tank units employed in the Middle East. Major Jones was named as the commanding officer of the depot.[23] The formation of the "A" Force Depot was timely because the British were planning a major offensive and the commanding general was eager to deceive the enemy.

In September Auchinleck formed the 8th Army under the command of Major General Alan Cunningham, a man who had distinguished himself in the East African campaign only months earlier.[24] Cunningham was particularly keen on the use of deception, which he himself employed in East Africa.[25] Shortly after his new appointment, Cunningham summoned Major Jones to his head-quarters to discuss opportunities for using Jones' dummies in preparation for Operation Crusader. The meeting resulted in yet another war establishment, this one for the Mobile Dummy Tank Regiment. The regiment, which grew into a dummy brigade in 1942, consisted of two mobile tank regiments, both made up of new Victor Mark IV Cruisers. The two units were to be employed with the 8th Army.[26] Thereafter, the new and more versatile mobile dummies would play an important role in future deception efforts.

Just prior to the launch of preparations for Crusader, the entire deception organization was reorganized. One of Wavell's last acts before he left the Middle East was to separate tactical from strategic deception—essentially creating a division between operations (Ops) and intelligence (I). According to the War Diary, "It was felt that the time had come to try and afford Commanders in the Field similar facilities for practicing deception to those already possessed by the Commander-in-Chief through the medium of the 'A' Force organization."[27]

To that end, a new tactical subsection, known as General Staff Intelligence (deception) (GSI[d]), came into being on July 2, 1941, under the leadership of Major A. D. Wintle. Its orders were to "look after 'measures of the deception of the enemy in the field . . . by means other than those employing camouflage or dummy units.'"[28] More specifically, it was to focus on the "planting of false information in the field and the general confusion and demoralization of the enemy by 'Fifth Column' methods."[29] "A" Force, which retained control of the strategic side of deception, as well as the use of camouflage, dummies, and its MI9 duties, fell under the command of Major Jones. Clarke oversaw both GSI(d) and "A" Force.[30]

Because numerous battles over control erupted between Ops and I, a further reorganization took place in October. Strategic deception remained under Clarke, but tactical deception, this time including camouflage, came under the direct control of a new chief deception officer of the 8th Army. Furthermore, special deception officers were appointed at the corps, division, and brigade levels to carry out the deceptive operations.[31]

Although its flaws were not immediately apparent, the split proved unworkable. First of all, Clarke opposed the idea of separating strategic and tactical deception. He saw the two as "different instruments in a single orchestra for which there had to be only one composer and one conductor."[32] Second, the division led to a loss of security because too many people were involved. As Michael Howard explains, "Once everyone knew about it, adequate security would become impossible. The success of 'A' Force had depended on only a handful of people knowing of its very existence and an even smaller handful knowing what it did."[33] Finally, the employment of deception officers required a significant amount of training. Since the chief deception officer had insufficient time to train new deception officers for the Crusader offensive, the attack, in Howard's words, "was launched and conducted without any tactical deception at all."[34]

The obvious shortcomings prompted Auchinleck to reunite tactical and strategic deception by February 1942 under Clarke's immediate authority, thus reestablishing a coherent unity of command. The experimentation in organization was unsuccessful, but it is not altogether surprising that it was attempted. Because "A" Force did not have a parent organization to base itself upon, the commanders were in many ways feeling their way along. They tried different approaches to running an efficient, albeit complicated, deception agency, but in the end they realized that "A" Force functioned best as it was originally designed.

One interesting experiment emerged from the temporary division, however. In mid-July 1941 Major Wintle proposed a plan known as the Coppers Scheme to doctor German and Italian ammunition by "emptying out the propellant and replacing it with a High Explosive."[35] When an enemy soldier fired his weapon, it would explode, causing either injury or death. Every high-explosive round, or copper, contained a slip of paper with a message to the enemy. Some messages were insulting toward Hitler or Mussolini and read, for example, "To Hell with Hitler!" They all contained the "V" sign with a crossed hammer and sickle.[36] The purpose was to "make it appear as if the filling were the work of some subversive organization in the enemy home country."[37] The deception team went to great lengths to distribute the doctored ammunition to places it was most likely to be discovered and used by the enemy.

The Coppers Scheme was not a traditional deception plan; in truth, it was closer to a war of nerves plan than a true deception operation. Its usefulness, however, is clearly described in the War Diary:

> The project was hardly Deception in the true sense of the word, but it had a more important object than the mere spreading of alarm and despondency or even of inflicting casualties. ROMMEL's forward troops were then some 800 miles from their base at TRIPOLI and, as always, supply considerations were the limiting factor to his Desert operations. If, under these circumstances, we could sow seeds of suspicion that certain "Lots" of ammunition were defective, it should have quite a disturbing effect upon his arrangements. But the COPPERS SCHEME went even further than that. By inserting inside each doctored cartridge-case an abusive message to HITLER or MUSSOLINI as the case might be, we hoped to arouse distrust and suspicion of whole factories in the home countries.[38]

The scheme appears to have worked. The British discovered a copy of Italian orders, dated November 16, 1941, asking for the reissue of machine-gun ammunition. The orders were accompanied by the message: "exhaustive experiments have shown that these cartridges can be used with safety if the guns are in good condition, and with these weapons they do not give evidence of their known peculiarity of blowing off the cartridge case."[39] Another bit of confirming evidence came in when the British discovered some abandoned weapons and ammunition in the Jalo Oasis. When investigated, the ammunition was found to include the doctored coppers.[40] The Coppers Scheme ran until April 1942 and produced a total of five thousand coppers.[41] It was the most notable operation carried out by GSI(d) in North Africa.

After Auchinleck took over the Middle East command, he began working on plans for a new offensive—Operation Crusader. The goal of Crusader was the same as that of Battleaxe—to clear the Germans and Italians from Cyrenaica and raise the siege of Tobruk. If the campaign was successful, Auchinleck hoped to push on to Tripolitania. Churchill wanted Auchinleck to resume the offensive immediately upon his appointment to the Middle East, but the new commander in chief estimated that the British forces would not be ready to launch an offensive until November. Although Churchill called the four-and-a-half-month delay a "mistake and a misfortune," Auchinleck saw it as the necessary amount of time to properly train and equip his troops.[42]

If Operation Crusader were to have a chance at success, the British had to achieve surprise. Of equal importance, the German and Italian forces could not be allowed to take advantage of the lull in fighting and attack the British during the preparation period. The plan, then, was to keep the enemy on the defensive. To ensure victory, Auchinleck called on Clarke. On July 17 Clarke and his team began preparing a strategic deception known as Plan Collect. The goal of Collect was to provide cover for the genuine military preparations for Crusader and to keep the Germans and Italians in a constant state of anticipation so that they would be unable to initiate an offensive of their own. The trick, therefore, was to make them think that the British were ready to take the offensive at any time.

The British were aided in their plans as Rommel had settled down defensively. Although Battleaxe had failed from the British perspective, it had nonetheless weakened the German and Italian forces considerably; furthermore, intelligence sources revealed that the enemy's supply situation was "increasingly precarious."[43] As a result, Auchinleck thought that he had some time before Rommel would strike again. The War Diary states that Auchinleck assumed Rommel "would not be in any mood to mount a serious spoiling attack for some time, and decided that the best way to upset his plans for the coming weeks would be to force him into urgent and premature defensive preparations for a supposed British offensive in August."[44] The objective, then, was to induce Rommel to believe that the British were going to commence a new campaign on August 9. The ninth was chosen because it was the earliest date by which troops from the Syrian campaign could return to the Western Desert. As the date approached, however, it was notionally postponed. A new offensive date was set for August 30 and then again for September 15. Finally, Clarke and his team intended to convey that the British would be unable to mount an offensive until after Christmas.

Throughout the course of the deception, Clarke fed false information through his established channels, spread rumors, and orchestrated leakages. He also had British commanders issue orders to support the ruse, "designed deliberately to deceive their own subordinates and units into thinking an early offensive was being planned."[45] Given the troops' tendency to speak freely without regard for secrecy, the commanders' orders were an almost foolproof way to ensure that the deceptive information made its way to the enemy. Clarke also warned local hospitals that they should expect casualties on dates corresponding with the notional offensive.[46] Collect was Clarke's first attempt at such a prolonged deception and the first time that he used the tactic of notionally planning and postponing an offensive.[47] Because of its success, this tactic became one of his signature methods of deception.

Multiple sources suggest that the first stage of Collect was a success. For one, German activities on or around August 9 and 30 and September 15 indicated that the Germans expected hostilities to begin. On September 14, for example, they conducted a rather large reconnaissance mission, presumably in anticipation of an imminent attack.[48]

Plenty of evidence also confirms that German intelligence received Clarke's planted information, although it was not always accepted as fact. On August 29 Rommel recorded in his diary, "There's a lot of blather about an imminent attack by the British, but it's probably pure gossip."[49] Rommel discounted the attack because he was aware of Britain's activities in Iran, its concern over the security of the Caucasus, and its uneasiness surrounding Japan's increasingly hostile attitude. In September German intelligence learned of the forward movement of South African and New Zealand troops, and on September 11 the Germans reported to Berlin that a British offensive could be expected within the next ten days.[50] In October German army intelligence warned all units that a British offensive was highly likely. On those occasions, however, reconnaissance failed to locate the invading forces or any signs of an impending attack at all.[51]

The lack of substantiating physical evidence uncovered a weakness in the deception planning. For the enemy to accept the threat as legitimate, verifiable proof had to support the rumors and leakages. Clarke had accomplished his mission from the strategic standpoint. He was able to get the story circulated among intelligence circles, and his disinformation reached the enemy as intended. From the tactical standpoint, however, little was done to support the strategic efforts and further the story. The tactical failure was most likely the direct result of the reorganization of "A" Force that had taken place in July. If Clarke had been in charge of the tactical preparations, there is little doubt that sufficient visible evidence would have been in place.

The lesson learned from this effort, and others to come, was that the deception must be carried out with the same degree of thoroughness and attention to detail as the actual military preparations; otherwise, it would fail. Similarly, both strategic and tactical measures were needed to pass along a believable deception. Nevertheless, even if the Germans did not always accept the information that reached them as accurate, they were still left guessing and remained on alert—and that was exactly what Auchinleck wanted and what Clarke had hoped to achieve. In that regard, Clarke had succeeded.

By the end of September the deception team was ready to take Collect to the next level. The second phase of the deception called for a double bluff—"A" Force's first double-bluff attempt.[52] This time Brigadier John Shearer, Auchinleck's director of intelligence, devised the plan. Shearer's intention was for the traditional channels to continue putting forth information to suggest an impending attack. A new source, one that was highly trusted by the Germans, was to provide information in direct contradiction of the others. Accordingly, Cheese, Britain's first double agent in the Middle East, passed along the following story: "The British purposely spread rumours that they intended to attack on the above dates because they were themselves apprehensive of being attacked by the Germans. After their abortive offensive in June, they realised that the Germans were considerably superior in tanks, both in respect of numbers and performance. . . . The British therefore put out the rumours that they were about to attack, to cover their own weakness, particularly while operations were proceeding in Syria and action was contemplated in Persia."[53] If everything went according to plan, the Axis forces would erroneously disregard any British offensive preparations that they observed, assuming them to be nothing more than harmless attempts at deception.

To further support the idea that the British were not planning a campaign for the fall, Cheese passed along information that they would be unable to launch an offensive until after Christmas. The reason for the delay, it was claimed, was equipment problems. To that end, the British claimed that they had encountered serious problems with the new American tanks: "The British are very dissatisfied with the new American tanks. The rubber tracks do not stand up to desert conditions. More British tanks were therefore demanded from the U.K., but the Home Govt. refused to sanction their release until after the invasion season in Sept. . . . Allowing for delays in transit, and the necessity for training and re-fitting on arrival, they could not be available for offensive purposes until after Xmas."[54] This information was, again, intended to induce the enemy to let his guard down and unwisely ignore the obvious signs of battle preparations.

The deception was extremely complex but was created in response to the unique challenges facing the deception planners. The British learned that the Germans had discovered some of their 38th RTR dummy tanks during a reconnaissance mission conducted on September 14; consequently, the enemy was aware that the British were using deception.[55] Similarly, as evidenced in Rommel's diary, Rommel doubted that the British were in a position to launch an offensive, regardless of strong evidence to the contrary presented by his own intelligence sources. The double bluff set out to confirm Rommel's suspicions, thereby blowing the older suspect channels, while simultaneously replacing them with a new, more reliable source. Cheese, who was gradually and meticulously built up in the enemy's estimation in the months before the fall offensive, was the perfect source to influence the enemy's high command.

It would be difficult to underestimate the value of Cheese to the deception organization. In fact, Cheese became the prominent source through which Clarke and his team passed the most crucial elements of the Collect deception plan. Likewise, the War Diary asserts that "the successful strategic surprise secured at the outset of the 'CRUSADER' offensive was in a very large extent due to 'CHEESE.'"[56]

From the perspective of Colonel Raymund Maunsell's SIME, the Cheese case began on June 3, 1940, when the War Office informed Cairo that a man named Renato Levi was on his way to Cairo from Italy.[57] The War Office warned SIME to keep a close eye on him. Levi, who the War Office curiously named as a British subject, was an Italian Jew and an "international adventurer."[58] By the summer of 1940, he was already working for both the German military intelligence service (the Abwehr) and the Allies.

Levi began his double-cross career in 1939, when a member of the German Schutzstaffel (SS), Dr. Hans Travaglio, approached him in Genoa. Travaglio asked Levi to go to France and work for the Germans as a spy. Levi promptly presented himself to the British consul in Genoa; there he was advised to continue on to France as instructed by Travaglio. While in France, Levi maintained contact with French military intelligence, the Deuxième Bureau.[59] Thus began Levi's work as a double agent.

When France fell, Levi returned to Genoa. He was again approached by Travaglio, who this time wanted him to travel to Cairo. Count Scirombo, the head of Italy's intelligence service, the Servizio de Informazione Militare (SIM), gave his consent to the plan.[60] The Italians made arrangements for Levi to stay in Cairo and promised to send him a wireless transmitter by way of the Hungarian diplomatic bag. He was accompanied by another man, Fulvio Melcher, whose job was to operate the machine.

The first leg of Levi and Melcher's journey to Cairo took them to Istanbul. Upon arrival in Istanbul, Levi immediately visited the British embassy. Suffering some bad luck, however, both men were arrested by the Turkish police on suspicion of passport fraud and dealing counterfeit money. After three weeks in jail, and with a little help from the British, the two were released. Melcher was so shaken by the experience that he returned to Italy, but Levi continued on to Cairo with the assistance of Maunsell's SIME.[61]

Now traveling on a British passport, Levi arrived in Cairo on February 19, 1941. Once there, he settled down in a hotel and proceeded to locate two contacts provided by Scirombo. In the meantime, he met with SIME agents daily. Both Levi and SIME eagerly awaited the arrival of the wireless transmitter that never came.

The lack of a transmitter posed a problem for SIME. The British had a unique opportunity to use Levi against the Germans and Italians, with the added benefit that Levi was already trusted by the enemy. Without a transmitter, though, they could not communicate with Levi's German controller at Bari. Not to be deterred, the determined men at SIME decided that they would have to make a transmitter for Levi themselves. A noncommissioned officer from GHQ Signals, Sergeant (and later Lieutenant) Shears, offered to build the device. Shears was a prewar amateur radio enthusiast, according to the War Diary, so he had the knowledge and ability to construct a transmitter that could not be traced back to the British. Shears also took on the responsibility of operating the machine, thereby impersonating Cheese.[62]

So that the Germans would not question how Levi came to own a transmitter, the British fabricated a story that he bought an old device from an Italian in Cairo for £200. Levi also claimed to have made contact with a man named Paul Nicossof, who he thought to be a Syrian, although the man's true ethnicity was unknown. The imaginary Nicossof had agreed to operate the wireless transmitter—for a handsome fee, of course—after Levi left Cairo. Shears, posing as Nicossof, began trying to send transmissions on May 25.[63]

Levi left Cairo for Italy on April 19. It was the last time SIME saw him until 1944. After only two months in his company, Levi's SIME case officer, Captain E. J. Simpson, described him as "a natural liar, capable of inventing any story on the spur of the moment to get himself out of a fix. He has very considerable intelligence and an inventive mind."[64] Although his craftiness did get him out of many serious predicaments, it could not save him from becoming a casualty of political infighting between the Germans and Italians.

As it so happened, Levi was arrested in Italy in October 1941 for "activities against the state" and sentenced to five years' imprisonment. Oddly enough, the Italian authorities did not appear to truly doubt his loyalty because the only matter they saw fit to question him about was his Jewish heritage. Nevertheless, it appears that both the Germans and Italians had their own reasons to want Levi out of the picture. The War Diary similarly records that "it seems fair to assume that his eventual imprisonment was intended more to keep him out of the way, for one reason or another, than to punish him for any specific act of treachery."[65] Thus, Levi remained confined until the British 8th Army overran his prison in October 1943. Although he provided the British with their first opportunity to employ a double agent in the Middle East, Levi's actual connection to the case was rather short lived.

After Levi's departure in April, the British began working to establish contact with the Germans. Their initial attempts in May failed, but after making some modifications, they finally made contact on July 14. Between July and October SIME worked diligently to build the Cheese channel up in the enemy's esteem. Most of the original messages were more technical in nature, but on July 21 the imaginary Nicossof informed his controller that he had befriended a "good South African contact."[66] On September 29 he revealed that the South African, referred to as Piet, was a noncommissioned officer who worked as a confidential secretary to Brigadier John Whiteley, head of the Operation Staff at GHQ, and was therefore privy to sensitive information. The Cheese file explains that Piet "proved a useful excuse for transmitting high-grade intelligence which would have been quite beyond the reach of [Levi's] associates."[67] The file further records, "Experience shows that the enemy is curiously unwary and eager to accept stories of the disloyalty of disgruntled Colonials, Irishmen, etc., and even of supposed ex-members of Fascist organizations in England."[68] Piet's motivation, according to Nicossof, was that he had serious problems with money and women. Like Nicossof, Piet spent much of his time asking the Germans for money.

Once SIME had meticulously established Nicossof's credibility, "A" Force took the opportunity to use the channel to directly influence the enemy's high command. Although SIME ran the double-agent network in the Middle East, the agents—and thus Cheese—fell under "A" Force's strategic control. As such, "A" Force was responsible for creating and approving the text of all messages and for determining the policy in regard to the specific employment of the double agents.[69] By October "A" Force was ready to include Cheese in the Collect deception. The Cheese file states, "In October–November, 1941, the organization of deception was rapidly developing. 'Advanced Headquarters, "A" Force' saw in CHEESE a possible opportunity for a decisive stroke. The information dispatched was gradually put on a far higher level, and close liaison was maintained between 'A' Force, S.I.M.E. and the Operational authorities."[70] Accordingly, Clarke decided to use the Cheese channel to pass on some of the more sensitive aspects of the deception, which could be relayed only by a highly trusted source.

On October 20, when the British were trying to convince the Germans that the 8th Army would be unable to go on the offensive until after Christmas, "A" Force instructed SIME to send the following message from Nicossof: "Very important news. Piet is desperate for money. He visited us yesterday. According to him Wavel visited Cairo secretly yesterday having come from Tiflis. Auchinles under pressure from Churchill has consented against his better judgement to send one armoured division and three infantry divisions to help the Russians in the defence of the Caucase. Wavel is going back to Iraq immediately to make the necessary plans for their reception."[71] Because this move would significantly weaken Britain's forces in the Western Desert, it clearly conveyed that the British would not be in a position to go on the offensive in the immediate future.

The information from Nicossof definitely made an impression on the Germans. In the conclusion of an intelligence appreciation of British intentions dated November 11, 1941, exactly one week before Crusader began, the Germans reported that there "are no apparent signs of preparations for an attack on

Cyrenaica." Among other supportive evidence, the conclusion was based on the following information: "Abwehr reports state that there are also differences of opinion between Generals Wavell and Auchinleck concerning strategy in the Middle East. Wavell advocates an attack into the Caucasus, but Auchinleck does not wish to move any more troops or equipment out of Egypt."[72] The fact that this piece of information made it into the German appreciation reveals the high degree of confidence the Germans placed in the notional Nicossof.

The role played by the Cheese channel was invaluable to the deception campaign, and many credit Cheese with the strategic success of Collect as a whole. A telegram sent to England on January 6, 1942, which refers to the Cheese channel by one of its aliases, Lambert, stated, "Have been officially informed that LAMBERT was main source by which successful deception recently achieved, resulting in complete strategic surprise at outset of Western Desert campaign. Without Lambert, main theme of deception plan which was put over on 20/10 & 27/10 could not have reached enemy before 18/11. This very satisfactory and completely justifies care and trouble taken."[73] Although SIME assumed that the Cheese channel would be blown after the offensive began, everyone involved considered it worth the sacrifice.[74]

Another aspect of the pre-Crusader strategic deception efforts was the Tripoli Plan. From July until the beginning of the campaign, Clarke worked to simulate a threat to Rommel's rear base at Tripoli, eight hundred miles behind his front-line positions. The Tripoli Plan was in essence a continuation of Plan A-R, which Clarke had initiated back in April. The port at Tripoli was the main source of supply for the Germans and Italians and their only viable lifeline in North Africa. The objective, therefore, was to create a threat to Rommel's supply lines and L of C, thus compelling the Axis forces to maintain sizable forces at Tripoli.[75]

To establish the threat, Clarke had a wireless message sent to the British consul in Spanish-held Tangier asking the consul to find and interview a British merchant seaman who, albeit a figment of Clarke's imagination, was said to have escaped Italian internment at Tripoli. Clarke directed the consul to ask the seaman three specific questions, all of which were designed to indicate that the British were planning an amphibious assault at the port of Tripoli. The message was sent over a compromised low-grade signal. Although it is difficult to discern exactly what effect the deception had, it is known that the Germans did not transfer a single new formation from Tripoli to the front.[76]

Whereas the strategic efforts to pass the Collect story generally met with success, the tactical component was less fruitful. In October, as the target date for Crusader neared, the 8th Army deception team began working to draw the enemy's attention to diversionary forces in the south. The plan was to simulate a concentration of forces in the southern sector in order to pin down substantial enemy forces far away from the intended line of attack. This portion of the deception effort was designed strictly to provide cover for the genuine campaign preparations. The areas chosen for the diversion were the southern oases of Jarabub and Siwa, positions at least a hundred miles south of Britain's left flank.[77]

General Cunningham ordered the Oasis Group, comprising the 6th South African Armoured Car Regiment and an infantry brigade, to transform Siwa into a fake forward base. On October 25 the forces were joined by the 38th RTR, fully equipped with fifty-two dummy tanks. The dummy unit made use of "A" Force's new track-simulator technology to create the impression of tank tracks in the sand, thereby providing visible proof of its journey.

British camouflage experts assigned to the 8th Army built fake camps to look as similar to genuine camps as possible. They included tents, cookhouses, latrines, shelter trenches, and bogus antiaircraft defenses. They erected stores and ammunition dumps, all poorly concealed for the benefit of aerial reconnaissance. The deception team also lit fires at night and transmitted phony radio signals to further support the existence of a troop buildup.[78]

Unfortunately for the British, the camouflage crew members had few resources at their disposal, forcing them to make do with whatever they could scrounge together. Geoffrey Barkas, the head of G(CAM), explained that the trenches, for example, were made by digging shallow slits and then using dark blankets or other material to create the impression of shadows. The buildings, latrines, and antiaircraft positions were created with nothing more than scrap material.[79] Barkas recalled, "Starved as they were for transport, labour, and materials, the Siwa and Giarabub schemes could never have produced much effect."[80] After the team converted Siwa into a fake base, it moved on to Jarabub and repeated the task—but the transfer took place two days after the Crusader offensive began.

The notional buildup did attract the enemy's attention. German reconnaissance noticed the activity and closely monitored it.[81] German intelligence documents recorded the British strength at Siwa and Jarabub as two infantry brigade groups and four to five armoured car units.[82] A captured Italian document from November 15 reveals that the Italians included an Egyptian camel corps in their estimation of British strength at the same location.[83] Neither G(CAM), the 8th Army's tactical deception team, nor "A" Force could claim credit for this mistake; no camels were used in the deception.

Although the Germans clearly took notice of the bogus concentration of forces in the south, it does not appear that it caused them much concern. In other words, they did not transfer any units to their southern flank to meet the threat; thus, the deception failed to achieve its objective. Charles Cruickshank explains the failure as follows: "It had been impossible to give the two chosen areas enough life to make them convincing, partly because some of the genuine troops which had been supposed to move through them did not turn up; and partly because there were too few vehicles to match the size of the formations simulated. There had been too few real trucks to carry the materials needed to make fake tents and vehicles; and, less excusable, the lack of operational direction meant that the synchronization of the deceptive plan with the genuine operation had been imperfect."[84] Because the army did not carry out the physical deception on the scale necessary, it failed to achieve its intended results. It appears that the military had yet to fully understand how much effort was required to successfully implement physical deception in the field. The attempt, therefore, exposed many weaknesses in the tactical organization in general.

On a positive note, the experience further reinforced a valuable lesson formalizing in the minds of the deception team that the same degree of effort and attention to detail must be put into the deception as was put into actual military preparations; otherwise, the deception would fail. Those in charge of tactical deception similarly realized that they could not skimp on deceptive operations in any way; the deception plans must appear as real as possible and be precisely coordinated with the genuine operation.[85]

Another tactical attempt to deceive the enemy took place at Capuzzo, with better results. Once the 8th Army began its thrust into Cyrenaica, it would need adequate transportation to carry troops forward and ensure a steady flow of supplies. That could be achieved only if the railhead at Capuzzo remained intact. Because the railhead would provide an all-too-inviting target for the Luftwaffe and was thought to be too large to camouflage, the decision was made to build a fake railhead and line to draw the enemy's attention away from the actual railhead.

To accomplish this task, Barkas' camouflage team created a dummy railhead at Misheifa, which the Germans obligingly assumed to be the main terminus of the Desert Railway.[86] His personnel also built a fake railway line and even supplied an immobile dummy train to add realism to the ploy. The deception succeeded, and the fake line was bombed on eight separate occasions. All told, the enemy dropped more than a hundred bombs on the decoy, whereas the Capuzzo railhead was never bombed.[87]

After several delays, Auchinleck committed to launching Operation Crusader on November 18. The timing could not have been more precarious, for, as the commander in chief well knew, Rommel was preparing his own offensive to capture Tobruk. Aware of Rommel's intentions, British intelligence carefully monitored the enemy's actions around the besieged port town. In July information became available suggesting that Rommel would be ready to begin his campaign by the end of October.[88] On September 17 the GC&CS finally broke the German Army Enigma, providing increased access to accurate information regarding Rommel's intentions, order of battle, and supply level.[89] The new source of information gave the British insight into Rommel's plans for Tobruk, although it was certainly not a complete picture. Nevertheless, by November Auchinleck knew that Rommel's offensive could occur at any moment. Finally, intelligence sources learned that the attack was set to take place within the last ten days of November. Rommel had traveled to Rome on November 1 and was planning to return to Libya on the evening of November 18.[90] Plans for Operation Crusader, therefore, went forward without the possibility of further delays.

When the British offensive began in the early hours of the eighteenth, it took the Germans and Italians by complete surprise. The British were able to move 100,000 men, more than 600 tanks, and 5,000 vehicles to the front on the sixteenth and seventeenth,[91] without alerting the enemy, for three main reasons: the determined activities of the RAF, the weather, and the deception campaign.

In the weeks before the opening of the campaign, the RAF made every effort to give Britain the advantage going into battle. Five weeks before the offensive, the RAF began flying regular reconnaissance missions, attacked the enemy's lines of supply on land and sea, and specifically targeted the German and Italian air forces with the intention of gaining air superiority.[92] The latter was of vital importance. To prevent the enemy from noticing the concentration of battle forces in the crucial days leading up to the offensive, the British had to have control of the skies. Their successful accomplishment of that goal played a decisive role in Britain's ability to achieve surprise.

The British were also tremendously aided by the weather. For days heavy rains descended on the region. Although the rain impeded the RAF's efforts as well, it successfully prevented the enemy from conducting aerial reconnaissance during the most critical period of buildup. German lieutenant general Fritz Bayerlein recorded, "As luck would have it, torrential rain put all of our airfields out of commission on the 18th November and no air reconnaissance was flown that day."[93] Had the skies been clear on the eighteenth and the preceding days, enemy aircraft might very well have been in a position to spot the massive concentration and deployment of battle forces.[94] F. H. Hinsley writes that since the enemy could not fly reconnaissance, its intelligence staff had to rely on monitoring the 8th Army's wireless transmissions. Because the army was careful not to increase its transmissions and maintained complete silence regarding the upcoming battle, the enemy was completely unaware that anything was afoot.[95]

As far as the deception was concerned, the hard work and dedication of everyone involved paid off handsomely. The greatest proof of the deception's achievement comes from the undeniable fact that the enemy was unprepared for the British offensive. As mentioned previously, a German intelligence appreciation from November 11 stated, "There are no apparent signs of preparations for an attack in Cyrenaica." The report went on to warn that there was a possibility of an attack during the next few months.[96] This suggests that the Germans were completely fooled by the Collect deception effort.

As further evidence of the success of both the deceptive activities and the endeavors of the armed services to divert the enemy's attention before the campaign began, Bayerlein recorded, "No supply dumps capable of supporting a major offensive were seen in the Egyptian frontier area. The enemy's approach march and deployment passed unnoticed by our reconnaissance. His concealment of preparations was excellent. The wireless silence which he imposed prevented our interception service detecting his approach march into the assembly areas. Our air reconnaissance . . . failed to spot his troops movements, probably because he only moved by night and laid up during the day under the protection of excellent camouflage."[97] The British efforts were so complete that even

Rommel failed to realize that a major offensive had begun; instead, he initially disregarded the action as a reconnaissance in force.[98] On November 19 he decided that the British advance was nothing more than an attempt to divert him from his own planned offensive. Barrie Pitt writes that Rommel "had not the slightest intention of reacting seriously to what he was certain was nothing but a diversion staged by the British Command in order to frighten the Italians at El Gubi and Bir Hakeim, causing them in turn to distract his attention from his main purpose, the final reduction of Tobruk."[99] According to I. S. O. Playfair, it was not until the evening of the twentieth that Rommel finally realized that the British had launched a well-planned offensive.[100]

Although Crusader was supposed to achieve a quick victory, it resulted in approximately two months of bitter combat. On November 21 British forces broke out of Tobruk and for the next three days found themselves engaged in some of the toughest fighting of the entire desert war.[101] In the meantime, the British suffered considerable damage to their armored units, depriving them of the numerical advantage with which they had entered the battle.[102]

By the evening of November 22 Cunningham was so concerned about the extensive losses to his armored forces that he questioned whether or not the British should call off the offensive. To prevent an unfortunate repeat of Battleaxe, Auchinleck intervened personally and ordered the offensive to continue. Because he thought that Cunningham was too defensive-minded, the commander in chief removed Cunningham from command on November 25. Auchinleck's own deputy chief, Major General N. M. Ritchie, was called in to replace Cunningham.[103] Rommel, for his part, had hoped that the British would retreat when faced with harsh opposition; only Auchinleck's intervention prevented that from happening.

By the end of November the momentum of the battle had swung in Britain's favor. Both sides had suffered heavy losses, but the British were able to bring in fresh reinforcements and supplies. Furthermore, Rommel's attempt to relieve his forces along the Egyptian frontier had failed. During the first week of December, the enemy position became increasingly threatened. Rommel was forced to pull his troops back to the Gazala line, where he hoped to establish a defensive position. On December 10 Rommel faced more disheartening news—the eight-month siege of Tobruk had come to an end. The reopening of the port was a major relief to the British. Not only was the exhaustive siege over, but now the British could use the port to supply their frontline troops much faster and more efficiently.[104]

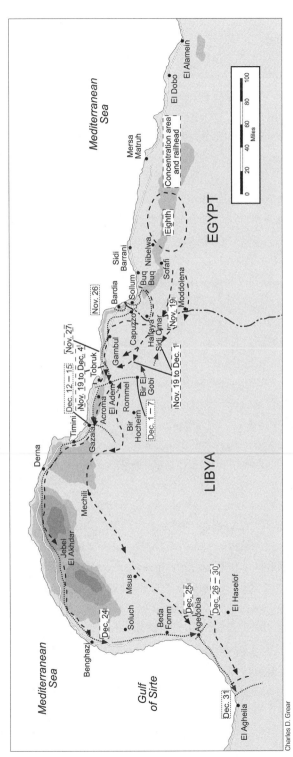

MAP 4. OPERATION CRUSADER, 1941: AUCHINLECK'S OFFENSIVE,
NOVEMBER 10–DECEMBER 31, 1941

Charles D. Grear

The situation continued to deteriorate for the Germans and Italians. Unable to maintain a viable defensive position at Gazala, Rommel opted to abandon the location on December 17. At the same time, the German commander made the decision to give up Cyrenaica altogether.[105] Because of the strategic significance of Tripoli, it was more important for the Axis powers to hold Tripolitania than Cyrenaica. From January 1 to 6, 1942, the Germans and Italians fell back to El Agheila under heavy attacks by the RAF.[106]

As the main Axis armies retreated, they left their frontier forces behind and completely cut off from supplies or reinforcements. The enemy troops at Bardia and Halfaya fought a determined delaying action, but they had insufficient resources to endure a prolonged engagement. On January 2 the Germans officially handed Bardia over to the British. The only enemy position remaining was at Halfaya. To bring about Major Wilhelm Bach's surrender at that locale, the British got creative.

Beginning late in December, the British tried their hand at deception to induce the surrender of Halfaya. On the night of December 24, they set out to convince the Halfaya garrison that a large tank formation was massing against it. To pull off the ruse, "A" Force employed an Egyptian film company, Misr Studios, to record the sounds of tank movements onto four separate sound tracks.[107] The recordings were broadcast over amplifiers for the benefit of the enemy troops. This was "A" Force's first use of sonic deception. In mid-1942 "A" Force employed a more sophisticated version of this ruse, using an armored sonic car, appropriately called "Sonia," to broadcast tank recordings.[108]

In the last days of December, "A" Force concocted yet another crafty plan to force the surrender of Halfaya. This time the deceptionists hoped to convince Major Bach that Rommel had authorized his capitulation. Thus, Plan Gripfix was a bold attempt to trick Bach into surrendering. To do this, "A" Force called on the services of its newly created Technical Unit, which was led by Mr. E. Titterington.[109] One of the "A" Force Technical Unit's specializations was creating forgeries, and that was exactly what Clarke needed.

Titterington did not have a sample of paper from Rommel's new headquarters, the Panzergruppe Afrika, but he did have a sample of a letter written on Rommel's old Afrika Korps stationery. Hoping that Major Bach would not question the use of Afrika Korps notepaper, Titterington forged a letter authorizing Bach to surrender. The English translation of the forgery read, "The heroic resistance of the defenders of Halfaya has now achieved its object. I can no longer hope to keep your forces supplied until the time when the Afrikacorps will advance again to relieve them. I have no wish to demand more sacrifices than are necessary from men who have already fought a tough fight against overwhelming odds. When you feel that further resistance can achieve no more, I give you formal permission to make an honourable surrender."[110] The letter, supposedly written and signed by Rommel, was placed in a captured German envelope, sealed with a German seal, and placed in a second envelope, which was sealed with captured rubber stamps. Three different copies were placed in three German message containers and dropped from British aircraft under the cover of darkness on the night of December 29. The timing of the drop was calculated to correspond with the assault on Bardia because Bach's wireless communications would likely be cut as a result of the battle.[111]

The RAF successfully made the drop, and Bach received the letter as planned. Although Bach attempted to inquire about the letter, wireless difficulties prevented him from personally making contact with Rommel's headquarters. Unfortunately for the British, however, Bach received a personal message from Hitler shortly after the British drop. Hitler expressed his confidence that the Halfaya garrison was making a significant contribution to the war effort and encouraged Bach to hold out as long as possible. In obedience to higher orders from the Führer, Bach held out until January 17. It is interesting that Bach never seemed to question whether the message from Rommel was authentic, although he did find it odd that Rommel wrote it on his old Afrika Korps stationery. Clarke called the operation a "near miss."[112]

With the surrender of Halfaya on the seventeenth, Operation Crusader came to an end. Crusader was a success: the eight-month siege of Tobruk was broken, and the British reclaimed Cyrenaica, thus relieving the immediate threat to Egypt. However, Crusader did not go as planned, and its mishaps revealed that the British still had a long way to go toward developing a sound armored strategy. David French explains that although the British had learned many lessons from the failure of Operation Battleaxe, they nonetheless failed to concentrate their tanks, which negated their numerical advantage during Crusader. Also, the British remained in the elementary phases of employing combined arms tactics, in stark contrast to the Germans' superior use of combined arms.[113] Because of these shortcomings, Britain's forces were at a disadvantage when fighting against the finer tactics of the Germans.

The offensive also took much longer than planned and resulted in tremendous loss of troops and matériel. Consequently, plans to continue on into Tripolitania were cancelled. All told, the British suffered 18,000 casualties and lost 278 tanks. The Germans and Italians combined lost 32,000 troops and 300 tanks.[114] The enemy clearly suffered greater losses, but the victory was extremely costly for the British and left them weak and vulnerable to a German counterattack.

Although 1942 would usher in a complete reversal of fortunes, the British ended 1941 on a positive note. Moreover, they had at least temporarily redeemed themselves from the failures of the Brevity and Battleaxe operations. While they still had much to learn as far as the employment of their armored forces was concerned, they were finally making progress and learning from their mistakes.

In the field of deception, on the other hand, the British were excelling. Under Clarke's exceptional guidance, the men at "A" Force were on their way to perfecting the art of deception. They had the vision to create such devices as tank-track simulators, track eliminators, and sun shields and the farsightedness to attempt the use of sonic deception—all of which clearly demonstrated the creativity and sheer genius that the deception planners possessed.

The advances in the design and employment of dummy vehicles and equipment provided many new opportunities for deception. Similarly, the creation of notional formations, such as the numerous dummy tank units, the 1st SAS, and the 7th Division, formed the basis of an entirely notional order of battle, which Clarke formally expanded in 1942. The fake units were all accepted as genuine by the enemy, which helped to create the impression of greater strength in the Middle East for the British—and for the rest of the war, Clarke moved his imaginary units all over the Middle East in support of his deceptions. The war establishments for Major Jones' "A" Force Depot and Titterington's Technical Unit also offered expanded opportunities for deception and unequivocally demonstrated that the use of deception as weapon of war was highly valued by the War Office.

The development of the Cheese channel gave the deception team a decisive advantage—essentially providing them a direct line to the enemy's high command—that truly catapulted "A" Force's deception work forward. Likewise, Clarke's success at establishing new contacts in Lisbon and Madrid between August and October provided additional channels through which he could pass deceptive information (discussed later). Closely related, Britain's ability to read the German

Army Enigma intercepts supplied Clarke and his team with better information on which to base their deceptions and feedback as to whether or not the enemy had swallowed the stories fed to him.

The experiences of "A" Force during its first year of operation had been invaluable and provided a solid foundation for future deception work. According to the War Diary, "We felt, in fact, on the eve of 1942 that we were beginning to know how to plan Deception, and that at last we had a well-oiled machine available to implement our plans. The organ was now built, its stops were ready for us to pull at will, and all we had to do now was write the music and gain a little more practice in playing it."[115] In less than a year, then, "A" Force had developed into a first-class organization that had achieved amazing stability, especially when one takes into consideration that it had no precedent. For all that "A" Force had accomplished, it is astonishing that the entire organization consisted of only twelve officers, seven of whom were devoted exclusively to MI9 activities.[116]

A true testament to the viability of "A" Force was that the small team managed to successfully implement the Collect deception even though Clarke was absent from the Middle East for the majority of the time that the plan was active. Clarke left the Middle East in August to travel to Lisbon and Madrid.[117] Because Portugal and Spain remained neutral, they proved to be fertile grounds for deception and intelligence gathering.[118] Clarke hoped to establish channels through which he could pass along his deceptions; to that end, he sought to befriend German Abwehr agents in those lands whom he could use as unwitting channels later. While in Portugal and Spain, he took full advantage of the opportunity to spread information connected to the Collect deception.

After leaving Western Europe, Clarke traveled to London to meet with members of the JIC, JPS, and Chiefs of Staff regarding the centralization of deception. This meeting led to the appointment of Oliver Stanley as the "controller" of global deception and then, in 1942, to the formation of the LCS.

Clarke finally returned to Cairo in November, coincidentally on the day that Operation Crusader began. In his absence, the deception machine had continued to function smoothly. The highly creative and independent staff at "A" Force had the ability to carry out their mission even when Clarke was not present to offer hands-on guidance. Clarke, of course, risked leaving during such a crucial time only because he knew that his staff had the skills to continue and succeed in his absence. Thus, Clarke had tremendous confidence in his men, and they did not disappoint.

As any new year does, 1942 brought many fresh challenges to the military and deception organizations. On the military side, the British experienced a devastating reversal of the Crusader gains as the enemy advanced frighteningly close to Cairo. Although Britain's supply situation had improved after the fall of Italian East Africa, Japan's surprise attack on the United States and British territories in the Far East stretched Britain's ability to supply its forces scattered across the globe and placed new demands on the Middle East command. As Britain's position in the Far East deteriorated, calls for troops, equipment, and vehicles from the Middle East increased. Moreover, the need to bolster Britain's Far East interests with resources from the Middle East coincided with Britain's hasty retreat in the face of Rommel's powerful advance.

Of course, the Japanese aggression was not all bad news for the British. Churchill was initially unaware of the extent of the damage inflicted upon the Americans at Pearl Harbor, but he admitted to feeling a deep sense of relief that the United States would now be fighting alongside the British. For him, the entrance of the United States into the war meant victory for the Allies. For the first time since the war began, the prime minister harbored no doubts that the Allies would pull through and that Britain would survive. He wrote, "Hitler's fate was sealed. Mussolini's fate was sealed. As for the Japanese, they would be ground to powder." With the British, Americans, and Soviets united, Churchill was confident that the Allies could overwhelm the Axis. On the night of December 7, Churchill "slept the sleep of the saved and thankful."[119] Both Britain and the United States declared war on Japan on December 8, and the United States declared war on Germany and Italy on December 11.[120] The United States was finally in the war, and by the end of 1942 it would have forces in North Africa.

Clarke and his team continued to cultivate the art of deception, devising new and more elaborate plans based on the experience gained from the previous year's work. By the end of 1942, they had established the blueprint that "A" Force, and subsequently London, would follow for the remainder of the war. It was the blueprint devised for the El Alamein deception that became the foundation for the most elaborate deception campaign of the entire war—Operation Bodyguard. Therefore, beginning with the success of Collect, Clarke's deceptions began to play a significant and indispensable role in Britain's victories. As a result, 1942 saw much advancement in the field of deception, and that would continue unabated throughout the remainder of the war.

—6—

The Great Allied Retreat: A Rough Start to 1942

For British forces in the Middle East, the outlook for 1942 was both favorable and daunting. In their favor, Operation Crusader ended by mid-January with the British again in control of Cyrenaica. Yet, although the campaign was a success, it took much longer than planned and turned out to be extremely costly. As a direct result of the material losses, human casualties, and excessive length of the campaign, the plan to follow Crusader with a drive into Tripolitania, known as Operation Acrobat, had to be suspended. Although the British had pushed the German and Italian forces all the way to El Agheila, they were too weak to consolidate their victory and continue the offensive from there.

Oddly enough, the situation at the beginning of 1942 was strikingly similar to that in the first month of 1941. In the opening weeks of both years, the British concluded offensive operations that positioned them on the western edge of Cyrenaica. In each case, however, Britain had exhausted itself, outrun its lines of supply and communication, and consequently missed the opportunity to follow up its victory with the complete destruction of the Axis forces in North Africa. In both instances as well, the commander in chief—General Archibald Wavell in 1941 and General Claude Auchinleck in 1942—had no choice but to hold the ground won with forces incapable of doing much more than providing a weak defensive front. Furthermore, in 1941 and 1942 the decisions to halt emerged from the faulty assumption that the Axis forces were too battered to mount a counteroffensive.[1] In the case of 1942, Auchinleck's intelligence underestimated the enemy's strength by more than 100 percent![2] Finally, the situations were exacerbated by events outside of the Middle East: in 1941 it was the impending German invasion of Greece, and in 1942 it was the entrance of Japan into the war.

The Japanese bombing of Pearl Harbor and assault on Southeast Asia had far-reaching consequences. For one, it brought the United States into the war, which was extremely advantageous for the British. The British, and especially Winston Churchill, were elated to have the United States formally in the war and fighting together with Britain against the Axis threat.[3] However, Britain also gained Japan as an enemy. As the Japanese struck Pearl Harbor, they simultaneously descended upon the British possessions of Malaya, Hong Kong, and Singapore. This aggression in the Far East prompted the British to declare war on Japan on December 8, 1941.[4] Thus, 1942 opened with Britain preparing for war against yet another opponent.

As one can imagine, the effort against Japan severely tested Britain's ability to supply its forces on multiple fronts. Just as quickly as the supply situation in the Middle East had improved in mid-1941, new demands were made and fresh challenges arose in 1942. Equipment and supplies destined to help rebuild the exhausted 8th Army were instead sent to India, Burma, and Singapore. Not surprisingly, Auchinleck was asked to release as many forces as possible for the protection of the Far East. According to the "A" Force Narrative War Diary, within the first days of January, the War Office ordered Auchinleck to part with 60,000 troops and 8,200 vehicles.[5] Additionally, reinforcements that were initially slated for the Middle East were instead diverted to the Far East. Finally, the RAF and Royal Navy were called upon to provide forces for the fight against Japan, which deprived the Middle East of much-needed support.[6]

In a case of history truly repeating itself, the gains made by Operation Crusader—just like those made by Operation Compass—were lost with bewildering speed. Only four days after Britain forced the surrender of Rommel's last stronghold at Halfaya, the Axis forces returned to the battlefield with the momentum entirely on their side. On January 21 Rommel launched a surprise attack against the British, catching the weak and incomplete units on the front completely off guard and utterly unprepared.[7]

Rommel's decision to take the offensive was strategic. On January 5, and again on the seventeenth, he received reinforcements of tanks and fuel. German intelligence accurately indicated that his forces around El Agheila and Mersa Brega were stronger than Britain's forward-most troops—around a hundred miles to the east—but that could change quickly if he allowed the British time to reinforce and rebuild their strength.[8] Therefore, he decided to strike while he still held the advantage.[9] Rommel ordered his troops to attack at 8:00 a.m. on January 21.

Ironically, the British misread the enemy's intentions and reached the same erroneous conclusion as Rommel had when the British launched Operation Crusader. General N. M. Ritchie, commanding the 8th Army, assumed the action to be a strong reconnaissance effort, or perhaps an attempt to reclaim some territory for security purposes.[10] Although Rommel had planned a limited action to regain lost territory, not a major counteroffensive, the German commander was a risk taker and would continue to advance as far as his army could take him. Regardless of Ritchie's miscalculations, the meager British forces left to defend the frontier were ill-prepared to ward off a strong Axis advance. The British had little choice but to give up land and try to establish a defensive base.

Although the British hoped to make a stand at Benghazi, the attempt failed and Rommel entered the city on the morning of January 29. As the British continued to fall back, the 8th Army decided to set up a defensive position at the Gazala line, less than thirty miles west of Tobruk. Because the Germans and Italians were short on fuel, their forward thrust came to a halt for the time being.[11]

On February 1 Auchinleck summoned Dudley Clarke to his headquarters in Cairo. At that meeting, the commander in chief asked Clarke to employ immediate deceptive measures to stop the enemy around the Derna-Mechili line. Clarke met with Ritchie the following day, but it was already too late. Rommel's troops were just then approaching the Derna-Mechili line, and the British army was quickly retreating to Gazala. The military situation necessitated a different deception plan, and so Clarke endeavored to convince Rommel that Tobruk was so heavily defended that it would be unwise to continue his advance. Operation Bastion, as the plan was known, hoped to buy the British three to four weeks' time—or until the beginning of March—to fortify the defenses at Gazala and prepare for battle.[12]

Clarke immediately began to implement Bastion, which was formally approved on February 8, but he was initially unable to do everything that Auchinleck asked of him. The reason, he informed his superior, was that he was not in charge of tactical deception. Tactical deception was the responsibility of the 8th Army's camouflage deception staff, which was part of the GSI(d) tactical deception organization formed by Wavell in July 1941. To confound the situation, G(CAM), the official camouflage organization headed by Geoffrey Barkas at GHQ, was in a period of training in Cairo and was therefore unable to participate in the deception. The War Diary states that Clarke was "forced to operate an urgent plan at 8th Army H.Q. with all the physical resources for implementing it under the control of another organisation back in CAIRO."[13] The situation was not conducive to success.

Auchinleck realized that Clarke's hands were tied and that the reorganization of "A" Force in 1941 had proved disruptive to the deception effort, thereby greatly limiting its efficiency. He also noted that the October 1941 expansion of GSI(d)'s responsibilities, which placed complete control of the means to carry out all tactical deception in the hands of an 8th Army chief deception officer, had failed to produce the desired results.[14] Auchinleck, therefore, reversed the decision and returned tactical deception to Clarke's direct authority on February 12, 1942.[15]

The 1942 reorganization led to an expansion of "A" Force, although it did not officially take effect until March 27. First, Clarke received the rank of full colonel. Second, "A" Force was divided into three sections: Control, Operations, and Intelligence. All three sections came under Clarke's command, and he received his instructions from the commander in chief. The Control Section was responsible for the administration, plans, and policies of "A" Force. Ops largely dealt with physical deception and supervised tactical deception in the field. Intelligence focused on deceiving the enemy's high command on both a strategic and tactical level, mainly by using established intelligence channels. Clarke intended for all future deception plans to employ strategic and tactical means of deception to the largest degree possible.[16]

Of the three, the dominant section was Ops. According to Clarke, Ops should naturally take precedent over I. He wrote, "Deception is a matter for Ops, not intelligence. Yes, intelligence has its own deception channels via direct communication with the enemy, but there has to be an overall plan and that comes from Ops. Also, deception requires far greater resources than 'I' can offer."[17] The War Diary further explains that it is "the Operations Branch who are the 'users' of Deception": "The 'O' Staff is the one which must originate the demand for a Deception Plan, and who alone can dictate the all-important 'OBJECT' which it is required to attain. It is they too who will direct the tempo of the plan as it develops, and who will eventually decide when it should be replaced by a new one."[18] "A" Force itself was officially transferred from I to Ops.[19]

With the reorganization came a much needed increase in personnel. "A" Force previously functioned with only twelve officers, seven of whom were assigned to MI9 duties.[20] MI9 received its own war establishment—GSI(N)—on February 25. Although it continued to function as a section of "A" Force, MI9 was granted its own permanent staff of six full-time officers committed specifically to escape and evasion duties.[21] The section was commanded by Tony Simonds.[22] As a result of the official recognition of MI9, "A" Force's N section no longer had to borrow officers from the deception staff. "A" Force, as a whole, saw a significant increase in staff as the number of officers rose from twelve to thirty-nine, not including Major Jones and his staff at the "A" Force Depot. Moreover, eighteen of "A" Force's officers were dedicated solely to deception.[23]

Because "A" Force's duties had multiplied many times over and quickly spread beyond Africa as the war expanded, the implementation of deception became increasingly complex. The area covered by "A" Force was considerable, and Clarke understandably could not be physically present everywhere to guarantee the proper implementation of his deception plans. Thus, he needed an efficient way to coordinate deception for the three armies under the Middle East command: the 8th Army in the Western Desert, the 9th Army in Syria and Palestine, and the 10th Army in Iraq. To accomplish this, "A" Force representatives were assigned to the headquarters of the three armies and the XIII and XXX Corps.[24] Through a highly secretive system of communication—which was itself deceptive—Clarke kept his representatives in the field, or suboperators as they were commonly called, informed of the overall strategic objectives and specifics of ongoing deceptions. The suboperators were then able to carry out "A" Force's deceptions in the field as Clarke had in mind.[25]

The new organization of "A" Force, which remained largely unchanged for the rest of the war, greatly pleased Clarke. With a firmly established unity of command, the organization was centralized under one authority, rendering the running of deception more secure and cohesive. The reorganization provided for an increase in officers that allowed "A" Force the personnel necessary to accomplish much more than it had previously. Finally, "A" Force became immeasurably more efficient at the tactical level.

Since Clarke had arrived in Cairo, the majority of his deception plans had been applied at the strategic level. Wherever possible, Clarke included physical means of deception to support his various plans, but at that early stage "A" Force did not have the staff or resources to implement extensive physical deception. Then, with Wavell's reorganization of "A" Force, which ultimately removed control of tactical deception from the group altogether, Clarke did not have the authority to employ physical deception.

Clarke, who always believed that for his plans to be truly believable, they ought to make use of multiple forms of deception, was ready to take the tactical side of deception to a new level. With Auchinleck's order of February 12 and the subsequent expansion of the "A" Force organization, Clarke finally had the authority, means, personnel, and leadership in position throughout the Middle East theater to plan and execute highly sophisticated deceptions using a combination of strategic and tactical means. That was the situation as Clarke began working on Bastion.

The goal of Bastion was defensive and aimed at preventing Rommel from taking to the battlefield for at least three to four weeks, thereby allowing the British time to strengthen their defenses along the Gazala line and bring up reinforcements—namely, the 7th Armoured Division and the New Zealand Division. Clarke hoped to accomplish that task by convincing Rommel that Tobruk was strongly defended and that the British were trying to lure him into a trap by inducing him to attack the highly fortified port. The deception contained the following points: (1) the British were poised to strike Rommel's troops but were waiting for the enemy to drive forward in order to cut him off and destroy his entire force; (2) the British were hoping that the Axis forces would attack the Gazala-Acroma position so that Britain's strong, reinforced armored forces could cut them off from their supplies; (3) tank formations were lying in wait at Tobruk, Jarabub, and Bir El Gobi for the counterstrike; and (4) Tobruk was designated as the forward base for British operations against Rommel's left flank. In addition, Clarke passed along information that Tobruk would be held at all costs.[26] In truth, Auchinleck had decided not to endure another siege.[27]

For the plan to succeed, "A" Force had to provide proof of Britain's strength at Tobruk; furthermore, it had to look as if the defensive positions were complete, not awaiting reinforcements. At the strategic level, this goal was accomplished by spreading rumors, organizing leakages, "losing" documents, and

ensuring that planted information traveled through the proper intelligence channels. Clarke arranged for SIME to spread rumors and send out wireless messages
reading, "Please counter suggestions that ROMMEL is advancing into a trap set
specially by us"; "Please counter leakages regarding arrival tank reinforcements
TOBRUK"; and "Please counter rumours that substantial reinforcements have
now reached Eighth Army in WESTERN DESERT."[28] The word "counter" was
code for "encourage." Thus, if the transmission was intercepted, it would not
expose the deception; to the contrary, the messages were written in a manner to
support the ruse. Additionally, administrative measures, such as making preparations for extending Britain's railway and rerouting convoys, were used.[29]

At the tactical level, "A" Force employed its dummy units and made extensive use of camouflage. As far as the dummy units were concerned, "A" Force
intended to simulate the existence of 300 additional tanks in the field. On
February 15 the 37th RTR of Major Jones' "A" Force Depot faked a concentration
of 150 tanks near Bir El Gobi, approximately 30 miles south of Tobruk. Oddly
enough, the 37th did so by using one of Rommel's known deceptive techniques.
Rommel liked to hide his tanks under Bedouin tents, but from the air the RAF
could always spot the tank tracks leading up to the tents. Therefore, instead of
using its dummy tanks, the 37th headed out with canvas material and track simulators.[30] On the night of February 15 Jones' crew set up 150 tents, complete with
telltale track marks in the sand. Only 4 dummy tanks were used, each poorly
concealed under a tent. Fires were lit, and the unit's wireless sets became active.
The hard work was rewarded when the Germans bombed the tents on February
16 and 22. The 37th then moved on and displayed its dummy tanks at Jarabub.[31]

On February 9 half of Jones' 38th RTR arrived at Tobruk with fifty-two tanks.
The formation was promptly bombed. The other half made it to Acroma on the
seventeenth to help supplement the XIII Corps' armored strength. The 101st
RTR provided an additional fifty dummy tanks to support the 1st Armoured
Division. Altogether, Jones successfully manufactured the appearance of three
hundred tanks in the target region.[32]

The camouflage teams also contributed greatly to the deception. Between
Gazala and Tobruk, they created the illusion of minefields, trenches, fortified
defenses, and gun positions. In Tobruk, where the camouflage experts had been
extremely active during the port's prolonged siege,[33] the crew helped to simulate

the appearance of strength and make it look as if the defense work was already completed. They also made every effort to ensure that the thinning out in preparation for a possible evacuation of Tobruk went unnoticed by the enemy.[34]

The War Diary reveals that one of the most important accomplishments of the camouflage team was to help increase the morale of the British troops in Tobruk. It asserts that in the "first days of February spirits were low in the former fortress. The rapid retreat from BENGHAZI after the victories of the previous month had started a wave of despondency." The narrative later states that the "activities soon appeared to have their effect upon the general atmosphere of the place . . . so that an officer who reported on the morale of TOBRUK two weeks later was able to say that it was 'greatly improved.'"[35]

The officers at "A" Force worked diligently to pass on every aspect of Operation Bastion to the enemy. With the momentum on the Axis side, Clarke and his men had to fight against the odds. To complicate matters, Clarke knew that it would be at least one week before the enemy began assembling the puzzle of information being fed to him through the various channels, and that it would take approximately three weeks for him to have a complete picture of the deception story. In the case of Bastion, Clarke assumed that the enemy would first be exposed to the deception by February 15, would be sufficiently under its influence by the twentieth, and would put the whole scenario together by the twenty-fifth.[36] Clarke could only hope that Rommel would buy into the deception before deciding to resume the offensive.

Only three days into the execution of Bastion, however, it appeared that the effort had failed before it really had a chance to get going. On February 15 the British learned that enemy formations were closing in on Gazala. The news was most unwelcome. Contrary to the story passed on to Rommel, the British were incredibly weak and in no way prepared to defend themselves at Gazala or Tobruk. Reinforcements from the Nile Delta had yet to arrive, and the defenses in the forward positions were not completed.[37]

Then, just as the British were preparing to meet the advance, the enemy stopped. On the sixteenth, the Axis forces returned to their original position. The War Diary comments that "what explanation lay behind this strangely un-German manoeuvre, we never discovered, and it still remains a mystery—though some of us would like to think that the Deception Plan had played a part."[38] There is little mention of this incident in other sources. F. H. Hinsley notes that Rommel intended for his forces to occupy the territory up to the Gazala line and that the move took place at the time reported in the War Diary. Hinsley does not mention the enemy's return to his original position but does explain that Enigma decrypts revealed that Rommel's troops had instead set up a defensive position and decided to rest and reorganize.[39] The action is not discussed at all in *The Rommel Papers*, although Rommel was preoccupied at that particular time with his desperate shortage of supplies.[40] If he had been convinced of Britain's supposed strength at Tobruk, that knowledge very well may have exacerbated his concerns. One can only guess, but it is plausible to suggest that Rommel might have been held in check by the deception efforts.

Whether the Axis halt had anything to do with Bastion is a matter of speculation. What is certain is that Rommel did not resume his attack on the Gazala position until the end of May, and that was remarkable considering that Britain's plan to keep Rommel at bay until the first week of March seemed highly optimistic at the time. Nonetheless, the lull enabled Clarke to see Bastion to fruition and to work on other deception plans. On March 15 all efforts associated with Bastion were suspended because the deception had fulfilled its objectives.

Clarke and his team benefited from the experience of each individual deception they attempted and extracted a number of lessons. The first lesson from Bastion was to ensure that the object of the deception reflected what the commander wanted the enemy to do, not what he wanted him to think. Correctly defining the object was not a new problem; in fact, the same issue had arisen during Clarke's first deception effort in Africa—Operation Camilla. During Camilla the Italians thought exactly what Wavell and Clarke had wanted them to think, but they acted in a manner that was the complete opposite of what the British had hoped to achieve.[41] Even though Clarke immediately resolved the problem of accurately defining the object after Camilla, it was an issue that continued to arise at "A" Force because military commanders had trouble expressing exactly what they wanted the enemy to do—it was much easier to articulate what they wanted the enemy to think.[42]

The second lesson from Bastion was that all deception plans needed sufficient time to play out if they were to achieve the intended results. The War Diary states, "It is no use telling a Deception Staff to try and influence an enemy 'at once.'" It continues, "We assumed as a rough rule that no deception measures would be likely to influence the enemy appreciably in less than a week from the date of their initiation, and that normally three weeks should be allowed before a plan could be expected to exert its full effect."[43] What that meant, of course, was that deception functioned at its best when it was offensive in nature and tended to thrive in situations in which the deception team enjoyed ample time for implementation. When the military situation was deteriorating and the army needed lifesaving deceptions hastily prepared on the spot, "A" Force could offer little help. That was almost the case when the Axis troops began moving toward Gazala only three days into Bastion; the effort was salvaged only because the enemy halted his advance.

The third point underscored by Bastion was the absolute need to combine tactical and strategic deception. When "A" Force could deceive both the eyes and the ears of the enemy, as likely occurred during Bastion, the deception had a much greater chance of success.[44] It only made sense that the more proof provided to the enemy, the more likely he was to buy into the ruse. From that point forward, with "A" Force again in control of tactical deception, the employment of physical deception in the field was considered just as important as, or even more so in some circumstances, strategic efforts.

With Bastion under way and the military situation calm for the time being, Clarke began work on another deception that was to become one of the most important—and successful—deceptions of the war. During 1941 Clarke had created a number of notional formations to supplement the appearance of Britain's strength in the field. Those formations were, among others, the 1st SAS, the 10th Armoured Division, the 7th Infantry Division, and the 37th, 38th, 39th, and 101st RTRs. In March 1942 Clarke determined to expand on his previous efforts to artificially enlarge Britain's order of battle. The plan, Cascade, was approved in its final form on July 5.

Part of Clarke's motivation at that particular time was the war's escalation. Although Britain's forces in the Middle East were engaged in combat only in the Western Desert, some feared that that might change in the near future. The British were most concerned about their northern front, namely, the areas of Syria and Persia, as the German armies in Russia were steadily pushing east. Germany's progress in Russia presented two specific threats. First, if the German offensive was successful, it might lead to a renewed focus on capturing Turkey. Second, if the Germans captured the Caucasus, along with its vast oil reserves, they could move against the British in the Middle East from the north. The latter scenario was particularly worrying. If the Germans managed to defeat the British in the Middle East, Britain would lose its major source of oil supply, and that could grind Britain's war effort to a near halt.[45]

Because Britain did not have sufficient forces to defend its northern front, Clarke opted to create them. The British had five armored and ten infantry divisions under the Middle East command, although Clarke proposed to notionally raise that figure to eight armored and twenty-one infantry.[46] Because the enemy "consistently over-estimated" Britain's strength by 30 percent, the addition of fourteen divisions was viewed as acceptable.[47] By providing evidence of Britain's strength in its northern front, the British hoped to ward off an attack in that region. The plan, therefore, was to contain the war by limiting it to the Western Desert; the official object of Cascade was to "discourage the enemy from launching any offensives against the Middle East during 1942, except from LIBYA."[48] In stark contrast to many of the other deceptions that "A" Force attempted, Cascade was clearly a resounding success.

Before the plan could ever get off the ground, however, Clarke had to convince the authorities in London and Cairo that the plan could work. The War Diary states, "The scheme itself had no precedent and was not at all easy to describe in cryptic 'Counteraction' signals; while an overworked Staff Duties Directorate at the War Office needed plenty of persuasion that the seemingly hairbrained idea could have real military value."[49] It took considerable administrative maneuvering, scrupulous record keeping, and meticulous attention to detail to run such a deception, but Clarke considered it to be of paramount importance. He realized the future potential of such a ruse and the versatility it could offer the deception planners. He wrote, "I cannot stress the building up of the false Order of Battle. This must be the first task of all Deception staff, and it must go on unceasingly. It is dull, hard slogging business, but it gets its reward from time to time in the shape of captured documents which show exactly what the enemy believes to be our own Order of Battle."[50] Unlike short-term plans, the order-of-battle deception ran throughout the entire war and proved invaluable to the Allied war effort.

The greatest challenge in bringing Cascade to life was administrative. Creating military formations from nothing but one person's imagination was not as easy as it might seem. Each unit had to have its own numeric designation, a specific insignia that would appear on uniforms and vehicles, a credible history, and an extensive trail of paperwork to support its existence. Once a unit received a name, its numeric designation had to be officially retired so that it could not be given to a real unit in the future. It would be harmful to the deception if, for example, a genuine 7th Division appeared in Syria at the same time the notional division was "active" in the Western Desert. The administrative sector had to take the same precautions when assigning insignia to the imaginary units.[51] The War Diary lightheartedly records that the "divisional signs . . . must have been a godsend to the enemy's Intelligence, for even the lowest grade of agent, whether he could speak English or not, could note without difficulty or risk the various vehicle signs appearing in different localities."[52]

Once "A" Force brought a new formation to life, the organization had to continue to provide detailed information and documentation of the unit's activities for the benefit of the enemy until the war's end. "A" Force could not create a unit and then abandon it, as that would arouse suspicion. Clarke explained, "Its main difference from any other form of deception is that it is a permanent daily dish—it goes on all the time. You must take a good deal of care in the false units you are going to create. It is necessary to stick to them and make every imaginary move a logical one."[53] Detailed records of the phantom units were kept in Cairo and London and had to be updated continuously. The entire operation was highly complicated but was successful because it was closely controlled by "A" Force.[54] Regardless of the work required, Clarke put forth the effort because he recognized what an asset the bogus formations could be to the war effort.

In 1942 Clarke created eight divisions and two armored brigades. In the first half of 1943 he added six more British divisions and a bogus American armored regiment. In May 1943 he formed two additional divisions, as well as the 12th Army and 14th Corps in December of that year.[55] In 1944 Cascade gave way to an expanded order-of-battle deception known as Wantage.[56] The later, well-known creation of the imaginary FUSAG in England, notionally commanded by Gen. George S. Patton, was the direct legacy of Clarke's success at building a bogus order of battle in the desert.

The success of Clarke's order-of-battle deception efforts is undeniable. As Clarke predicted, captured enemy documents provided irrefutable proof that the enemy had accepted the false order of battle as authentic. In December 1941, before work on Cascade had even begun, the British recovered enemy documents that included the 10th Armoured Division, 7th Infantry Division, 38th RTR, and 39th RTR in the enemy's estimations of British strength. In May 1942, with Cascade fully under way, captured documents revealed that the enemy had overestimated Britain's strength in the Middle East by 30 percent and had accepted the 8th Division, 12th Division, 2nd Indian Division, 101st RTR, and a parachute battalion of the 1st SAS as real.[57]

In November 1942, after the Battle of El Alamein, the British discovered sufficient enemy records to know that the Germans believed seven of the original eight Cascade divisions to be genuine formations. The findings also included a U.S. tank regiment and officially listed the British dummy tanks regiments as an armored brigade. All told, the enemy overestimated Britain's infantry forces by 45 percent and its armored strength by 40 percent.[58]

Finally, the discovery that the Germans had bought the deception and obligingly included the notional forces in the British order of battle gave "A" Force a significant advantage over the enemy. After each discovery, Clarke knew that he could safely use the identified formations in future deceptions. In fact, the bogus units became a staple of just about every one of Clarke's deceptions from that point forward. The painstaking and laborious work necessary to create a fictitious order of battle from Clarke's imagination reaped great rewards.

At first the use of bogus forces was employed defensively—to provide a facade of strength when the British were in reality extremely weak. As the military situation slowly changed and Britain's situation improved, Clarke was able to use his false order of battle offensively. The offensive nature of his work can be seen from mid-1942 to D day.

During the spring of 1942, the war ground to a halt. The Axis forces needed to rebuild their strength after reclaiming the majority of Cyrenaica but were experiencing delays in receiving supplies. The British 8th Army had taken a severe mauling during its retreat to Gazala-Tobruk but was trying to rebuild and plan for a summer offensive. Auchinleck originally hoped to have the 8th Army ready to launch another campaign by the end of May, but he soon pushed the date back into June. In the meantime, the commander in chief asked Clarke to prepare an offensive deception that would mislead Rommel as to the exact time and location of the impending action. To achieve surprise, Clarke was to convince Rommel that the British were in no position to attack before August. To render the enemy vulnerable at the focal point of the attack in the south, "A" Force set out to demonstrate that the main thrust would come in the north.[59] Plan Fabric—which combined strategic and tactical measures—was approved on April 4, 1942.

The tactical aspect of Fabric sought to establish that the British were planning to launch their future offensive at the enemy's northern frontier, thus forcing him to make faulty adjustments to his defensive dispositions. The strategic part of the plan focused on convincing Rommel that the British would not attempt an offensive until August at the earliest. August was chosen to provide some leeway in the plan because Auchinleck had doubts that Ritchie would be able to mount an offensive in June.[60] So, it fell to "A" Force to put forth a plausible explanation for the delay.

A number of reasons were proposed. First, according to the deception story, the British expected an attack elsewhere—either at Cyprus or along their northern front—thus, they had little choice but to reinforce those sectors at the expense of the 8th Army. Second, the British would not be able to attack during the particularly hot and windy months of May, June, and July, commonly referred to as the khamsin period; it was implied, largely through the press, that the British assumed that the enemy would also be prevented from staging an offensive owing to the unfavorable climate.[61] Finally, the British claimed that they were unable to use their new American Grant tanks (that were essential for the campaign) because the proper ammunition had yet to arrive from the United States.[62]

There is evidence that the Germans not only received the planted information but also believed it to be true. For instance, Rommel specifically recorded in his papers that the British had been reinforced with some Grants from the United States but that they lacked ammunition. He therefore discounted them as a factor in the upcoming offensive. Not surprisingly, he was caught completely off guard when he encountered the Grant tanks in battle in May.[63]

To offer visual proof that the British were not planning to strike, "A" Force simulated a weakening of Britain's forces at the front. That was, of course, quite contrary to reality because the British were preparing for an offensive and were rapidly reinforcing their frontline positions. The trick, then, was to simultaneously hide the genuine preparations and create the illusion of a withdrawal.

To provide the proper visual evidence of a withdrawal, Clarke called in Major Jones' dummy units. For the first time, Jones put together an entire dummy brigade. The notional 33rd Armoured Brigade, which was just formed in May 1942, was ordered to move to the front under the cover of darkness for complete secrecy.[64] Next, it was to leave the front and head east during the day, when it could be observed by enemy reconnaissance. If the plan worked, the enemy would deduce that the British were withdrawing a large portion of their armored units from the front.

In that same regard, the policy concerning the movement of genuine formations was to conceal those moving to the front, but not those leaving. As an example, Clarke specifically issued the following order regarding genuine troop movements taking place: "We must not hide from the enemy the withdrawal of the New Zealand and Polish Bdgs. and 4 Ind. Div., but must conceal as much as possible the forward move of the 5 Ind. Div."[65] By doing this, Clarke hoped to create the appearance of a general thinning out at the front.

To help support the ruse, everything possible was done to create a "peaceful atmosphere."[66] Among other things, 8th Army soldiers were granted leave, "leave trips" were organized for personnel, arrangements were made for war correspondents to tour the Western Desert, officers were asked to accept any invitations they received for future social engagements, and wireless silence bans were lifted.[67]

These measures were accompanied by Plan Maiden, which sought to further the impression that nothing was brewing in the Middle East. Accordingly, full arrangements were made for Auchinleck to visit London during the days immediately preceding the offensive. It was understood by those involved in the deception that the visit would have to be cancelled as time drew near, but in the meantime, the commander in chief's departure from Cairo certainly indicated that the 8th Army was not planning an attack.[68]

Although Clarke and his team labored tirelessly to implement the deception, they encountered many difficulties with Fabric. Part of the problem Clarke faced was that his orders from GHQ to create the impression of weakness at the front ran counter to the 8th Army's desire to show strength in order to keep Rommel at bay. Thus, while Clarke was working to demonstrate that the 8th Army was not in the active stages of planning an offensive but was instead relocating formations to protect Britain's northern front, Ritchie was planning a series of strong raids into Axis territory to interrupt the offensive preparations under way at the enemy's camp. In May, when it became clear that Rommel was planning an offensive, Ritchie completely abandoned the policy to simulate weakness. From that point on, the 8th Army commander did everything in his power to project strength in order to delay the attack.[69]

The constant change in policy complicated matters for Clarke and left him with no alternative but to try to integrate the 8th Army's fluctuating plans into the deception on an ad hoc basis. To explain the raids, for instance, he hastily spread rumors that the army was initiating the attacks in an attempt to cover their actual weakness.[70] To confound the problems, the War Diary reveals, "War Correspondents at the Front were starting to belittle the weather difficulties of May, to speak of increasing strength and reinforcements, and generally rattle the saber."[71] Then, to make matters even worse from the deception standpoint, the transport of reinforcements to the front, which was supposed to be concealed, was duly noted by enemy reconnaissance.[72] On the whole, the general circumstances made upholding the ruse difficult for Clarke.

Despite "A" Force's best efforts, Fabric was falling apart, and it all came to an abrupt end before it had really gotten off the ground. The plan had to be abandoned in late May after Rommel launched an offensive to capture Tobruk on the night of May 26.[73] The British learned of the coming attack well in advance, so all work on Fabric ceased as defensive preparations took precedence.[74] What was particularly frustrating for the deception team was that the majority of the plans associated with Fabric were never even implemented.

From the beginning, Fabric was plagued by difficulties. For one, the overall plan was written at GHQ, but the tactical side of the plan should have originated at the 8th Army headquarters, as the army was in a better position to know what it needed in the field. Clarke wrote, "I think the lesson for the future is that GHQ. should avoid preparing an 'Army' cover plan and assist only in the 'putting over' of a story which has been devised by the Army HQ. An Army HQ. will be more in the picture of a cover plan they have drawn up themselves and can better tell GHQ what help they want. It will be preferable to GHQ. telling them what to do to 'cover' their own operations and, with the additional GSO.I's [general staff officers (grade 1)] now in the saddle, this should not be over-burdening the Armies."[75] The GSOIs Clarke referred to were the "A" Force field representatives appointed to the army and corps headquarters. During Fabric, the 8th Army did not yet have an "A" Force representative in place because "A" Force had only recently reassumed complete control over tactical deception. In the future, however, "A" Force organized the strategic planning of its deceptions from Cairo, and the "A" Force representative at army headquarters helped to develop and execute the tactical side of the plan.[76] Thus, the tactical deception plan originated with the army instead of GHQ, and that move proved most effective.

An additional problem with Fabric worth mentioning is that the plan called for "A" Force to run the tactical deception from April until August. The time frame was based on the assumption that the military situation would remain constant for four months. Because that assumption was not even remotely realistic, the deception team had to constantly rework Fabric to meet the ever-changing circumstances in the field. If nothing else, this experience convinced Clarke that tactical deception plans could be planned only on a short-term basis.

In an overall assessment of Fabric, it appears that its greatest flaw rested with the object that was provided by GHQ. To achieve surprise, the British wanted Rommel to think that they were weak and not planning an offensive. The strategy might have been good if the 8th Army was in a position to launch an offensive in the near future and was simply trying to buy a few weeks' time, but that was not the case; nobody at GHQ or at 8th Army headquarters knew for certain when the army would be ready to take the offensive. It seems that instead of thwarting an enemy attack, the British may have enticed Rommel to strike by emphasizing their weakness when they were incapable of withstanding a vigorous enemy assault.

Although Fabric was dogged by troubles, many of its elements were used in the deception for the major offensive at El Alamein. The El Alamein effort was a resounding success, and one can argue that it greatly benefited from the lessons learned from Fabric. In other words, the kinks of learning how to effectively combine strategic and tactical deception over an extended period were worked out just in time.

Finally, Fabric may not have gone as planned, but it would be incorrect to argue that it failed completely. Although it is true that the deception failed to prevent Rommel from taking the offensive, he was thoroughly surprised at how strongly defended the British line was. One account records,

> Rommel's plan for the attack on the Gazala Commonwealth position was based on evaluations of the enemy which were somewhat different from reality. Axis intelligence units had failed to identify certain Allied units and

positions on the eve of battle. The 22nd and 32nd Armored brigades were thought to be far from the Gazala line. The 3rd Indian Motorized brigade south of Bir Hacheim and the 29th at Bir el Gobi were also surprises, as well as the 201st brigade at the Knigthsbridge strongpoint. The 150th brigade box at Gor el-Ualeb would be a great surprise and block Axis supply and communication for part of the battle before finally being cleared.[77]

It is also known, as previously noted, that Rommel was caught off guard by the appearance of the American Grant tanks in battle.

It can be deduced that Rommel was deceived by Fabric. He certainly did not realize that in choosing to attack Britain's southern section—from which the British planned their own offensive to begin—he was sending his forces up against one of the more strongly defended sectors of the Gazala line. Because of Rommel's faulty estimations of British strength, his forces encountered much tougher fighting than anticipated. Consequently, their advance consumed far more resources than expected and took considerably longer than planned. In fact, Rommel intended to take Tobruk on the fourth day of his offensive; instead, it took him nearly a month.[78]

Throughout May Rommel made preparations to retake the offensive by the end of the month. For the first half of 1942, the Germans had put forth a determined effort to rectify their supply situation by neutralizing Britain's air and naval activity at Malta. Under heavy air attacks, the British were unable to harass the enemy's shipping as they had in the past. By April, then, Rommel's supply situation had greatly improved because his lines of supply were protected and greater numbers of convoys had arrived in Africa intact.[79]

For the British, the attacks on Malta were distressing. The first, most immediate concern was that they were unable to prevent the enemy from reinforcing. Second, the increased presence of the Luftwaffe made it nearly impossible for the British to receive shipping through the Mediterranean, so Britain's supply convoys had to make the long and arduous journey around the cape. By the end of May, however, Malta was showing signs of recovery.[80] Rommel realized that he needed to strike the British as soon as possible, while he had fresh supplies and before Britain had sufficient time to strengthen its forces.

Rommel launched his attack on May 26. Using his own deception, he sought to make the British believe that the main weight of the assault was coming to the northern part of the Gazala line.[81] To mislead the British, he sent the Italian infantry with German armor to the north on the twenty-sixth. The infantry's tanks and trucks were to "drive in circles day and night behind the front," and at night the Italians were instructed to make as much noise as possible to simulate a large concentration of forces. Another unit, the 90th Light Division, was equipped with "dust-raisers" to "feign the presence of massed armour in the area."[82]

Although Britain's knowledge of the enemy was incomplete, its intelligence agencies discovered evidence of the impending offensive in early May. From Enigma decrypts, the British learned that the campaign would begin in the latter part of May and that Tobruk was the immediate objective. Despite the forewarning, the British were unaware of the operational details of Rommel's offensive.[83] Nonetheless, Rommel failed to attain surprise or to deliver the knockout blow he had hoped for.

The Battle of Gazala began on May 26 and lasted until June 15. Although the British knew that the attack was coming, they fell for Rommel's deceptive moves and expected the main thrust in the north.[84] Regardless, the enemy did not initially achieve his goals, and the effort to break through Britain's defensive positions failed. In those first days of battle, the British suffered heavy losses to their armor, revealing that they still lacked a solid understanding of how to properly employ their armored units on the battlefield. It was unfortunate because the British entered the battle with the numerical advantage in tanks. There is no greater condemnation of Britain's misuse of its armored forces than that provided by Rommel:

> Ritchie had thrown his armour into the battle piecemeal and had thus given us the chance of engaging them on each separate occasion with just about enough of our own tanks. This dispersal of the British armoured brigades was incomprehensible. In my view the sacrifice of the 7th Armoured Division south of Bir el Harmat served no strategical or tactical purpose whatsoever. . . . The principal aim of the British should have been to have brought all the armour they had into action at one and the same time. They should never have allowed themselves to be duped into dividing their forces before the battle or during our feint attack against the Gazala line.[85]

Despite their armored blunders, the British still managed to check the initial German and Italian thrust.

By May 29, after suffering heavy losses of his own, Rommel found his army surrounded in the "cauldron" south of Gazala. The situation might have ended badly for the Germans and Italians, except that Ritchie's counterattack on June 5–6, which aimed to destroy the Axis forces in the "cauldron," failed disastrously. Not only did Rommel see it coming, but the attack also provided him with the opportunity to break out. David French insists that the British effort "revealed the depths to which the British had sunk in carrying out combined arms operations."[86] Auchinleck reportedly remarked that the "unsuccessful counter-stroke was probably the turning point of the whole battle."[87] If nothing else, it certainly led to a shift in the momentum.

On June 10 the Axis forces took Bir Hacheim, and by the fifteenth the British had to abandon the Gazala line. The 8th Army then began a full retreat to the Egyptian border. In a matter of weeks, the British lost Gazala; their months of planning and preparing defenses had amounted to nothing.

Rommel's next move was to take Tobruk. As early as February the three commanders in chief of the Middle East had agreed not to undertake yet another siege of Tobruk. If it looked as though the port was going to be invested, the British intended to withdraw.[88] However, the prime minister disagreed with the policy and wanted Tobruk "held at all costs."[89] By June 18 the enemy had surrounded Tobruk. Because the port was so well supplied, though, Auchinleck assumed that it could hold out for at least three months until his forces were able to mount a counterattack.

Tobruk had served as a great source of embarrassment for the Germans in 1941, and there was no way that Rommel could afford to carry out another prolonged siege of the port. Therefore, he planned to take Tobruk as quickly as possible. On June 20 the battle for Tobruk began. It was over by the twenty-first. The enemy took approximately 33,000 troops prisoner and laid claim to vast amounts of abandoned food, water, equipment, supplies, and fuel.[90] The loss was devastating for the British, but Churchill was particularly shaken by the surrender. He wrote, "This was one of the heaviest blows I can recall during the war. Not only were its military effects grievous, but it affected the reputation of the British armies. . . . Defeat is one thing; disgrace is another."[91]

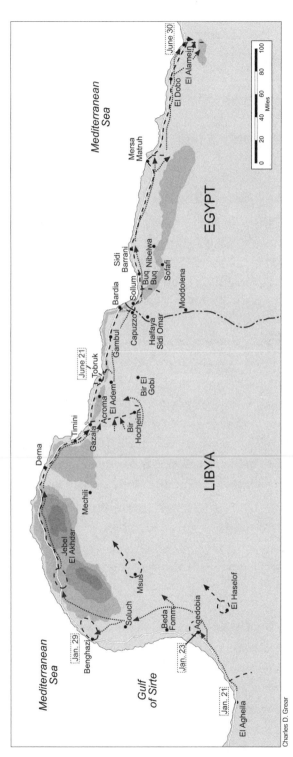

MAP 5. NORTH AFRICA, 1942: ROMMEL'S SECOND OFFENSIVE,
JANUARY 21–JULY 7, 1942

Charles D. Grear

As for the victors, the reaction at the Axis camp was quite joyous, and Rommel was generously rewarded with a promotion to field marshal. But the German commander was not finished with the British yet. Given that the 8th Army was weak and on the run, Rommel wanted to pursue it into Egypt. On June 23 Hitler agreed that Rommel should continue the advance. Three days later Rommel was granted formal permission to pursue the British as far as El Alamein.[92]

Unable to establish a defensive line along the Egyptian border quickly enough, the British fell back to Mersa Matruh and El Alamein. On June 25, when facing possible defeat, Auchinleck assumed personal command of the 8th Army. He then made the decision to hold his forces at El Alamein. The narrow passage at El Alamein between the Mediterranean Sea and the Qattara Depression—an area consisting of salt marshes and quicksand—provided a favorable position for defense. Jon Latimer explains that to "outflank the natural barrier to the south would require a massive detour and crossing the shifting sands of the Sahara. Here was the one place with secure flanks that precluded the tactics that had brought Rommel to the verge of Cairo."[93]

Of even greater significance, El Alamein was essentially the last place that the British could make a stand. It was approximately forty miles from Alexandria, and from there the enemy would have a clear path to Cairo.[94] If the German and Italian forces managed to break through the El Alamein defenses, they would likely be at the gates of Cairo in only twenty-four hours.[95]

At no other point in the war in the Middle East had the British come so close to defeat. Even in the summer of 1940, when the British stood completely unprepared for war against a massive Italian army, they remained hopeful that they could protect Cairo. Now, with Rommel's forces barreling down on El Alamein, it looked as if all might be lost. Geoffrey Barkas poignantly recalled,

> It was not a battle, but a war that hung in the balance. The ultimate prize lay almost within the German grasp. They had swept forward some five hundred miles. Another sixty, and then the Mediterranean would truly be their lake. Alexandria would be theirs. Looking southward, an intoxicating prospect would beckon to them across the caramel-pink salt marshes fringing the city. The Delta, Cairo, Suez, the huge depots and workshops, the ports and railways, airfields, factories, and supplies. Port Said, Suez,

the Canal itself. The gate would be thrown wide open to the Red Sea, the Indian Ocean, and the Persian Gulf; to India and onward to a meeting with the Japanese. The oil of the Middle East would be theirs. All these juicy fruits would be ripe for the plucking if only the Afrika Korps could burst through the defences of Alamein while Eighth Army was still tangled in the chaos of a long retreat.[96]

The situation appeared so critical that the British began burning their documents and making preparations to evacuate Cairo. The War Diary records,

> Inside the city itself hasty defences were being manned on the West banks of the NILE, civilian evacuations were under way, and G.H.Q. and the Embassy began to burn their records. A rapidly-improvised "DELTA FORCE" under General REES was brought into being to defend the NILE crossings, and General AUCHINLECK with a small staff prepared to open his Battle Headquarters in the hills to the East of CAIRO. Meanwhile the Main Headquarters of the 8th Army had arrived outside the Pyramids at MENA, with its Advanced Headquarters not many miles behind up the CAIRO-ALEXANDRIA road. The threat to CAIRO had suddenly become very real, and all offices were ordered to prepare for sudden evacuation.[97]

Thus, the entire war in the Middle East hinged upon the 8th Army holding at El Alamein.

On June 29 the enemy captured Mersa Matruh—along with all of its supplies—and on the thirtieth Rommel's troops reached the El Alamein line. Rommel had no intention of allowing the British to establish a strongly forti- fied defensive position, so his soldiers were not allowed time to rest.[98] On July 1 he ordered them forward; again, however, tremendous improvements in intel- ligence gave the British forewarning of the attack.[99]

For three days in a row the enemy attacked, but the 8th Army held firm. For the entire month of July, the two sides engaged in a bloody confrontation that some consider the first Battle of El Alamein. Both sides suffered tremendous casualties, but the enemy had the greater difficulties of supply and reinforce- ment. The British were steadily provided with supplies and fresh reinforce- ments, and accordingly, the British gained the advantage.[100] In the end, the 8th

Army held fast to its position, giving up only a few strongpoints along the El Alamein line. Rommel wrote that his "chance of over-running the remainder of the Eighth Army and occupying Eastern Egypt at one stroke was irretrievably gone."[101] Although the 8th Army had finally stopped the Axis advance, it was weak, battered, and suffering from low morale. Yet, because the enemy remained so close to Cairo, the army could not afford to let its guard down. In other words, the immediate crisis had passed, but the threat remained.

During the intense fighting of July, Clarke began work on another deception, Plan Sentinel, which was to run from mid-July to the end of August. Sentinel was a defensive deception designed to dissuade the enemy from resuming the offensive by convincing Rommel that the area west of the Nile Delta was strongly defended along the Natrun line.[102] As Barkas put it, "The stronger he thought we were, the greater the force he would feel compelled to muster for the assault. The bigger the build-up, the longer the time. The longer the time, the better for us."[103]

Because the stakes were so high, the deception experts set out to use every resource at their disposal. In spite of that, efforts to use Jones' dummy tank formations were limited. The 33rd Armoured Brigade, which had participated in Fabric and then accompanied Britain's genuine armored units during the retreat to El Alamein, had returned to Cairo to refit on June 30. The depleted brigade was reconstituted and renamed the 74th Armoured Brigade. Two of its regiments, the 101st and 102nd RTRs, both of which employed the new mobile Grant dummies, were hastily put together and sent to the Natrun line beginning on July 15. Because the need at the front was so pressing, the two regiments were redirected to El Alamein. Furthermore, because the dummy formations had suffered such extensive damage during the period of retreat, "A" Force did not have additional dummy units available for deployment.[104]

Given that Clarke was unable to make greater use of Jones' dummies for the deception, he turned to his phantom Cascade formations. Using his intelligence channels, Clarke passed along the story that the 6th New Zealand Division and 3rd South African Division (both notional) had arrived at the Natrun line. To provide visual proof of their existence, "A" Force needed the help of camouflage.

Barkas was thrilled to be called in at the beginning of a deception plan, and he took great delight in creating the phantom forces and defenses. His team began by erecting tents to simulate camps. From those camps "smoke began to rise from cookhouses and incinerators. Dust clouds sprang from the new networks of tracks connecting the camps with the tarred main road. Trucks, guns, light tanks, dumps of stores, began to show themselves. 'Canteens' did a brisk but imaginary trade with the imaginary drivers of the dummy vehicles parked outside."[105] The camoufleurs also helped to provide the appearance of greater strength at genuine defensive positions and patched a weak spot in the 8th Army's line.[106] Barkas succeeded in creating the impression of extensive defenses for the benefit of enemy aerial reconnaissance. He would repeat his effort on a much grander scale only months later in preparation for the El Alamein offensive.

As usual, Clarke used his intelligence channels to pass along the deception; one, however, requires special mention. After Operation Crusader, most everyone at "A" Force and SIME assumed that the Cheese channel was permanently blown. One man, Cheese's case officer, disagreed; he thought that the channel could be revived. Captain E. J. Simpson (a prewar novelist) argued that it was not Paul Nicossof's fault that he had received bad information from his contact at GHQ. By shifting the blame, the imaginary Nicossof could again be built up in the enemy's esteem.[107]

Evidence that the Germans were suspect of Nicossof came to the attention of SIME in January 1942. From January until July, then, Nicossof played a negligible role in Britain's deceptive activities. But Simpson was not discouraged. To the contrary, he expected the Germans to question Nicossof, especially because they put so much weight on the information that he provided them prior to the Crusader offensive. Simpson's plan was to keep the channel alive in an effort to regain the Germans' trust, even if it was not of deceptive value for a time. Thus, Nicossof maintained contact with his Axis controller, although for months the enemy did not appear to trust him and rarely approached him for information. Nicossof, for his part, mainly complained of his financial troubles. In this way, Simpson gradually reassured the Germans of Nicossof's reliability and restored his reputation as a trusted agent.[108]

On July 2 it appeared that Simpson's determination had paid off. Nicossof received a message to be on alert and was asked to begin sending daily signals. In December 1941 British officials at Bletchley Park had broken the Abwehr Enigma. From that point forward they could "verify the credibility of their own double agents and see which of the messages they planted commanded credibility and which did not."[109] Abwehr messages sent between July 4 and 12 proved that the Germans considered Nicossof to be "credible" and "trustworthy" again.

The Germans likely changed their minds because they desperately needed intelligence as they advanced east.[110] Besides, they had not discovered any concrete evidence to suggest that Nicossof had deliberately misled them.

This turn of events was readily exploited by SIME and "A" Force. The fictional Nicossof began to "picture himself as 'the man who brought Rommel into Egypt'"; he dreamed "of the entry of the Panzer Armee into Cairo" and imagined "high German Officers hastening to his hotel to thank him, pay all his debts, and load him with money and medals."[111] Mostly motivated by the potential for material gain, Nicossof welcomed the opportunity to help the Germans again. Fortunately for the British, the channel was reestablished just in time to help pass along the Sentinel deception.

On July 31 Plan Sentinel was revised when British intelligence learned that the Germans were preparing to strike. The new story, promptly passed to the enemy, was that the British were trying to encourage Rommel to attack the 8th Army when the British would have the upper hand, specifically, between August 10 and 20. The timing was crucial because Rommel would not have received substantial reinforcements yet. The 8th Army was strong in antitank weapons, and by the tenth, according to the story, the British would have reinforced the army's troops to the extent that they could withstand an enemy attack. Similarly, if the Axis forces attacked during that period, they would have to fight in Britain's extensive minefields. So, the most advantageous time to lure the Germans into a premature offensive was between the tenth and twentieth. The deceptionists hoped that Rommel would conclude that the situation was no longer favorable for an attack after the twentieth as by then the 8th Army would be strengthened appreciably by the Delta defences. In a further attempt to forestall Rommel's attack, they added to the story that after August 20 Britain intended to launch its own offensive; Clarke hoped this would force Rommel into a defensive posture.[112] British intelligence learned that Rommel personally received the revised version of Sentinel on August 22.[113]

Sentinel was a success, although it is impossible to gauge to what degree. The enemy's reconnaissance observed the "buildup" between El Alamein and the Nile Delta, which led him to "grossly" overestimate British strength in the region.[114] Furthermore, the enemy offensive that appeared to be imminent did not materialize until August 30. It appears that Sentinel may have played a part in delaying the attack. Ultimately, Rommel's offensive at Alam Halfa failed (as discussed in chapter 7). Having achieved its objectives, Sentinel was cancelled. The British then began planning for a major offensive at El Alamein.

By July 1942, after Auchinleck oversaw the retreat of the 8th Army from the western edge of Cyrenaica to El Alamein, Churchill determined that the Middle East was in need of new leadership. Churchill liked and respected the commander in chief, but he was no longer confident that Auchinleck was the right man to command the theater at such a critical stage in the war. Moreover, the need for victory in the Western Desert had never been greater: at the end of July the Germans were only weeks away from reaching the Caucasus, which they did on August 9, and India had good reason to fear an invasion by Japan.[115]

Churchill decided to pay a visit to Cairo in the beginning of August. To help ensure his safety, "A" Force devised a plan, Grandiose, to misinform the enemy. Clarke knew that it would be impossible to hide the trip from the enemy, so "A" Force set out to spread deceptive information regarding the exact timing of the visit and the specifics of Churchill's whereabouts. Back in the enemy's confidence, Cheese participated in the ruse. For the most part, the information "A" Force passed along was accurate, but about two days late.[116]

Churchill arrived in Cairo on August 4, 1942. General Jan Smuts flew in from South Africa, as did General Wavell from India. The primary reason for Churchill's trip was to make a decision on the question of leadership, and he thought that he needed to visit Cairo in person to do so. He was at that moment still undecided, although his visit to the desert quickly confirmed his suspicions that a change was needed. Churchill's eventual decision to remove Auchinleck was difficult. He recalls that "in dealing with a commander of the highest character and quality, of proved ability and resolution, such decisions are painful."[117] Still, the prime minister was convinced that the Middle East needed fresh leadership and new ideas. He did not approve of Auchinleck's hasty retreat to El Alamein and had argued that the commander in chief should have taken personal command of the army much sooner than he did.[118] Similarly, the prime minister was shocked to learn that the 8th Army could not resume the offensive until September—Churchill wanted an attack without delay. According to Latimer, the postponement of the attack was ultimately Auchinleck's undoing, and Churchill made the difficult choice to appoint a new commander in chief.[119]

The irony of the situation, as Latimer points out, is that Auchinleck's successor came to the exact same conclusion—that the offensive could not take place until September at the earliest. In fact, it was pushed back until October 23. Latimer concludes, "Like Wavell before him, [Auchinleck] was compromised by the disasters that had occurred on his watch."[120]

On August 6 Churchill made the following changes to the organization and command structure: To begin, he divided the Middle East into two separate commands. The "Near East command" consisted of Africa, Palestine, and Syria and had its headquarters in Cairo. The "Middle East command" included Iraq and Persia and on August 21 became known as the Persia and Iraq command (PAIC). Churchill asked Auchinleck to accept the position of commander in chief of the PAIC, but he refused. Auchinleck disagreed with the division of the Middle East into two commands; he viewed the formations in the region as one cohesive unit. The position was subsequently offered to General Maitland Wilson, who was at that time commanding the 9th Army in Syria—he accepted. Auchinleck went on to become the commander in chief of India exactly one year later, when Wavell was appointed viceroy of India.[121]

To replace Auchinleck in Cairo, Churchill appointed General Harold Alexander to the position of commander in chief of the Near East command; he officially took command on August 15. On the sixth, General W. H. E. Gott was named as the new commander of the 8th Army, and General Bernard Law Montgomery was chosen to help plan and coordinate Operation Torch (the Anglo-American landings in French North Africa). In a stroke of misfortune, Gott died the next day when his plane was shot down by the enemy. Churchill, therefore, placed the 8th Army under Montgomery's command.[122]

Montgomery brought immediate changes to the 8th Army. Although he was not supposed to take control until August 15, he assumed command on his own authority on August 13 after visiting the army and realizing what terrible shape it was in. Montgomery was struck by the drab and uncomfortable living conditions the troops had to endure. He recalled, for example, that they ate on the bare ground and slept under the open sky. The army's morale was understandably low, and the troops seemed confused by the absence of clear orders.[123] Alexander noted that although the troops retained their determination, they did not understand why they had been ordered to withdraw from land they had defended resolutely. To restore morale, the new commander in chief informed the army that "no further withdrawal was contemplated and that we would fight the coming battle on the ground on which we stood."[124]

The long retreat from western Cyrenaica to El Alamein had clearly taken its toll on the troops. Auchinleck had always intended to maintain the integrity of the 8th Army, so when he was faced with the choice of losing the entire army or pulling back, he chose to retreat. On August 12 Montgomery met with Auchinleck. Auchinleck explained that if the enemy were to attack in force, the 8th Army was under orders to retreat to the Nile Delta and then, if Cairo were lost, south along the river. Montgomery, like Alexander, absolutely disagreed with the policy of retreat, which he forbade upon his assumption of command the following day. He reiterated Alexander's order and made it clear to the army that he expected them to stand their ground. He wrote, "I issued orders that in the event of enemy attack there would be *no* withdrawal; we would fight on the ground we now held and if we couldn't stay there alive we would stay there dead."[125] He also ordered the cessation of all efforts to fortify the Nile Delta. Because the army was not to take a single step back and the defense of Egypt depended on El Alamein holding, all defenses would be concentrated at El Alamein.[126] Alexander issued orders to the same effect.[127]

Upon his arrival at the 8th Army, Montgomery immediately realized that the army and air force needed to work in closer unison. The two headquarters were miles apart and not in close contact. According to Montgomery, the two forces appeared to be fighting two different wars.[128] In an effort to form joint operations with an integrated system of command, he relocated the army headquarters near the sea at Burg el Arab, where it was in close proximity to the Desert Air Force (DAF) headquarters. Living conditions at the new headquarters were greatly improved, as were those of the army itself. Tents were promptly erected and furniture added to the mess so that the troops could "be as comfortable as possible"—Montgomery could see no reason for them to be miserable, which did nothing to improve their morale.[129]

Montgomery also made a point of visiting with the troops, and his visible presence had the desired effect of reenergizing the 8th Army. He promised reinforcements, reassured his troops that the worst times had passed, and asked them to have faith. Playfair describes Montgomery's approach and its effect: "All this and more was put over with a Cromwellian fervour, and the effect was electric. By a strenuous programme of tours and visits, with the objects of seeing and being seen and heard, of getting to know and becoming known, the new Commander strove to impress his personality upon his whole Army. He certainly succeeded."[130] Montgomery's ability to show his resolution, convey his strategy in no uncertain terms, and express his confidence that the British would succeed went far toward building a bond between the new commander and his troops.

By bringing in reinforcements, Montgomery was able to strengthen the army and, most important, to increase its overall confidence. He also made significant changes to the way the army fought. Over and over the 8th Army had been mauled by Germany's armor and powerful antitank guns, even when it had an overwhelming numerical advantage. The problem was that the British had yet to learn how to fight a modern armored war. Montgomery carefully studied how the Germans organized their armored formations, and he set out to create a panzer army of sorts at the 8th Army. From then on, the British would not disperse their tanks but would concentrate as a division, like the Germans did. Montgomery steadily worked to rebuild, reequip, and train the army so that Britain could resume the fight; once it was ready, Montgomery intended to "hit Rommel for six right out of Africa."[131]

With the change in command and a new focus that was clearly offensive, the situation in the Middle East began to show signs of marked improvement. On August 19, having returned to the Middle East after a trip to Moscow, Churchill again visited the 8th Army. This time, he found the situation much improved. He described the scene when he arrived: about a thousand soldiers were bathing in the sea, bronzed from the sun, and apparently enjoying themselves.[132] In a telegram dated August 21 he wrote, "A complete change of atmosphere has taken place. . . . The highest alacrity and activity prevails. . . . The roads are busy with forward movement of troops, tanks, and guns. . . . Our army will eagerly meet the enemy should he attack and I am satisfied that we have lively, confident, resolute men in command working together as an admirable team under leaders of the highest military quality."[133] The prime minister was clearly pleased with the progress and with his choice of leadership for the Middle East.

Thus far, 1942 had been a particularly rough year for the British in the Middle East; however, the recent changes in leadership, the determined focus on taking the offensive, and the active efforts to strengthen, train, reorganize, and reenergize the army brought a renewed sense of hope and purpose to the 8th Army. With Montgomery's steadfast resolve to transform the army into an imposing force capable of outfighting and outsmarting the Germans, the air of defeatism that previously prevailed faded, and victory again seemed possible.

As the army prepared for the next major offensive, so did the deception organizations. The Battle of El Alamein would be the largest battle yet fought in the desert, and it called for the greatest deception effort of the war up to that point in time. Having had close to two years of practice and ample opportunity to learn from their mistakes, the deceptionists felt confident that they could deceive the Axis on the grandest scale yet attempted. "A" Force, its representatives in the field, the 8th Army, G(CAM), SIME, and the intelligence services came together to implement the most successful deception of the desert war, one that helped to ensure British victory. Moreover, the deception campaign resulted in the formulation of the blueprint for all future Allied deceptions of the Second World War.

It almost seems providential that the military and deception teams worked out their kinks at the same time, and at the exact moment when it was most needed. The military had struggled with its inadequate combined arms tactics and, to a lesser degree, with inferior equipment. "A" Force, once reorganized, had to learn how to effectively combine strategic and tactical deception in a timely manner. Thus, by the fall of 1942 both the military and deception organizations had identified their shortcomings and made the necessary adjustments to improve their performance. The 8th Army that took to the battlefield in October looked like a new force. Likewise, the deception effort was successful beyond expectation because it avoided the mistakes of the past. With the military and the deception machine functioning at their best and strategically synchronizing their efforts, they proved to be a formidable foe.

After the Battle of El Alamein, the British—joined by the Americans—steadily forced the Germans and Italians out of North Africa. The year 1942 may have begun on a disastrous note, yet it ended triumphantly. The quest for victory continued, and in 1943 victory was achieved in North Africa. The military—and deception organizations—continued its fight against the Axis, but this time on European soil.

–7–

Victory in the Desert:
The Deception Blueprint Revealed

By August 1942 Britain's military situation was at long last showing promising signs of improvement. After a grueling retreat through the desert, the British had checked the Axis advance at El Alamein in July. Throughout the month of July, the 8th Army successfully thwarted subsequent attempts by the enemy to strip the British of their last viable defensive position before Alexandria and Cairo. Although the army was weak and battered, it had survived.

By July Britain's intelligence community had made tremendous strides toward securing its communications procedures, thus depriving the enemy of valuable intelligence that he had become quite dependent on. The leaks mainly came from the 8th Army, RAF, and the U.S. military attaché in Cairo. The army and RAF had a relatively lax system of security, and they regularly transmitted their messages in a field code easily broken by Captain Alfred Seeböhm, Rommel's chief cryptographer.[1] Col. Bonner Fellers, the U.S. military attaché, unknowingly used a low-grade cipher system that was well-known to the enemy and commonly referred to as the "Black Code" to send regular reports on the British military situation to the United States.[2] Thus, through multiple sources the Allies had unwittingly provided Rommel with accurate and timely intelligence. Improvements in procedure, which were completed by 1943, led to secure communications with immeasurable benefits for the British military and deception planners.[3]

With the intelligence gaps identified and largely repaired, the military services could proceed with reasonable confidence that the enemy was no longer privy to their plans and state of readiness. For the deceptionists, the changes brought enormous relief. Until the fall of 1942, most of Clarke's efforts to deceive the enemy met with only limited success. There is absolutely no doubt that the enemy had been duped repeatedly by Clarke's attempts to misinform, but all too often the results fell short of their potential.

There are multiple explanations for the shortcomings. For one, the deceptionists were learning as they went along. There was no precedent to follow or deception handbook to read. Therefore, most of the early deceptions were implemented on a trial-and-error basis. Clarke and his staff at "A" Force rightly learned from their mistakes and applied their knowledge and experience to each new deception campaign. The team collectively did the best it could with the resources at its disposal, but its resources were meager during its first year of operation. It was not until 1942 was well under way that the resources allocated to deception became plentiful.

Another reason for deception's slow start was its organization—or attempts to alter its organization—and the resulting implications for the conduct and control of deception. In the beginning, "A" Force had the means to practice strategic deception only. When, by mid-1941, it became increasingly possible to employ tactical measures of deception, "A" Force was reorganized, and tactical deception became the responsibility of the army. That allocation having failed, tactical deception was again placed under Clarke's direct authority in early 1942. Once both means of deception were reunited under one head and sufficient resources made available, "A" Force had to make up for lost time and learn how to effectively employ tactical deception. The team learned quickly but did not avoid all growing pains.

Probably the greatest cause of "A" Force's setbacks, however, was the lack of proper intelligence security when it came to communications. "A" Force could try to convince the enemy that the army was weak or strong, preparing an offensive or planning to remain on the defensive, and so on, but when Rommel received accurate intelligence to the contrary courtesy of the 8th Army, RAF, or the U.S. military attaché in Cairo—who was in a position to have access to that level of information—the deception measures were not as effective as they could have been. Unfortunately for Clarke, that scenario played out repeatedly from 1941 to mid-1942.

It must also be mentioned that the deceptionists were at the mercy of the military itself. When the military was weak and on the defensive, deception was unlikely to succeed.[4] "A" Force could try to artificially strengthen the appearance of the military, or attempt to delay an enemy offensive, but it was unable to do much more. Moreover, the deceptionists needed time to put their plans into motion. When the army was facing an imminent threat or in the process of retreat, "A" Force did not have sufficient time to carry out adequate deceptive maneuvers.

Finally, the military and deception organizations had to work together in absolute unison for deception to reap its greatest rewards. The military leadership could not suddenly alter the overall strategy or objective without adversely affecting the deception effort.[5] General Archibald Wavell understood the concept of total cooperation between the two organizations, but that degree of unity was not maintained after his departure from the Middle East command. Not until Bernard Law Montgomery assumed command of the 8th Army did the army and "A" Force become closely integrated again. With the military situation improving and the intelligence gaps plugged, the deception machine was in position to achieve unprecedented success.

In August 1942 changes in leadership brought fresh faces and ideas to the Middle East command, along with a renewed sense of hope and energy. General Harold Alexander replaced General Claude Auchinleck as the new commander in chief, and Montgomery took over command of the 8th Army. Alexander and Montgomery approached war in a like manner. They were absolutely determined to achieve victory, and neither would entertain the idea of another retreat. Similarly, both were determined to see that the 8th Army was well trained and adequately equipped before delivering the decisive blow to the German and Italian forces in North Africa.[6]

Under new leadership, the 8th Army prepared to go on the offensive. On August 19 Alexander issued the following directive to Montgomery:

1. Your prime and immediate task is to prepare for offensive action against the German-Italian forces with a view to destroying them at the earliest possible moment.

2.   Whilst preparing this attack you must hold your present positions
       and on no account allow the enemy to penetrate east of them.[7]

Although Alexander and Montgomery focused on taking the initiative as soon
as possible, they also realized that Rommel would likely strike before the end
of August. The British were rapidly reinforcing and, because of their position
at El Alamein, were extremely close to their supply base. At the other end of
the spectrum, Rommel's forces were approximately twelve hundred miles from
their base at Tripoli and dangerously short on supplies.[8] If the German commander entertained any hopes of defeating the British, he had to act immediately
before his adversary became too strong. Rommel, who was aware that the British
were expected to receive "immense reinforcements" in early September, wrote,
"The balance of strength would then go so heavily against us that our chances of
mounting an offensive would be gone for good. So we intended to strike first."[9]
Rommel planned to launch an outflanking maneuver on Britain's southern sector (which he assumed to be weak) in late August.

Montgomery's intelligence correctly predicted that Rommel would target
the area of the Ruweisat and Alam Halfa Ridges; sigint confirmed the suspicions.[10] In the short time preceding the battle, Alexander ordered reinforcements
to Alam Halfa Ridge, and the 8th Army extended its protective minefield on the
southern perimeter. By the time Rommel attacked on the night of August 30, the
southern sector was strongly defended by nearly 400 tanks (most of them dug
in), more than 300 antitank guns, close to 250 field guns, and an extensive minefield. Moreover, Rommel had clearly lost the advantage of surprise.[11]

While anticipating the Axis move, Montgomery made full use of deception.
Once aware of Rommel's intentions, he hoped to delay the attack for a fortnight
while the 8th Army prepared for a defensive battle. On August 19, after receiving
his orders from Alexander, Montgomery called Clarke to his headquarters to
discuss what "A" Force could do to assist. "A" Force was already involved in Plan
Sentinel, which was designed to delay an attack by convincing Rommel that the
British had established strong reinforcements in the area between El Alamein
and the Nile Delta. To provide further assistance, Clarke decided to revive a
previous deception, Plan Rayon, which threatened an invasion of German-held
Crete. Michael Howard describes the deception effort: "Dummy landing-craft
were assembled in Cyprus harbours to simulate an amphibious threat, dummy

gliders were displayed on Egyptian airfields to suggest airborne support, and the Greek forces in the Nile delta were put on stand-by. . . . In addition, a dummy support line was constructed behind the main British positions, manned by two of the notional divisions created as part of Operation *Cascade*. Plentiful visual evidence was provided for curious observers in the way of minefields, trenches and tracks."[12] It is unknown whether the plan had a significant impact on the Germans, but they did refrain from sending reinforcements from Crete to Egypt, where they were most needed, during the month of August.[13] At the very least, Clarke's efforts helped to limit the reinforcement of the enemy in Africa.

In another ploy to trick Rommel, Clarke sent out a wireless message on August 20 to the effect that the British were trying to coax the Axis armies into an attack that would pin their armor down in Britain's minefields, where it could be destroyed by antitank fire. In Clarke's view, the best way to prevent an enemy attack was to make the enemy think that this was exactly what the British wanted. As Clarke anticipated, the message was intercepted by enemy intelligence. In a letter to Brigadier F. W. de Guingand, Montgomery's chief of staff, Clarke reported that the message was intercepted at Athens and reached Rommel at Panzerarmee headquarters on the twenty-second.[14]

Consistent with most deceptions of that time, "A" Force made optimal use of its dummy tanks in anticipation of the attack at Alam Halfa. Major Victor Jones' dummy 74th Armoured Brigade joined the genuine 7th Armoured Division to inflate its size. It appears that the ruse worked and had the effect of "imposing caution" on the Germans, who were alarmed at the apparent strength of the armored force.[15]

Another deception device used was the planting of a fake map. To plant the map, the British blew up an armored car in a minefield facing the enemy.[16] In the destroyed vehicle was a "going" map of the Alam Halfa Ridge area. According to Alexander, the map "showed an area of very bad going extending across the route we did not wish the enemy to take."[17] Conversely, it showed a stretch of good land that the British hoped would guide the enemy into a trap. Alexander wrote that after capturing General Wilhelm von Thoma, commander of Afrika Korps, in the Battle of El Alamein, "we learned that this ruse had been effective; the enemy had intended to outflank the ridge to the north-east but had altered his plan on the basis of this false information."[18] Although it appears that the 8th Army orchestrated the scheme, it is unclear what exact role "A" Force played in the ruse. What is certain is that if "A" Force was not directly involved, it was at least aware of the venture.

The deceptive efforts, along with the extensive defensive preparations, had the desired effect and the battle did not go nearly as Rommel had planned. It took significantly longer to pass through the minefields than anticipated, the enemy found Alam Halfa Ridge defended in much greater strength than he expected, and the invaders came under heavy artillery and air attacks. Moreover, the German and Italian forces were critically low on supplies and ran out of fuel on the battlefield. By September 1 Rommel was forced to establish a defensive posture; on September 2 he ordered a withdrawal. The Battle of Alam Halfa was officially over on September 7.[19]

As the Germans withdrew on September 3–6, Rommel realized that he had lost his only opportunity to destroy the British. He wrote, "With the failure of this offensive our last chance of gaining the Suez Canal had gone. We could now expect that the full production of British industry and, more important, the enormous industrial potential of America, which, consequent on our declaration of war, was now fully harnessed to the enemy cause, would finally turn the tide against us."[20] Alexander remarked that the withdrawal was the first step backward for the enemy; unknown at the time, the German retreat would finally end in Tunis.[21] After Alam Halfa the tide of war began to change, and for the first time the momentum shifted irretrievably to the British side.

The British victory at Alam Halfa might appear minor juxtaposed against the broader context of the war, but its importance should not be underestimated; its implications were far-reaching. For an army that had endured an arduous retreat from western Cyrenaica to El Alamein, the success of not only holding off the enemy advance but thwarting it provided a tremendous boost to morale. Further, the victory was instrumental in increasing the army's confidence in its new leadership.

As for Montgomery, he had proven himself on the battlefield. On this occasion, he demonstrated that he could go head-to-head with Rommel in a defensive battle and win. Also of great importance, he employed new tactics with exceptional results. Instead of allowing his armor to be coaxed out into the open just to be mauled piecemeal by the enemy's powerful antitank guns, as had happened over and over again in the past, Montgomery ordered his tanks to remain fixed in their positions and to force the enemy armor to come to them.[22] The new tactics worked and raised the spirits of an army that had been repeatedly outmaneuvered and beaten by superior German tactics.

Another new feature of the battle was the close ground-air support. One of Montgomery's first decisions when he took command of the 8th Army was to move his headquarters near that of the DAF and ensure that the army and air force would fight with a single objective in the coming battles. In their first test at combining air and ground operations, the union proved to be happy. Montgomery wrote, "Army and Air Force worked on one plan, closely knitted together, and the two headquarters were side by side."[23] The DAF inflicted heavy casualties on the enemy at Alam Halfa and on Axis lines of supply throughout the desert and Mediterranean.[24] Rommel decided to withdraw solely because his forces could not endure the heavy air attacks and had not received the supplies they needed to fight the battle.[25] After the tremendous success of combined operations at Alam Halfa, the ground and air arms continued to work in unison for the remainder of the war.

The mere existence of the 8th Army had been at stake when the Battle of Alam Halfa commenced. If the British had failed to repel the Axis advance, the likely result would have been the complete destruction of the army and subsequent loss of Egypt. Montgomery had no choice but to prevail. The victory significantly increased the feeling among the troops and leadership that Rommel could be beaten, that the war could and would be won, and that Montgomery was the man to lead them to success. Charles Richardson, the GSOI (Plans) at the 8th Army who was to coordinate the military's side of the deception in preparation for the upcoming Battle of El Alamein, commented that with Montgomery's "'uncanny' foresight, his clarity and poise, and his professional stage-management of the battle he had saved Egypt, and inflicted on Rommel his first defeat. We were ready for the offensive, and prepared to follow him."[26]

It is interesting to note that the enemy retained some of the minor gains he won during the battle, one of which was the peak of Himeimat. From the peak, the enemy had a clear view into Britain's southern sector. Although it might appear that this gave the enemy an advantage, it was not quite the advantage he thought given that Montgomery intended to exploit it for the purposes of deception.[27] Everything the enemy was allowed to observe from the peak was part of the most elaborate deception of the desert war.

After the Battle of Alam Halfa, Alexander and Montgomery resumed their focus on getting the army ready for the upcoming offensive. Operation Lightfoot, as it was known, was set to begin on October 23. To ensure that the army was ready to fight in the unique conditions of the desert, Montgomery paid special attention to its training and quality of leadership. At the same time, the army was reinforced and sizable reserves created.[28]

Unlike previous campaigns in the desert, the attack would have to take place on a rather narrow front of only forty-five miles at its widest. Since El Alamein was positioned between the Mediterranean Sea in the north and the impassable Qattara Depression in the south, the British were unable to attempt an outflanking maneuver. Hence, the only option was to launch an all-out frontal assault.

The British were at an advantage because they clearly outnumbered the enemy in every aspect, but it could not be ignored that they were facing a highly skilled opponent who had twice overwhelmed the 8th Army when it was superior in strength and matériel.[29] Furthermore, Rommel was confident that the El Alamein position favored the defender, because it could not be outflanked, because it was protected from a surprise attack in the rear, and because the attacker would have to maneuver his way through massive minefields while the German and Italian armies could bring up their reserves. In fact, the Axis forces were positioned behind approximately 500,000 mines.[30] Moreover, because the British had to first clear paths through the extensive minefields before they could engage the enemy in direct combat, they had to attack under a full moon—which worked to the enemy's benefit as well. Facing such challenging conditions, Montgomery readily embraced deception to give his troops the maximum advantage.[31]

It would be virtually impossible to hide British preparations for the offensive; yet, through the medium of deception, Montgomery sought to achieve surprise by misleading the enemy as to the time and exact location of the attack. The British plan was to convince Rommel that the main thrust was aimed at his southern flank.[32] The "A" Force Narrative War Diary provides a succinct explanation of the military situation before the battle and the intended plan of attack:

> Before the Battle the line was held in the North by the 30th Corps
> and in the South by the 13th. Behind them, in reserve to the South of

ALEXANDRIA, was the newly-formed 10th Armoured Corps. General MONTGOMERY's Plan was to make his major attack in the North with a subsidiary attack in the South. The role of the 30th Corps was to make two gaps in the enemy's minefields and defences, through which the 10th Corps's Armour was to pass. In the South the 13th Corps was to make a single gap for the 7th Armoured Division, and then to do all it could to divert enemy attention away from the North.[33]

The placement of the 7th Armoured Division in the south must have been strategic because the enemy had considerable experience with that division and would expect it to spearhead any major British offensive—just as it had in the past.

Between September 5 and 12 an "A" Force representative toured the front line to gain perspective on the general situation. In his opinion, the enemy would be receptive to efforts to mislead him. According to his report, "the main characteristic of the enemy was his extreme nervousness and fear of attack. He was thus in an extremely favourable receptive mood for deceptive measures and scare tactics. This mood may be expected to occur given similar conditions and deceptive possibilities should, therefore, be exploited."[34] The deceptionists were more than accommodating.

An interesting feature of the operation was that the deception agencies were brought into the discussion at the beginning of the planning phase, clearly demonstrating that Montgomery realized what a vital role deception could play in securing the army's success. The deception campaign to accompany Lightfoot was the largest of the desert war. In addition, it was a highly integrated effort: "A" Force, G(CAM), and the 8th Army—strongly supported by the intelligence agencies—all participated in the ruse from the start.

In accordance with Montgomery's directive, the attempt to deceive the enemy as to the time of the attack was the main focus of the strategic planning. Plan Treatment, a strategic deception, was an "A" Force operation largely carried out through intelligence channels. The plan to mislead the enemy as to the location of the main thrust was the responsibility of the tactical planners, namely, the 8th Army and G(CAM).[35] Clarke assumed overall command of the deception effort as a whole.

In his capacity as the GSOI (Plans) with the 8th Army, Richardson was charged with developing military plans—both genuine and deceptive. Moreover, as the GSOI (Plans), Richardson served as "A" Force's representative in the field for deceptive purposes. He was responsible for devising and implementing the tactical plan known as Bertram.[36] Thus, Bertram was an army plan carried out by the 8th Army and additional forces placed at its disposal—namely, G(CAM) and Jones' dummy armored brigade.[37] Throughout the deception campaign, Clarke (or Noël Wild in Clarke's absence), Richardson, and Geoffrey Barkas maintained close contact with each other; in what turned out to be a fully collaborative endeavor, they combined their skills, resources, and energy to ensure the 8th Army's success on the battlefield.

On September 14, 1942, Montgomery met with Clarke to discuss the possibilities of deception to cover Lightfoot. By the sixteenth Clarke had finished writing his draft for Treatment, which was accepted on the twenty-sixth. Shortly after completing the draft, Clarke left the Middle East for the United States to help coordinate the deceptive activities to cover Operation Torch, the Anglo-American invasion of French North Africa. In his stead, his deputy and second in command, Lieutenant Colonel Noël Wild, took over implementation of Treatment.[38]

The main story that Clarke intended to plant on the enemy was that the British were becoming increasingly concerned about the security of their northern front as a result of the recent German advance into the Caucasus. Thus, the British would not consider major offensive action in the desert until winter had commenced in Russia and the threat was minimized. In the meantime, the British were still preparing for an invasion of Crete.[39] In the desert, they were supposedly planning a minor offensive to establish a stronger ground position. The limited action would take place under the cover of darkness on November 6.[40] To give support to the tactical plan, the story included information to the effect that the attack would begin with a feint to the north, while the main thrust was launched in the south.[41]

Under Wild's direction, the cover story was passed through the usual means of rumors and leakages, as well as through Clarke's channels in Turkey. In addition, top military and political leaders in Cairo were asked to discreetly drop hints in "susceptible circles" in support of the story. Some were instructed to mention problems with the new Sherman tanks—problems that would inevitably delay preparations for an attack. Others were to speculate that the offensive could not possibly begin until November.[42]

Wild also employed tactics that were originally key components of Plan Fabric but that were not carried out to fruition after Rommel's attack at Gazala in May 1942 brought the deception to an untimely end.[43] The first of these tactics was to create an atmosphere of peace so that the enemy would naturally conclude that nothing was amiss. To that end, British officers in Cairo were asked to schedule social engagements and vacations for the end of October; some well-known 8th Army generals had hotel rooms booked in Cairo for the end of that month; and the last week of October was set aside as a leave week for the 8th Army.[44]

The second tactic was fashioned after Plan Maiden, a subcomponent of Fabric. Because German agents were known to be particularly active in Persia, the plan was to schedule a conference in Tehran between Alexander, General Archibald Wavell, General Maitland Wilson, Air Marshal Arthur Tedder, and Minister of State Richard Casey. The meeting, supposedly called so that the men could discuss upcoming plans for the northern front, was scheduled to take place on October 26, three days after the opening of Lightfoot. Although those in attendance were supposed to be the only ones aware of the conference, each dropped indiscreet hints regarding their plans.[45]

Although the few involved leaked subtle hints about the conference, they maintained absolute secrecy as to their true plans. In a letter to Wilson, Alexander confirmed, "None of my staff will be aware that the arrangements are not for a genuine meeting."[46] To that end, and to achieve absolute realism, arrangements for the conference proceeded exactly as they would have had the conference been real. The meeting was set to be cancelled on October 24.[47]

Not surprisingly, SIME's most successful double agent, Cheese, played a leading role in passing along the Treatment cover story. Between October 13 and 15 Cheese reported that an invasion of Crete was planned for early November. On October 17 he alerted his controllers to the commanders' conference scheduled for October 26.[48] The following day he predicted that the British offensive in the desert would commence in November. To SIME and "A" Force's delight, the Abwehr responded to the message by requesting more information regarding Montgomery's plans to attack in the south.[49] Two days later Cheese reported that the attack on Crete was to take place on November 8 and would likely be accompanied by a simultaneous advance in the desert.[50] Gravely concerned about the threat to Crete, Hitler repeated a previous order to reinforce the garrison there on October 21.[51] He did not, however, express any concern for the situation in Egypt, where the German and Italian armies could have used the reinforcements that were needlessly sent to Crete.[52]

While the strategic efforts to misinform the enemy as to the timing of the attack were under way, the 8th Army and G(CAM) were busy implementing physical measures designed to mislead the enemy as to the location of the offensive's main thrust. In early September Richardson received his orders to devise a tactical deception plan in support of Lightfoot. On September 17 Richardson and de Guingand met with Barkas, the head of G(CAM), to discuss the role of camouflage in the forthcoming operation.[53] They specifically wanted to know if G(CAM) could help to (1) conceal the preparations in the north, (2) create the impression that the attack was to be mounted in the south, (3) minimize the appearance of the buildup in the north once concealment was impossible, and (4) make it appear as if the offensive preparations would not be completed until after the campaign was scheduled to begin.[54]

Barkas was thrilled to have a key role in the deceptive operations and to be involved in planning from the beginning, but he was understandably overwhelmed by the size of the effort and the amount of resources required. In his words, the "sheer material problem of providing and moving the gear needed for concealment and display was frightening."[55] Although G(CAM)'s stores of resources were limited, Barkas was confident that his organization could pull the deception off if the army provided it with the necessary supplies and personnel. The military command, alert to the need for deception, was quick to agree to all of Barkas' requests. Alexander, for example, commented, "I decided that we must go to all lengths to make this deception plan a success and no effort was spared to that end which ingenuity could suggest."[56] With the assistance of two fellow camoufleurs, Tony Ayrton and Brian Robb, Barkas got to work.

Bertram consisted of numerous components. The first and most immediate was to hide the preparations taking place in the north. One of the first steps to prepare for the actual campaign was to transfer supplies to the front. Therefore, the army needed to position supply dumps in close proximity to the front line, but these supplies had to be concealed from the enemy because their mere existence was a good indicator that an offensive was near. It fell to G(CAM) to hide the dumps. All told, more than six thousand tons of supplies were hidden at two locations. At El Alamein Station, only five miles from the front, 600 tons of supplies (food and commodities), 2,000 tons of petrol, and 420 tons of engineer stores were hidden. At Imayid Station, some twenty miles from the front, 3,000 tons of ammunition and 600 tons of ordnance supplies were dumped and concealed. The camoufleurs used great ingenuity to make the supplies invisible—all the while working right under the enemy's nose.

At El Alamein Station, Ayrton and Robb discovered a hundred slit trenches, already built and lined with masonry. The team deduced that they could stack tins of petrol on both sides of the existing wall—thereby thickening the wall, yet not changing its appearance from the air. Barkas recalls that British "air observers were invited to locate the dump. They tried, and failed."[57] Using the open-air slit trenches had the added benefit of allowing for adequate ventilation. Because the enemy was already aware of the trenches and their appearance did not change from the aerial view, they provided the perfect camouflage for the petrol. All the work was done at night, so the enemy was unable to observe the activity.[58]

In many cases it was impossible to actually hide the dumps, but they could be concealed by disguising them as something less ominous. At El Alamein Station, the camoufleurs concealed the army's stores of food and commodities by disguising them as three-ton trucks. They stacked and positioned the boxes in the shape of a truck and covered the "vehicle" with camouflage netting. They also erected makeshift tents, to resemble bivouac tents (bivvies), next to the vehicles in order to accommodate any overflow of supplies. From the air, the enemy would be able to spot a "congregation of thin-skinned vehicles," which he was unlikely to view as any cause for immediate concern.[59]

To make the area appear more alive, a small unit set up residence there and periodically drove vehicles around the camp to simulate normal camp activity. The army also occasionally diverted genuine motorized units through the camps to add realism to the facade. An air test proved that the dummy vehicles were indistinguishable from trucks from the air.[60]

At Imayid Station, the camoufleurs had to hide three thousand tons of ammunition. To do so, they stacked the ammunition in piles at twenty-five yard intervals. After the piles were made, the teams shoveled sand around the sides to prevent shadows that would be visible from the air. Next, they covered the piles with sand and hessian (burlap). The entire dump covered three square miles of desert but was camouflaged with such precision as to render it invisible from the air. The ordnance stores at Imayid were disguised as trucks and bivvies, just like the food supplies concealed at El Alamein Station.[61]

Supply dumps were not all that had to be hidden in the north. Engineers of the 8th Army were in the process of bulldozing a track that would allow the 10th Armoured Corps to travel from its staging areas in the rear to the front line. The track could not be completely hidden, but Ayrton suggested that it be made in stages and in widely separated sections. All the sections of the main track would finally connect as one right before the attack, but until that time the enemy would not realize that the work was all part of one continuous track leading to the front. Where possible, Ayrton also advised the army to clear the track in terrain that would naturally render it less obvious from the air. According to Barkas, the trick worked in that "the enemy did not appear to attach significance to the work until it was too late."[62]

In addition to the approach track, the camoufleurs also had to hide more than four hundred 25-pounder field guns—twice. First, the guns had to be concealed at their concentration area just south of El Alamein Station, known as Cannibal 1. Just before the attack they had to be hidden yet again, this time at their barrage positions along the front line at Cannibal 2. The shape of the guns made them hard to hide, and the presence of massed artillery would undoubtedly put the enemy on high alert. The easiest solution was to disguise them as harmless trucks. G(CAM) had a plentiful stock of dummy three-ton trucks constructed of a simple canvas frame; although wheel-less, they appeared perfectly realistic from the air. The camouflage experts decided to place the guns under the truck frames. Barkas comments that it actually made the dummy trucks appear more realistic because the wheels from the gun, its limber, and its quad (tractor) appeared to belong to the trucks. The contraption was known as a "cannibal," hence the names of the concentration areas.[63]

Each individual gunner was instructed on how to take down and reconstruct his cannibal. The moves into Cannibal 1 and Cannibal 2 went according to plan. The crews moved into their locations at night just before the offensive was set to begin, and by the morning all four hundred guns were camouflaged as trucks. The enemy did not become aware of the gun positions until the gunners threw off the disguise and opened fire.[64]

An additional task in the north centered on the placement of the actual assault and armored forces that would spearhead the offensive. The enemy was well aware of the 13th and 30th Corps, which were positioned defensively along the front, but the British wanted to hide the role of the newly formed 10th Armoured Corps, which was selected as the main armored assault force for the attack in the north. Understandably, the deceptionists decided it would be impossible to hide an entire corps. Instead of hiding it, they opted to stage a massive concentration of vehicles in the assembly area of Martello in plain sight as early as possible. They hoped that the enemy would become so accustomed to seeing the idle formation of thin-skinned vehicles that he would soon disregard its presence. No armored vehicles were included in the group, however, because that would have caused the enemy great concern and likely led to increased vigilance and reconnaissance efforts on his part.[65]

All told, the army massed 4,000 real vehicles and 450 dummies at Martello by October 6. In addition, between October 1 and 20, camouflage crews erected 722 sun shields—one for each tank. The use of sun shields, or canvas covers shaped as trucks and designed to fit over specific tanks, proved to be an ingenious technique for disguising tanks.[66] Moreover, by placing the sun shields at the assembly site, the army was later able to move its tanks forward into position without the enemy ever realizing that Britain's armor had begun massing along the front. Each sun shield was given a number corresponding with a specific tank. Thus, when the tank crews of the 10th Armoured Corps began arriving at Martello during the night of October 20, they found their assigned sun shield waiting for them.[67] As with the cannibals, the tank crews were instructed in the use of their sun shield. According to Barkas, the entire undertaking was a "long and detailed job, but when the order came to move up, each tank knew where to go, what to do, and how to get out of sight before dawn."[68] And the hard work paid off. The enemy never realized that the 8th Army was positioning itself for the attack.

While the deception teams were busy concealing all signs of offensive preparations in the north, their counterparts in the south were trying to simulate pre-offensive activity. If it was difficult to hide that activity in the north, it was equally challenging to manufacture it on such a grand scale in the south. Barkas initially estimated that he could produce the effects of two armored brigade groups; Montgomery greatly expanded the project when he requested that Barkas create an entire armored corps instead.[69]

One of the first steps to make it appear as though preparations were under way in the south to support a major offensive was the laying of a water pipeline.

There was already a pipeline in the north that traveled southward to Bir Sadi. The plan, referred to as Diamond, was to extend the existing pipeline an additional twenty miles farther into the south. Thus, it would appear as if the British were making arrangements that would enable them to provide provisions for a significant military buildup in the southern sector. The pipeline extension was, of course, a fake.

Between September 26 and October 22 army engineers and camouflage teams worked together to lay the dummy pipeline. The army company began by digging a five-mile trench. In open view the so-called piping was laid alongside the trench. The piping was made by lining up four-gallon petrol tins in a row. Barkas describes the petrol cans as "so useful for almost every purpose except that for which it was intended."[70] At night, the fake piping was moved farther south and the trench filled in. Once five miles of pipeline were completed, the crews began on the next five-mile stretch. Although the plan was to make it appear as if the pipeline could not be finished until November, the crews actually completed their work a few days before the offensive began.[71]

To add realism to the pipeline, camouflage crews built three dummy pump houses. There were also overhead water tanks and filling stations at two of the sites and a reservoir at the third. Dummy vehicles and troops were posted at the watering points and regularly moved around for the benefit of the aerial observer. Finally, the army diverted traffic to travel along the pipeline.[72] Barkas concludes that although the Diamond operation appeared crude from the ground, it was "good value for the money by reason of its very special significance."[73]

Another sign that the British were planning to strike from the south would be the placement of supply dumps in that sector. While the camouflage teams went to great lengths to conceal the dumps in the north, they worked just as diligently to construct fake dumps in the south. The operation was named Brian after the camoufleur Brian Robb. Brian began on October 7.

Just to the east of the southern end of the dummy pipeline was a nine-square-mile stretch of desert set aside specifically for the dumps. There the camouflage crews constructed 700 stacks that would appear to hold approximately 9,000 tons of supplies. The stacks were intentionally designed with revealing characteristics to indicate that they contained certain types of supplies.[74] For example, the Bertram file suggests that the crews created the appearance of 3,600 tons of ammunition, 4,200 tons of petrol, 700 tons of supplies (food and commodities), 400 tons of engineer stores, and 100 tons of ordnance stores.[75] The simulated dumps were completed by October 21, despite sandstorms and what Barkas calls an "invasion" of British tanks. As it so happened, the tanks of the 10th Armoured Corps were taking part in deceptive maneuvers designed to draw the enemy's attention to the south. Barkas comments that the telltale track marks they left behind in the dump zone actually helped support Brian.[76]

Yet another scheme intended to coax the enemy into focusing on the southern sector was the use of dummy artillery in the south. While the deception teams had to hide the 25-pounder guns in the north, they allowed the enemy to observe their artillery in the south. Although dummy artillery was placed all along the southern front, the Munassib effort stands out from the rest as it has the unique distinction of being a rather clever double bluff.

The purpose of Munassib was to mislead the enemy as to the time and place of the actual attack in the south, with the benefit that it helped swell the appearance of Britain's forces in that sector. To that end, Brian Summers of G(CAM) saw to the erection of three and a half field regiments of dummy artillery at the Munassib Depression—in close proximity to the front line—beginning on October 15. The fake artillery was created to appear real and provided with camouflage. However, the camouflage was not maintained, and the enemy was able to determine that the guns were in fact dummies. After the enemy had sufficient time to conclude that the site was part of a deceptive hoax, the dummies were replaced by real guns. As confirmation of the plan's success, enemy troops staged an armored counterattack on the Munassib sector a few days after Lightfoot began, only to be heavily bombarded by guns they assumed to be dummies.[77]

To the vast array of visual effects produced in the south as evidence of the "buildup," "A" Force added audible proof by way of sonic deception. For that purpose, "A" Force positioned its sonic units—equipped with sonic cars—along the southern front. The sonic cars were made by fitting a Marmon-Herrington armored car with sound transmission devices capable of broadcasting from distances up to fifteen hundred yards. Between October 15 and November 5 the sonic units operated in the 13th Corps' sector. When called upon, they broadcast sounds of tanks and motorized vehicles to create the impression of strength and imminent offensive activity. They played a crucial role after the offensive began in keeping the enemy's armor tied to the south in expectation of a powerful British advance.[78]

While the vast assortment of strategic and tactical deception plans was in full operation with the goal of keeping the enemy misinformed, the 30th Corps (north) and 13th Corps (south) held the front. The main armored assault force, the 10th Armoured Corps, comprising the 1st and 10th Armoured Divisions, was held fifty miles east of the front in the area of Wadi Natrun. With the exception of some deceptive maneuvers in the south, the armored corps remained in its training zone until orders came for it to begin its move to the front.[79] On October 19 the 10th Armoured Corps began its journey forward to three separate staging areas: Murrayfield (north), Murrayfield (south), and Melting Pot. The move was made in the open and done in such a way as to support the deception by, yet again, drawing the enemy's attention to the south. Instead of trying to conceal the move, the British actually hoped that the enemy would notice the concentration.[80]

The three staging areas were positioned along a set of tracks leading to the southern sector. From the aerial view, it would appear obvious that the armored forces intended to follow those tracks south. Yet, as Barkas reveals, to the west the decoy path was intersected by other tracks leading to the Martello assembly point. The real challenge was transferring an entire armored corps to its assembly zone in the north without it being noticed.[81]

The move to Martello presented two specific challenges. First, the army and camouflage teams had to work in unison to hide the corps' arrival at Martello. That challenge was made easier because the assembly zone was already prepared for its arrival. All the tank crews had to do was locate their assigned sun shields and hide their tanks. The motor vehicles simply took the positions that the stand-in vehicles had held for them.[82]

The second challenge was to prevent the enemy from noticing that the corps had left the staging areas. Barkas wrote, "The advantages of this would be hard to exaggerate. So long as he thought the armour was still in the Staging Areas, it would be a fair assumption on his part that it would take at least two days to move the Armoured Corps up into assault positions."[83] The reverse of this statement is, of course, if the enemy noticed the move forward, he would expect the offensive to begin at any moment.

On October 18 Richardson decided that the Melting Pot staging zone would come under the command of Major Jones. As the 10th Armoured Division of the 10th Corps moved out of Melting Pot, Jones' dummy 74th Armoured Brigade took its place. Jones arranged with the division for its cookhouses and latrines to remain in place so that the scene would appear as unchanged as possible. On October 22 and 23 the Germans flew reconnaissance flights over Melting Pot.[84] There is no indication that they noticed any change, such as the complete absence of the 10th Armoured Division.

The effort to simulate the presence of the bulk of the 10th Armoured Corps presented tremendous difficulties for G(CAM), which was responsible for the two Murrayfield staging zones. Barkas and his team estimated that they would need to erect four hundred dummy Grant tanks, a hundred dummy guns, and approximately two thousand dummy vehicles to act as stand-ins for the 10th Armoured Corps in the two Murrayfields.[85] The most pressing problem was that the need far surpassed G(CAM)'s resources. Because G(CAM) did not possess the dummies and Jones' dummy brigade was already put to use at Melting Pot, the only viable solution was to manufacture them—quickly.[86]

Because time was limited and resources scarce, the camoufleurs looked for materials that would be suitable and readily available. They decided to use panels of split palm that the locals used for making bed frames and packing cases. John Baker, a newer member of G(CAM) and an architect, created a dummy tank prototype in thirty-six hours using nothing but palm hurdles, hessian, thread, and paint. The British ordered "unbelievable numbers of bed components" from local laborers, who dismissed the whole matter as a classic example of "English craziness."[87] Using the assembly-line method and workers from three native pioneer companies, the dummies were mass-produced and ready to move into position when G(CAM) received word on October 20 that the 10th Corps would be heading to the front that night.[88]

As the 10th Armoured Corps made its move to Martello under the cover of darkness during the nights of October 20–21 and October 21–22, the camoufleurs filled each tank vacancy with a dummy and made every attempt to erase the tracks of the genuine tank movements from the landscape. On the morning of October 22, even though an entire armored corps had moved to the front right under the enemy's nose, the scene appeared unchanged. Barkas wrote,

> From the enemy's point of view on that morning of 22nd October, 1942, MARTELLO must have looked precisely as he had become accustomed to seeing it for the past few weeks—a fairly dense concentration of

thin-skinned vehicles with nothing specially menacing about it. Down in the south, he could see that the new pipe-line was finished. He could put his own interpretation on the recent dumping of thousands of tons of petrol, ammunition and food, and on the appreciable massing of artillery at Munassib. In the Staging Areas, astride the system of tracks leading southwards, he could still see the whole array of our armour and take what comfort he could from the fact that so long as it stood there he still had some days of grace. The blow could hardly fall for another two days, or even three.[89]

Barkas concluded by writing that all signs pointed toward an attack in the southern sector, yet everything the enemy could see in the south—the armor in the staging areas, the guns, dumps, and pipeline—was nothing more than "stick and string, tin and canvas." In reality, the stage was set in the north. The dumps were stocked with everything the army needed; the guns were in position; the armor was carefully hidden under sun shields and ready to strike; and the army was prepared to advance.[90] After the 10th Armoured Corps moved up to Martello and its place in the staging areas filled with dummies, G(CAM)'s job was over.[91]

The tactical deception campaign was a resounding success. It had called for absolute cooperation between G(CAM) and the army, and both rose to the occasion. Had either failed to do its part, it is doubtful that the effort would have succeeded as it did. Moreover, Bertram, which holds the distinction of being the largest camouflage effort of the desert war, made excellent use of the army and G(CAM)'s years of experience. When resources were not readily available, the two organizations came together to buy, manufacture, and transport the materials needed for the specific task. It is a true testament to the ingenuity of the camouflage personnel that they were able to use such creativity and make skillful use of the natural environment when that was all they had to work with.

In addition to the strategic and tactical efforts, one other deception deserves mention. Beginning in September, the 8th Army employed a wireless deception to help ensure that the 10th Armoured Corps could move to the front unnoticed. The operation, known as Canwell, was an army plan. On September 24 the army established a bogus signals network for the 10th Armoured Corps called "Mock Main H.Q. 10 Corps." The army's wireless specialists ran the scheme from Wadi Natrun from September 24 through October 20, and during that time the enemy became familiar with the bogus signal and could identify the unit by its specific call signs. All the while, the 10th Armoured's genuine wireless system remained silent. On October 8 the corps headquarters moved to the front ahead of the unit. Because the enemy was tuned in to the mock radio signal, he was unaware of the headquarters' relocation.[92]

On October 20 the "Mock Main H.Q. 10 Corps" began transmitting from the three staging areas the 10th Armoured had just vacated. It remained at the staging areas until October 23, by which time the 10th Armoured Corps was located at Martello and preparing for the offensive to begin. All together, the army used twenty-five wireless sets for the ruse.[93] Moreover, wireless deception had become more important to the Germans since the British had closed their intelligence gaps and deprived Rommel of vital sources of information that he had come to rely upon.

The deception effort in preparation for Operation Lightfoot was a massive undertaking. The entire venture called for absolute cooperation between the army, G(CAM), and "A" Force. The "A" Force Narrative War Diary states, "The whole programme represented a vast effort. In addition to the '74th Armoured Brigade', it employed four Camouflage Companies, four of Pioneers, five of Engineers and one of transport, with the additional labour of several infantry battalions. The devices which were used numbered 722 'Sunshields' for disguising tanks, 360 'Cannibals' for disguising guns, 500 dummy tanks, 150 dummy guns, and nearly 2,000 dummy transport vehicles of all kinds. There was also the 'substitute M.T.' employed in the plan which totaled over 6,000."[94] Given the scale of the deception campaign, it is astounding that secrecy was maintained throughout.

If the enemy had discovered that any part of the deception effort was indeed a hoax, the entire operation might have been fatally exposed. As a result, it was of paramount importance to maintain absolute secrecy. Thus, only a few people knew of Montgomery's intentions to attack on October 23, and only a handful knew of the massive deception program. That might seem odd given the sheer number of troops who participated in the various deceptive operations, but most were unaware of the specifics of their work. For example, the 8th Army provided countless vehicles for the transport of deceptive devices and material, but it is doubtful that the drivers were aware of the contents of their load. Similarly, the drivers were ordered to navigate certain courses or transfer to specific areas without being told that their task was part of an extensive deception plan. Furthermore, many of those who provided labor for the various camouflage operations had little knowledge of the overall effect being produced.

In situations where it was impossible to hide the nature of the deceptive activity, extra measures were taken to ensure security. A prime example of this was when G(CAM) had to produce hundreds of dummy tanks to fill the Murrayfield staging areas. There was no way to conceal from the workers that they were producing fake tanks. Therefore, all leave was cancelled, and the camp was intentionally situated deep in the desert, a great distance from any roads or tracks.[95]

Just as the deception crews had to maintain secrecy, so too did the army itself. To that end, Montgomery did not inform his brigadiers of Lightfoot until September 28, unit commanders until October 10, and commanders of companies or batteries until October 17. The remaining officers and troops learned of the offensive on October 21. Whereas the majority of the army knew that the attack was imminent by the twenty-first, the troops stationed closest to the enemy, and especially those conducting patrols, were not made aware of the plans until the day of the attack.[96] An additional measure of security dictated that after the assault forces had moved into position under the cover of darkness, the troops had to lay hidden and silent all throughout the day.[97] On October 21 all leave was officially cancelled, but quietly and without written orders. The story provided was that leave was cancelled because the British expected an enemy attack during the full moon period.[98]

As far as the enemy was concerned, full moon periods always posed a threat, but on this particular occasion, no immediate signs indicated that the British were prepared to advance. Of course, because the RAF dominated the skies, the enemy was not able to conduct extensive reconnaissance missions from October 18 to 23.[99] Yet, from what he could observe, the 10th Armoured Corps had not moved up to the front. As long as the 10th Corps remained in the three staging areas, the enemy would assume that the offensive could not begin for another two to three days. As far as the enemy could discern, the telltale activities associated with an imminent offensive had yet to commence.

As absolute proof that the Germans did not expect an attack, Rommel was not even in Africa when Lightfoot began. Increasingly plagued by illness, Rommel had left Africa on September 23 to seek medical treatment in Germany. General Georg Stumme arrived in Egypt on September 19 to relieve Rommel.

Had the Germans had any inkling that the offensive was imminent, Rommel certainly would have returned to the desert immediately.

By early October Stumme thought the offensive might come at any time, but he mistakenly believed it to be directed toward the northern sector of his southern front; in other words, he bought the deception.[100] Furthermore, although he thought the attack could come soon, no evidence suggests that he expected it on October 23. From the German perspective, October 23 was "just another day like all the rest on the El Alamein front."[101] The enemy was caught completely off guard by the attack.

At 9:40 on the night of October 23, the quiet and unassuming British positions erupted in a barrage of artillery fire reminiscent of the First World War. More than a thousand guns, most of which had been perfectly concealed before the attack, pounded away at the enemy for fifteen minutes. At precisely 9:55, the shelling stopped. At that time, the infantry of the 13th and 30th Corps prepared to advance. Its job was to clear a path through the minefields for the armor to pass. At 10:00 the British guns again opened fire—the signal for the offensive to begin. The Battle of El Alamein was under way.[102]

The British blanketed the enemy with artillery fire for five and a half hours. The RAF also pounded away at the enemy positions from the air, mainly focusing on antitank gun positions and L of C. In the meantime, the infantry began its task of clearing the minefields. According to Montgomery's plan, the infantry of the 30th Corps was to clear two paths through the minefields in the north for the 10th Armoured Corps. In the south, the infantry of the 13th Corps was to clear a single path for the 7th Armoured Division.[103] The British had 1,200 tanks for the offensive; the Germans and Italians had roughly 525 combined.[104] Rommel's armor was equally divided between his northern and southern sectors, so the aim of the attack by the 13th Corps was to pin down the 21st Panzer Division and Ariete Armoured Division in the south, thereby preventing them from reinforcing the enemy's northern front.[105]

British efforts to clear the minefields were time consuming. By first light on October 24, little progress had been made. To make matters worse, Montgomery was displeased with the conduct of his armored forces, which he believed were being too cautious. The 10th Armoured Corps was supposed to establish a bridgehead between the first and second mine belts by dawn, but it fell far short of its objective.[106]

The British spent the next few days trying to clear paths through the mine-fields and so reach open country. In the meantime, the RAF provided continuous air support. On October 24 the RAF flew almost a thousand sorties. The U.S. Army Air Force (USAAF) flew an additional 147. On the night of the twenty-fourth, while the army resumed its attempt to clear the minefields, the RAF dropped 137 bombs on enemy positions.[107] By the twenty-sixth, the army had established the bridgehead, but the armor was still unable to pass into open country. By that time, the offensive had lost much of its initiative. Montgomery decided to temporarily establish a defensive position while he regrouped his forces and created reserves.[108]

Although the Axis forces were stunned by the opening of the offensive and powerful artillery barrage, they put up a tremendous fight. Because the British failed to penetrate the Axis positions during the initial advance, the enemy believed that he could hold off further penetration of the front by organizing a series of armored counterattacks. On October 24 and 25 the Axis launched successive set-piece counterattacks, but in the end the attempts only provided the British the opportunity to destroy the enemy's armor piecemeal.[109]

The counterattacks also played into the hands of the deceptionists. One of the armored assaults was launched in the south at Munassib, where camouflage crews had allowed the enemy to observe dummy gun positions. After the offensive began, the British replaced the dummy guns with genuine guns. When the enemy counterattacked at Munassib, he unexpectedly found himself under heavy artillery fire.

Another opportunity for deception presented itself on October 25. In the early days of the offensive, it was crucial to keep the enemy's armor in the south from reinforcing the north. To that end, "A" Force's sonic unit joined forces with the 50th Division in the south. The plan was to use the sonic unit to make it seem as though a major armored attack was under way in the south. Beginning at 10:00 on the night of the twenty-fifth, the sonic unit broadcast the sounds of tanks to simulate an entire armored brigade. At 12:01, the unit created the impression that the brigade was advancing toward the enemy. The "A" Force records state, "Within ten minutes of running the sound track a fairly heavy concentration of shells fell on the ridge where the Sonic Unit was located."[110] The operation was considered to be a great success. The sounds, according to the file, were heard from two miles away.

In general, the efforts of the 8th Army and deception units to convince the enemy that the main attack was aimed at the south achieved the intended objective. The intelligence services also contributed to the ruse by feeding the enemy false information. Because the British had tightened their intelligence security and the RAF prevented the Luftwaffe from conducting aerial reconnaissance, Rommel had no choice but to rely heavily on the little information gathered by his intelligence sources. Owing to the broad campaign of misinformation, Rommel did not shift his focus to the north until October 26.

Rommel had returned to Africa on October 25 to find the situation bleak. On the twenty-fourth Stumme suffered a fatal heart attack while he attempted to tour the front. Oddly enough, nobody even knew what had happened to him until his body was discovered the following day. As a result of his death, the Axis armies lacked cohesive leadership at a most precarious time. In addition, the army was facing a critical shortage of fuel and ammunition that severely limited its maneuverability and freedom of action. For example, the scarcity of ammunition had prompted Stumme to issue an order forbidding his artillery to fire on the British during the initial offensive. Hence, the British were able to take part of the minefield and inflict heavy casualties on the Axis forces at little cost to themselves.[111] Rommel tried to remedy the situation by launching counterattacks to check the British advance, but to no avail.

By the evening of the twenty-sixth, Rommel had accurately deduced Montgomery's plans and determined that the main British thrust was coming at the north near Sidi Abd el Rahman. To meet the threat, he transferred the 21st Panzer Division to the north. Because of his fuel shortage, however, he knew the division would not be able to return.[112]

By October 29 Montgomery had learned that all the German forces were concentrated together in the north and the Italians were isolated in the south. He immediately changed his plan to attack at Sidi Abd el Rahman and instead focused on the gap between the German and Italian positions, with the brunt of his force aimed at the Italian sector. To keep Rommel's attention on the northern sector, Montgomery ordered the 9th Australian Division to attack northward toward the sea. In the meantime, he ordered his regrouped forces forward for the breakout, known as Operation Supercharge. Because he knew from intelligence that Rommel's forces were severely weakened and facing critical shortages of fuel and ammunition, Montgomery was all the more convinced that the renewed offensive would succeed.[113]

Operation Supercharge began on the night of November 1–2. As the 8th Army focused its weight in the gap between the German and Italian positions, the 50th British Division carried out a feint operation in the south to prevent the two sectors from linking up. A total of two hundred dummy tanks and twelve guns were erected at Alam Nayil in the southern sector opposite the Italians. On the night of the first, genuine vehicles moved forward and sounds of tanks were broadcast over loudspeakers. In addition, flash simulators were set off to induce the enemy to overestimate the size of the attack.[114]

At 9:15 p.m. on November 1 the RAF began an eight-hour raid. In a letter to his wife dated November 2, Rommel lamented, "Air raid after air raid after air raid!"[115] On the ground the Axis again put forth stiff resistance. German and Italian troops successfully checked the advance, but at irreparable cost to themselves. The damage was so great that the commanders knew they would be unable to withstand another British thrust.

By the evening of the second, Rommel knew that he had no choice but to begin a withdrawal. Facing imminent defeat, he sent the following message to Hitler:

After ten days of extremely hard fighting against overwhelming British superiority on the ground and in the air the strength of the Army is exhausted in spite of today's successful defence. It will, therefore, no longer be in a position to prevent new attempts to break through with strong enemy armoured formations which is expected to take place tonight or tomorrow. An orderly withdrawal of the six Italian and two German non-motorized divisions and brigades is impossible for lack of MT [motor transport]. A large part of these formations will probably fall into the hands of the enemy who is fully motorized. Even the mobile troops are so closely involved in the battle that only elements will be able to disengage from the enemy. The stocks of ammunition which are still available are at the front but no more than nominal stocks are at our disposal in the rear. The shortage of fuel will not allow for a withdrawal to any great distance. There is only one road available and the Army, as it passes along it, will almost certainly be attacked day and night by the enemy air force.

In these circumstances we must therefore expect the gradual destruction of the Army in spite of the heroic resistance and exceptionally high morale of the troops.[116]

With the withdrawal under way on November 3, Rommel received orders from Hitler to stand firm. On the fourth, Rommel again asked for permission to pull back, and this time it was granted.[117] By the night of the fourth, what remained of the Axis forces was in full retreat to Fuka. Incidentally, Rommel recorded that he learned the lesson of obedience from the experience—from then on he ignored orders to hold firm when the battle was already lost.[118]

With the Axis retreat, the Battle of El Alamein officially came to an end, and the threat to Egypt vanished. The desert war was not yet over, but ultimate victory was in sight. It was no longer a matter of if, but when.

Although the British entered the battle with the odds in their favor given their numerical superiority, victory was never a foregone conclusion. They still faced a determined enemy who made them fight for every gain. All told, the British suffered 13,560 casualties and had 500 tanks damaged (most were repairable). The Axis forces suffered devastating losses. Rommel had only 36 of 249 tanks left. The Italians lost almost all of their 278 tanks and three entire divisions. Exact casualty figures are unknown, but 30,000 enemy troops were in British hands by November 11.[119]

While credit for the victory must first go to the troops who fought and died, it cannot be denied that the air and deception campaigns played a significant role in the battlefield success. The RAF dominated the skies before, during, and after the battle. Altogether, it flew a total of 10,405 sorties in direct support of the army. The USAAF flew 1,181 sorties. In addition, the RAF flew continuous missions aimed at the enemy's shipping in an effort to prevent him from receiving the supplies of fuel and war matériel that he so desperately needed. The success of that effort rendered the enemy unable to continue the fight.[120] The close cooperation between the air and ground forces was carried out on an unprecedented scale.

The deception effort should receive full credit for the attainment of surprise, without which the British might have encountered much stiffer resistance from the onset. Without deception, it would have been impossible to hide such a massive buildup of forces and invasion matériel from the enemy. The value of the deception plan's success can hardly be underestimated.

Although the Battle of El Alamein was over, the fighting continued as the British followed the retreating enemy forces into Libya. The British were unable to pursue the enemy as quickly as they might have liked owing to heavy rains and disorganization in the army, but by November 11 no enemy forces remained in Egypt. On the thirteenth the British regained possession of Tobruk, and on the twentieth they entered Benghazi. As the 8th Army approached El Agheila, where the enemy had established a defensive position by November 27, Montgomery was determined not to let history repeat itself for a third time.[121]

On the two previous occasions that the British took possession of Cyrenaica, they stopped short of their goal of Tripoli because they had overextended themselves, thus rendering the army weak and vulnerable. In both cases, the enemy counterattacked before the British were ready and all gains were quickly lost. But this time Montgomery intended to maintain the initiative and advance quickly. To alleviate the risk of shortages, he called a temporary halt to regroup while he made extensive arrangements to ensure that the army would have adequate supplies when it resumed the fight.[122]

In addition to the military preparations, Montgomery again sought the aid of deception. He believed that the enemy's situation was so desperate that he could induce the Axis to withdraw from El Agheila without a fight. He met with Clarke, who quickly thereafter began developing Plan Windscreen.[123] First, the plan was to allow the enemy to observe the offensive preparations under way. Second, Clarke hoped to use dummy parachutists to threaten Rommel's communications in the rear and dummy landing craft at Benghazi to simulate the appearance of a planned seaborne attack behind the front.

Despite the plans, Windscreen barely had time to take effect. The British learned that the enemy was already withdrawing, and this forced Montgomery to speed up the date of his advance. As Montgomery ordered his troops forward on December 13, Rommel led his troops in another full retreat, this time to Buerat.[124] The enemy endured a costly fighting retreat but made it to Buerat by the seventeenth.

Windscreen was then altered to pose a threat to Rommel's base at Tripoli. According to the new story, the army was facing administrative problems that

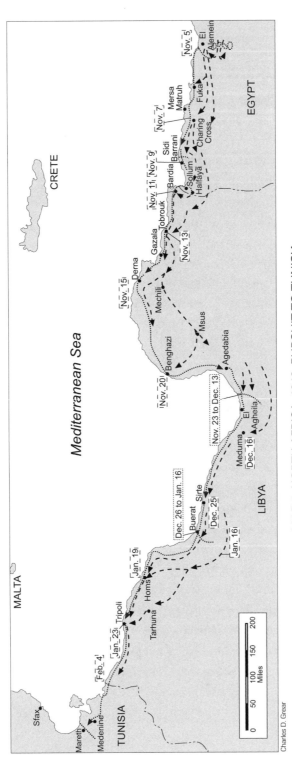

MAP 6. NORTH AFRICA, 1942: PURSUIT TO TUNISIA,
NOVEMBER 1942–FEBRUARY 1943

Charles D. Grear

would prevent it from advancing; instead, the British planned to divert the forces originally slated to invade Crete to Tripoli instead. The goal, of course, was to convince Rommel of the need to withdraw from Buerat in order to protect Tripoli.[125] On January 7, 1943, Rommel began to pull his nonmotorized Italian forces back and by the fifteenth was in the process of yet another retreat. The British remained on the enemy's heels. On January 23, exactly three months to the day after the Battle of El Alamein began, the 7th Armoured Division entered Tripoli unopposed.[126]

By the beginning of February the enemy was cleared from Libya. The British had advanced twelve hundred miles from Alamein to Tripoli, but as Major General I. S. O. Playfair contends, it was more of an administrative coup than a military one because the army did very little fighting during the pursuit.[127] Even though the long sought after objective of Tripoli was finally in British hands, the desert campaign was not over. The 8th Army continued the pursuit into Tunisia, but it was no longer fighting alone. On November 8, 1942, the British and Americans had pulled off a surprise landing in French North Africa. Rommel found himself facing Montgomery to his east and the Anglo-American forces to his west.

After the United States entered the war, the Americans embarked upon a "Europe-first" policy.[128] They began working with the British on plans to open a "second front" in accordance with the wishes of Josef Stalin. Although the Americans favored a cross-channel invasion of France, the British were convinced at that time that it would fail. At the Second Washington Conference in July 1942, plans for an Anglo-American invasion of French North Africa were worked out.[129] The operation, officially accepted on July 24, was dubbed Torch.[130]

Although the Americans viewed Torch as an indirect approach, it had legitimate benefits. If successful, it would placate Stalin and reopen the Mediterranean for Allied shipping. Moreover, it required fewer landing craft than an invasion of France, would provide a friendlier battleground for the fresh American troops, would facilitate the Allied blockade of Germany, and would hopefully bring the French back into the war on the Allied side. Gen. Dwight D. Eisenhower was chosen as the commander in chief of the Allied Expeditionary Force (AEF) on August 6.[131] The invasion was scheduled for November 8, 1942.

The Allies shared concerns over a potential negative French reaction to the invasion, but the more immediate source of anxiety revolved around how to transport such large invasion forces by sea without the enemy noticing. For that, the Allies turned to their trusted and proven secret weapon—deception. For the first time, the deception was not spearheaded by "A" Force. This time it came under the control of the newly formed LCS headed by Lieutenant Colonel John Henry Bevan. Torch, as it turned out, represented the LCS's first attempt at deception.

With the ultimate objective being the achievement of surprise, the LCS attempted multiple schemes. The first was known as Operation Overthrow. The goal of Overthrow was to pin down sizable German forces in northwest France by threatening a seaborne invasion aimed at the Pas de Calais. To accomplish this, the LCS used both visual means of deception and double agents. The visual aspect of the plan had little effect—thus highlighting the inexperience of the LCS—but the use of double agents proved fruitful. Under the control of MI5's B1A section, the agents passed along information in support of the ruse. Most important was a trusted agent code-named Garbo who reported troop movements in southern England. He also warned that the British were spreading rumors deliberately designed to mislead the Germans regarding their intentions.[132] Hitler accepted the report as credible and ordered the reinforcement of Cherbourg. The German forces under Field Marshal Gerd von Rundstedt remained in a state of alert for a total of four months as a result of the ruse. Hence, Overthrow was viewed as a great success.

Another plan, known as Solo I, was created to convince the enemy that the British intended to launch an invasion of Norway. It was likely that the Germans would learn of the concentration of ships to be used for Torch, but they would have no indication of where the fleet was headed until it left port. Thus, the LCS organized a host of deceptive activities to lure the Germans into believing that Norway was the intended target. The RAF flew reconnaissance missions over Norway, the Royal Navy cleared passages through minefields for the invasion forces, extensive radio traffic was simulated in Scotland, and MI5's double agents reported on troops "training for mountain warfare, the purchase of snow-chains and anti-freeze in large quantities, and a subtle rumor that Lascar seamen on vessels in the Merchant Navy were being offered large bonuses if they agreed to serve in waters north of latitude 60°N."[133] All indicators pointed toward Norway.

In response, Hitler ordered Norway reinforced by an additional infantry battalion, the bulk of the German navy remained in Norway, and on November 2 Norway was put on a full state of alert.[134]

The next phase of the deception was to mislead the enemy as to the destination of the assault convoys once they set sail (between October 22 and 26). The British fleet would have to sail a total of 2,760 miles; the U.S. fleet would travel 4,500. Although it was possible that the fleets might go undetected in the beginning of their individual journeys, it was unlikely that they would evade notice indefinitely. Therefore, the LCS proposed to suggest that they were headed anywhere other than French North Africa. Operation Kennecott provided the enemy with multiple plausible destinations, such as French Dakar, Sicily, and Italy.[135] Clarke and Bevan considered including the ports of Tripoli and Benghazi in the operation, but decided against it as they assumed the enemy would not think these ports a feasible option given the narrowness of the Sicilian Channel.[136]

In a particularly crafty scheme, dubbed Solo II, British planners sought to deceive the assault forces themselves. British troops were told that they were headed to the Middle East but would first take the port at Dakar. American troops were led to believe that they were heading to the Caribbean for training exercises—they were even given vaccinations to prevent tropical diseases.[137] Of course, such measures were necessary to avoid leaks.

After the two fleets linked up in the Atlantic and turned east for the Mediterranean, the deception effort came under the jurisdiction of "A" Force. Clarke devised Plan Townsman as part of Kennecott. The goal was to reinforce the suggestion that the convoys were headed for Sicily with the ultimate goal of establishing a bridgehead to Italy. Clarke included the threat of a diversionary attack on Crete in Townsman.[138] Hitler took the threat to Crete seriously and ordered it reinforced by the 22nd Division.[139]

By the time the deception was transferred to Clarke's sphere of control, it could be implemented only through means of intelligence. Clarke was confident that Operation Lightfoot, set to begin on October 23, would provide natural cover for the Torch convoys because the enemy would be focused almost exclusively on the battle under way. Thus, Clarke suggested that "A" Force conduct the bulk of its intelligence implementation approximately one week before the landings.[140] As early as seventeen days before Torch was set to begin, however, Cheese had already sent his first warning of the threats to Italy and Crete. On October 31 he sent a "strong warning" of the threat to Italy and added that in his opinion, Crete was not the main objective. Throughout the first week of November, he repeatedly reported on American plans to carry out air raids over Italy.[141] Furthermore, rumors were spread about the "demand for Italian interpreters and guide-books, the printing of Italian money, the attachment of Roman Catholic chaplains to units on the strength of their knowledge of Italy, and the imminence of heavy air raids on Italian cities."[142]

One final aspect of the deception was Britain's attempt to provide an explanation for the concentration of troops and war matériel at Gibraltar. It was almost certain that the enemy would notice the buildup of air forces, landing craft, and supplies there. To ward off speculation, the LCS put forth the story that the buildup was intended to help supply Malta. Given the enemy's heavy attacks on Malta throughout 1942, it was certainly a believable story. However, because the presence of landing craft was not consistent with a relief effort, the LCS spread additional information that the craft were to be used for an attack on Dakar.[143] The enemy conducted one reconnaissance flight over Gibraltar in the crucial period before the landings, but the pilot must not have noticed the concentration because he did not attempt to bomb the site, did not return, and apparently did not report any unusual activity.[144]

With the deception effort under way and the convoys en route as scheduled, there was nothing left to do but wait. The British expected the convoys to be discovered at any time, especially after they entered the Mediterranean through the Strait of Gibraltar, but that was not the case. Clarke called it a stroke of luck, for which he credits the enemy's focus on the ongoing battle at El Alamein.[145] The ships were finally spotted by the Luftwaffe on November 6, but they were assumed to be heading to either the ports of Tripoli-Benghazi, Sicily, or Sardinia, in addition to resupplying Malta (this was accepted by the enemy as a given); thus, no immediate action was taken.[146] The fleet destined for Algiers suffered the only casualty of the voyage, and that was from a single torpedo strike hours before Torch began.[147] "A" Force saw the attack as a sign of the deception plan's success: "No air attack took place until the ALGIERS convoy had actually put into harbour. This appears to be a certain indication that it was expected to pass through the SICILIAN STRAITS and that the convoy was to be dealt with in the same way as previous MALTA convoys. These were always attacked for the first time East of ALGIERS, generally in the sea area off BOUGIE."[148] What the attack clearly shows is that the enemy did not expect the fleets to go ashore where they did.

On November 4 the amalgamation of ships had split into two fleets again—one headed for Casablanca in Morocco and the other for Oran and Algiers in Algeria. The Morocco-bound forces were American; those landing at Oran and Algiers were a combination of British and American troops. To support the deception effort, the Oran and Algiers fleets maintained a course consistent with a Malta-bound convoy until the last moment, when they suddenly turned south.

The Torch landings took place as planned in the early hours of November 8. Although the invasion forces encountered some resistance from the French, it was generally mild. The heaviest fighting occurred at Morocco. On the morning of November 10 Admiral Jean François Darlan, who happened to be in North Africa by chance, issued a cease-fire order that effectively ended French opposition.[149]

Based on the achievement of surprise and the limited opposition encountered, the cover plan for Operation Torch can be considered a resounding success. General Alfred Jodl, the German chief of staff, admitted, "When the African landings were made they were a complete surprise, the first news received was by air reconnaissance from the GIBRALTAR area. Even then it was assumed that the operation was directed towards a landing in ROMMEL's rear."[150] Playfair contends that "secrecy had been well guarded, cover plans cleverly baited, and a large measure of surprise achieved."[151] Michael Howard calls it the "first major success for strategic deception," which was to "foreshadow many more."[152] To further illuminate the success, the entire effort represented the first attempt to combine the strategic efforts of London (LCS) and the Middle East ("A" Force). It proved to be a workable union and excellent practice for the forthcoming campaigns in Europe.

With surprise achieved and the landings largely unopposed, the invasion forces could begin their move east. The Allies headed toward Tunis and Bizerta as soon as the coast was neutralized, but the Germans beat them to Tunisia. That meant the Allies would have to fight and the war would not be over by Christmas as they had hoped. It also meant that the enemy could be reinforced and resupplied from bases in Naples and Sicily. Many scholars see this as a great failure of Torch. The general argument is that the landings were too far west to enable Allied troops to reach Tunisia before the enemy. By allowing the enemy to get

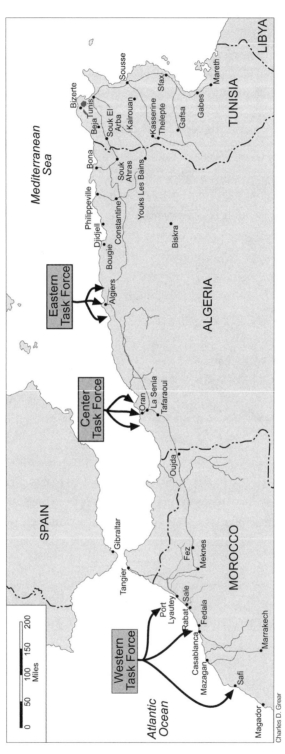

MAP 7. OPERATION TORCH, 1942: THE ALLIED INVASION,
NOVEMBER 8, 1942

Charles D. Grear

there first, the Allies became bogged down for an additional six months in war against an enemy that should have been defeated.[153] Although the Germans had gained a second wind, Rommel was not deluded into thinking that victory was still possible. Having learned of the landings, he frankly acknowledged, "This spelt the end of the army in Africa."[154]

When the British and Americans landed in North Africa, Hitler sent the 5th Panzer Army under Colonel Hans-Jürgen von Arnim to Tunisia. On the one hand, Arnim held a central position that would force the Allies to come to him and fight. On the other hand, he found himself facing Montgomery's 8th Army to his east and to his west the newly formed British 1st Army under Lieutenant General Kenneth Anderson and the U.S. II Corps under Major General Lloyd Fredendall. The German and Italian forces under Rommel were in the middle of their retreat from El Alamein, but they too would be in Tunisia by the end of January 1943.

Having established a strong defensive position at the Mareth line along the Tunisian border, Rommel advocated fighting the fresh British and American troops first, before Montgomery could resume the offensive and drive into Tunisia. While Arnim focused on the British forces, Rommel launched an attack against the Americans in mid-February. Rommel eventually took the Kasserine Pass, although he had to relinquish his gains in short time. Nevertheless, the offensive revealed the II Corps' lack of training, inadequate leadership, poor discipline, and inexperience at desert warfare. To rectify the problems, Eisenhower relieved Fredendall and placed the II Corps under the command of George S. Patton.[155]

Aware of the difficult position the Americans were in, Montgomery began putting pressure on Rommel at the end of February. On March 6 the 8th Army repulsed two enemy attacks at Medenine. Finally, on March 20 Montgomery began a major offensive against the Axis at the Mareth line. The Battle of Mareth lasted until the twenty-seventh and ended in victory for the Allies.[156] Noticeably absent from the battle was Rommel. After trying to convince Hitler that the continued defense of Africa was futile, Hitler personally removed Rommel from his command on March 10. General Giovanni Messe assumed overall command of the combined German and Italian forces.[157]

By April 8 Montgomery had joined forces with the Americans. On May 6 the 1st Army, with some 8th Army units on loan, captured Tunis. On the seventh the

American II Corps took possession of Bizerta. The last German resistance came to an end on May 12, and the Italians under Messe surrendered on May 13. The Allies took a total of 248,000 prisoners upon the Axis capitulation.

The final victory came some six months after the Battle of El Alamein, when the Axis retreat first began. In that time, the 8th Army advanced two thousand miles in pursuit of the enemy.[158] As for the Axis, the defeat was total. Furthermore, given that the German 6th Army had surrendered at Stalingrad earlier the same year, the loss of Africa was all the more bitter. In response, Hitler ordered ten German divisions to the Balkans and another seven to Greece to defend against the possibility of an Allied attack in southern Europe.[159]

The German folly in deciding to defend Tunis is aptly described by Douglas Porch: "The Axis decision to reinforce Tunisia had proven disastrous. Between them, Hitler and Mussolini had offered two new Allied armies a place where they could learn to fight at low risk." Porch goes on to quote Lt. Gen. Omar Bradley, who wrote, "In Africa we learned to crawl, to walk—then run."[160] Because the new armies worked out their kinks in Africa, they were much better prepared to fight on the European continent in 1943.

On May 13 Alexander sent the following message to Churchill: "Sir, it is my duty to report that the Tunisian campaign is over. All enemy resistance has ceased. We are masters of the North African shores."[161] After three full years of war, the battle for North Africa was over.

Conclusion

For three long years Britain fought to defend Egypt against the determined armies of Germany and Italy. The British began the war utterly unprepared for a major land battle, a by-product of the interwar policies of a country reeling from the effects of the First World War. Because the British army was ill-equipped, poorly supplied, and greatly outnumbered, the situation was precarious from the moment Italy declared war in June 1940. Over the next two years, Britain's military made many costly mistakes against a tactically superior enemy; however, the British army eventually developed a sound strategy and tactics of its own, enabling it to defeat the highly esteemed Field Marshal Erwin Rommel and his Italian allies. Similarly, the British went to great lengths to rectify the supply situation in order to provide the armed forces with the resources needed to fight a large-scale war.

Once Bernard Law Montgomery took charge of the 8th Army, he made immediate improvements. Montgomery saw to the proper training of his troops, ensured quality leadership, organized a steady flow of supplies and reinforcements to guarantee that the British would have the numerical advantage, and developed new battlefield tactics more consistent with those employed by the Germans. He also organized the air and ground arms into a more closely integrated joint operations command. After years of failures and defeats, the British were finally prepared to fight the Axis armies at the Battle of El Alamein. The 8th

Army, in particular, had finally come into its own and was now a force capable, not only of stopping the Axis forces, but of defeating Rommel.

The Battle of El Alamein was without doubt the turning point of the war in the Middle East. It was, furthermore, of paramount importance for the British—not only because the survival of Egypt was at stake but because it was the first true British victory in the war against Germany. Although the British had secured a number of smaller successes in the past, none proved to be lasting. As Churchill declared, "Before Alamein we never had a victory. After Alamein we never had a defeat."[1] General Harold Alexander similarly proclaimed, "It proved to be the turning point of the war. This great battle was the fore-runner of a series of victories which never ceased until the enemy were finally cleared from the African continent."[2] If the Battle of El Alamein and subsequent drive to Tunis was the turning point of the war in North Africa, it was equally a turning point for the morale of the British government, the armed services, and the people of England. Churchill recalled that in London "there was, for the first time in the war, a real lifting of spirits."[3]

The efforts in preparation for El Alamein represented the defining period for British deception as well. Up until El Alamein, it can be argued that the deceptionists were merely feeling their way along. The official organization responsible for the coordination of all deception efforts in the Middle East, "A" Force, was learning as it went given that there was no adequate precedent for its activity. In the meantime, "A" Force had to overcome experiments with its organizational structure and difficulties in coordinating its efforts with those of the military. After years of trial and error, however, Dudley Clarke felt confident that "A" Force had developed into a "well-oiled machine."[4] His assumption proved correct, for "A" Force, along with G(CAM) and the 8th Army, pulled off the largest deception of the desert war in the weeks and days preceding the Battle of El Alamein.

The deception campaign succeeded for a number of reasons. First, the top military leadership recognized the value of deception and ensured that every resource was made available to the deceptionists—and in a timely manner. Second, the various deception and intelligence agencies worked together, harmoniously, from the beginning. Third, all parties involved accomplished the incredible feat of maintaining absolute secrecy throughout the duration of the deception. Fourth, the effort was built upon years of experience that taught the deceptionists how to deceive effectively. Although it might seem that some of the previous deception efforts had failed, and thus wasted precious time and effort, that conclusion could not be further from the truth. The El Alamein deception succeeded only because the deception teams already knew exactly what would work and what would not. That knowledge came from experience, and the deceptionists learned just as much—if not more—from the failures as they did from the successes.

David Mure, a deception suboperator under Clarke, described the great deception coup as the "first full-scale integrated deception plan, using a majority of the devices so painstakingly developed over nearly two years."[5] As Mure suggests, for nearly two years before El Alamein, the officers at "A" Force had taken advantage of the opportunity to practice their craft and used every spare moment to design devices and other aids to deception that were all put to full use at El Alamein. By the time of the battle, "A" Force had worked out its kinks. The "A" Force Narrative War Diary states, "From an uneasy start, in which problems of organisation and control had handicapped the earlier Deception plans, it closed with the success at El ALAMEIN and NORTH AFRICA in which the attainment of Surprise had been undisputed. To 'A' Force this seemed to show that the machinery forged during 1941, and tempered in the fire of the Summer battles, was now the finished product, ready to meet whatever calls 1943 might make upon it."[6]

What emerged from the entire effort was a perfect blueprint for deception that served as the foundation and model for all future deceptions. According to Mure, "It was the complete blueprint of all the plans that were to come. Here the ingredients of strategic deception—bogus order of battle, double agents' reports, misleading W/T [wireless telegraphy] traffic, concentrations of bogus landing craft were to be combined for the first time with the tactical measures—camouflage, dummy tank and artillery formations, sonic devices; and, combined for the first time, they worked like clockwork."[7] The El Alamein deception campaign was the most comprehensive, integrated, and successful of "A" Force's deceptions up to that point in the war. Furthermore, the ability to achieve surprise on such a narrow front as existed at El Alamein clearly demonstrated the worth of deception for any skeptics and ensured that it would remain an integral part of the military's strategy after the war moved beyond North Africa.

As the war made its way to Europe, the British and American armed forces, along with "A" Force, continued to practice deception on an increasingly expanding scale. Although tactical maneuvers still accompanied the military's campaigns, the strategic efforts of "A" Force and the LCS were instrumental in the deceptions practiced during the remaining years of war. There was a difference between the type of deception employed in North Africa and that in Europe, however. The deception of the early years was primarily defensive. Beginning with El Alamein, both the military and deception efforts evolved from being defensive to offensive in nature.

At the end of 1942 the question of who was responsible for deception had to be answered. More specifically, the LCS had to clearly define the domains of responsibility before the deceptionists could proceed. The LCS had the task of coordinating global deception. It then issued general directives to both "A" Force in the Middle East and GSI(d) in India, both of which were given a free hand to develop deception plans so long as they aligned with the strategic goal put forth by the LCS. During this same time, "A" Force was expanded to cover the whole of the Mediterranean (upon General Eisenhower's specific request), Persia and Iraq, East Africa, and South Africa.[8] Clarke established an advanced headquarters for "A" Force in Algiers under the command of Lieutenant Colonel M. H. Crichton. A tactical headquarters headed by Lieutenant Colonel David Strangeways was created to accompany General Alexander's newly formed 18th Army Group. Clarke remained behind at the main headquarters of "A" Force in Cairo.[9]

In 1943 "A" Force was called upon to help provide cover for Operation Husky, the upcoming invasion of Sicily, set for July of that year. Since Sicily was the most logical target of an Allied attack, the deceptionists had to suggest another plausible location to divert attention away from the island. Clarke wrote the actual deception plan, code-named Barclay, which was approved in London on April 10. Barclay had multiple components involving London and the Middle East. The London-based deception headed by the LCS aimed at keeping as many German troops in Norway and France as possible.[10] It achieved limited results, however, as the enemy naturally expected the attack to come in the Mediterranean and tended to discount evidence to the contrary.

"A" Force took on the responsibility of keeping German forces tied down in the Balkans and southern France. To accomplish this goal, Clarke provided the story that the British planned to invade the Balkan Peninsula by way of Greece.

The deception story also purported that American forces intended to take both Sardinia and Corsica with a view toward establishing a bridgehead into France. The enemy expected the attack to come at Sicily. Thus, Clarke spread information that the Allies had decided to neutralize Sicily and Italy by air, but because they were unwilling to become bogged down in heavy fighting in the mountainous terrain of Italy, both would ultimately be bypassed.[11]

"A" Force implemented the plan based on the model provided at El Alamein. Genuine forces in Syria, reinforced by dummies, were moved around to suggest a possible strike into Turkey. Bogus radio traffic from the phantom 12th Army, notionally stationed in Cairo, filled the airways. "A" Force arranged for Greek units in Egypt and French units in Algeria to practice amphibious operations, providing evidence that preparations were under way for the forthcoming invasions of Greece and southern France, respectively. Similarly, Major Jones had his dummy tanks and landing craft positioned on the beaches of Cyrenaica to indicate an impending seaborne assault toward Greece.[12] To cover the activities of the genuine units that might give evidence of their ultimate destination, camouflage was employed to hide their movements. As one would expect, "A" Force also made use of its double-agent network, which had been greatly expanded over the previous six months, to send reports in support of the ruse.[13] Finally, "A" Force organized extensive administrative measures, spread rumors, and initiated a detailed propaganda campaign.[14]

In addition to "A" Force's activities in the Mediterranean, London orchestrated one of the more fanciful deceptions of the entire war—Operation Mincemeat. Under the guidance of Flight Lieutenant Charles Cholmondley and Lieutenant Commander Ewen Montagu, the British determined to drop a corpse (supposedly Major Martin of the Royal Marines) in Spanish waters carrying important documents that identified Greece as the target of the upcoming invasion. The body was released from a submarine off the coast of Spain and, shortly thereafter, discovered along with the documents in a briefcase attached to the body. As hoped, the documents were copied and handed over to the Germans. Clarke's role in the hoax was to help write the draft of the crucial "Greek" document when he met with Colonel John Henry Bevan of the LCS in March.[15]

The combination of "A" Force's efforts and Operation Mincemeat appeared to have achieved the stated objectives. As proof, the "A" Force Narrative War Diary records,

On the 9th March there were 8 complete divisions in the BALKANS (6 in YUGO-SLAVIA, 1 in GREECE and 1 in CRETE). By the 10th July the total had risen to 18. . . . Of these 9 were in GREECE and 7 in YUGO-SLAVIA. It seems fair, therefore, to claim a net 10 Divisions as having been added to the German BALKAN Armies during the period of operation of the "BARCLAY" Plan. The Garrison in SOUTHERN FRANCE had been increased simultaneously by 2 to 3 German Divisions, while 2 more had been sent to occupy SARDINIA and CORSICA.[16]

From all accounts, it appears that Barclay was a success. The Allies did achieve surprise, and the Germans had only two divisions stationed on the Sicilian island to assist the Italians at the time of the attack.[17]

"A" Force was involved in multiple deceptions throughout 1943, but Barclay was by far the largest campaign of the year. Throughout the remainder of the year, Clarke and his team continued to manufacture threats to the Balkans in order to force the Germans to remain committed to the region's defense. Clarke states that should the Germans "discover that the EASTERN MEDITERRANEAN was never intended to become a major battlefield again, vast numbers of German Divisions might well have been released from GREECE, ALBANIA, and YUGO-SLAVIA to bolster up the fronts in EASTERN or WESTERN EUROPE."[18] Thus, "A" Force saw as its overriding task from 1943 on to keep the Germans pinned down in the Balkans using any means possible. The majority of the work was accomplished through the use of double agents and Clarke's bogus order of battle.

By the end of 1943 the Allies were making plans for a cross-channel invasion of France; as a result, the military and deception organizations became increasingly focused on Western Europe. In December the LCS devised Operation Bodyguard to cover plans for Operation Overlord. It would be impossible to hide the fact that an invasion was being planned, but the deceptionists could try to mislead the enemy as to the exact time and location of the attack—just as they did at El Alamein. Bevan, however, was short on personnel and needed men who already knew how to plan and implement a successful deception to take the lead in planning Bodyguard. For that expertise, he naturally turned to "A" Force. As Clarke put it, "Before 1943 was out there started a noticeable exodus of "A" Force officers from the MEDITERRANEAN to the UNITED KINGDOM."[19]

Perhaps the most important transfer to London was that of Lieutenant Colonel Noël Wild. Wild arrived in London on December 17 to take command of Ops B, the deception section of the newly formed Supreme Headquarters Allied Expeditionary Force (SHAEF). Although Eisenhower had requested Clarke for the position, Clarke declined and sent Wild in his stead. Wild recalled, "I found myself appointed the 'Head' of a scarcely existent organisation at SHAEF charged with planning and executing a cover and deception plan in support of the forthcoming Normandy landings timed to take place in June."[20] In addition to being Clarke's deputy and second in command at "A" Force, Wild had been responsible for organizing and seeing to fruition the strategic deception in preparation for the Battle of El Alamein in Clarke's absence. Therefore, Eisenhower had at his disposal a man who brought with him to London all the knowledge, experience, expertise, and efficiency of "A" Force. As Mure put it, "The erstwhile apprentice turned the blueprint of four experimental years into a working machine."[21] That the Bodyguard deception was modeled after the "A" Force established blueprint, then, should not come as any surprise.

Whereas the LCS created the overall deception plan, Ops B, under Wild, supervised the two London-based plans, Fortitude North and Fortitude South.[22] Wild organized Ops B in true "A" Force fashion with a division between operations and intelligence; he appointed J. A. Jervis-Read to head the tactical section and Roger Fleetwood-Hesketh to handle all intelligence matters.

The first of the plans, Fortitude North, generated a threat to Norway. According to the deception, the attack was to be carried out by the fictitious Fourth Army stationed in Scotland. The deception was passed largely through the double-agent channels, simulated radio traffic, and diplomatic maneuvering with the Swedish government. Although the Germans accepted the possibility of an attack on Norway as probable, they made no attempt to reinforce the region because they steadfastly believed that the most urgent threat was to France.[23] Thus, as Clarke might argue, the Allies persuaded the Germans to think in terms of the deception, but not to act as they had hoped. In that respect, Fortitude North failed.

If it can be argued that Fortitude North failed, Fortitude South was a resounding success. The overriding goal of Fortitude South was to divert the Germans' attention away from Normandy and make it appear as though the attack could not take place until the latter part of summer. David Strangeways, a former "A"

Force representative then serving under Montgomery at 21st Army Group headquarters, played a pivotal role in Fortitude South by ensuring that the deception centered on the Pas de Calais. Hitler and his generals were in agreement that the Allied focus had shifted to Western Europe.[24] Although it would be futile to claim that the Allies were not focused on France, the deceptionists could still try to divert German forces away from Normandy specifically. The key to that task, argued Strangeways, was to convince the Germans that the Allies intended to attack the Pas de Calais and that any other action—such as a landing at Normandy—was nothing more than a diversion intended to draw forces away from the genuine target.

The crucial factor in keeping the Germans committed to the defense of the Pas de Calais was setting aside a force in England specifically identified as the main invasion force. Ideally, this decoy force would be larger than the actual Overlord forces. Of course, the Allies did not have a spare army sitting around, so they simply created one in true "A" Force fashion. FUSAG already existed in skeletal form. "R" Force, under Strangeways, developed a plan to notionally transform the barely existent U.S. force into a first-class army of 150,000 troops.[25] To make the army appear genuine, it was placed under the command of George S. Patton. Because the RAF dominated the skies and it was therefore unlikely that the Germans would be able conduct aerial reconnaissance, the existence of FUSAG was largely put over by the double agents and bogus radio traffic.[26]

To keep the enemy focused on the Pas de Calais after the D day landings, information was fed to him suggesting that FUSAG would not be ready to attack until after the D day landings had in fact taken place. Similarly, and probably of the greatest consequence, Garbo, MI5's most successful double agent—and the agent most trusted by the Germans—sent a message on June 9 that caused the German 15th Army to maintain its post at the Pas de Calais. Garbo warned,

> From the reports mentioned it is perfectly clear that the present attack is a
> large scale operation but diversionary in character for the purpose of estab-
> lishing a strong bridgehead in order to draw the maximum of our reserves
> to the area of operation to retain them there so as to be able to strike a
> blow somewhere else with ensured success. I never like to give my opinion
> unless . . . I have strong reasons to justify my assurances. Thus the fact

that these concentrations which are in the East and South-East of the Island are now inactive means that they must be held in reserve to be employed in the other large scale operations. The constant aerial bombardment which the area of Pas de Calais has suffered and the strategic disposition of these forces . . . give reason to suspect an attack in that region of France, which, at the same time, offers the shortest route for the final objective of their illusions, which is to say, Berlin.[27]

The fact that FUSAG remained stationary in England, as Garbo claimed, provided the Germans with overwhelming proof that the Normandy landings were indeed part of a great diversion. Consequently, they continued to expect the "main attack" to come at the Pas de Calais until August. There can be no doubt that Fortitude South achieved its goals.

At the same time that London was working on misleading the enemy as to the time and location of the attack, "A" Force was busy implementing its side of Bodyguard in the Mediterranean—Plan Zeppelin. The goal of Zeppelin was to help prevent the reinforcement of Normandy by diverting the Germans' attention to the Mediterranean for no less than twenty-five days after D day.[28] Clarke had his work cut out for him at a time when the stakes could not have been higher. To accomplish such a tremendous feat, he used every trick he had developed over the previous years. Charles Cruickshank explains, "The programme included virtually every known deceptive ploy, and Dudley Clarke manipulated all branches of the Allied forces in the Mediterranean like a master puppeteer. Navy, army, air force, administration, camouflage experts, propagandists, saboteurs, even the Commander-in-Chief himself, were all expected to play their part."[29] Fortunately for Clarke, the Germans believed the British to be considerably stronger than they were because of the remarkable success of his continual efforts to devise and maintain an extensive bogus order of battle.

Zeppelin was divided into two plans—Turpitude and Vendetta. The first of the plans, Turpitude, created an artificial threat to Greece and the Balkans.[30] The deception story sought to convince the Germans that the Allies would be unable to launch their cross-channel attack until late summer. In the meantime, they would strike the Balkans beginning with a landing at Crete and the Peloponnese and followed by an invasion across the Adriatic Sea aimed at the Istrian Peninsula and northern Dalmatia. The attacks were to be mounted by the notional 12th

Army stationed in Egypt and the genuine U.S. Seventh Army in Algiers, respectively. Once the bridgehead was established, the Allies would link up with the Soviets, who were coordinating their actions with the British and intended to land at Varna in Bulgaria.[31]

"A" Force brought the deception to life by spreading rumors, employing its double agents to spread misinformation, displaying dummy aircraft on airstrips and landing craft at various ports in North Africa, moving genuine formations around in support of the deception—including the largely notional 9th Army in Syria—and simulating radio traffic.[32] Essentially, the tactics meticulously cultivated by "A" Force during the first years of war and brought to maturity by the time of the El Alamein campaign were all replicated for Turpitude. In stark contrast to past efforts, the plan was carried out with complete disregard for the future. Clarke explained, "In the past when nearing the climax of any plan we have been at pains to conserve our machinery for another day, this time that policy will no longer hold." He continued, "Once we have entered the month of June all considerations regarding the safety of our channels (outside Italy) are to be subordinated to the demands of the plans on which we are now working and every risk accepted which can further the success of these plans."[33] Fortunately for the Allies, the risk was not in vain. According to the "A" Force Narrative War Diary, "The task did not end until after 'D-Day' in NORMANDY, which found over 600,000 Germans, including over twenty complete Divisions, engaged upon an entirely fruitless defensive task in YUGO-SLAVIA, ALBANIA, and GREECE alone. It is inspiring to reflect how History might have changed had they been employed instead upon the beaches of NORTHERN FRANCE or the Western boundaries of RUSSIA."[34] Whereas the efforts aimed at the Balkans met with tremendous success, those directed at southern France achieved less impressive results.

The purpose of Vendetta was to force the Germans to maintain a strong defensive force in southern France by threatening an invasion in that region.[35] According to the deception, the U.S. Seventh Army in Algiers was planning a seaborne invasion of Narbonne on June 19.[36] "A" Force went to considerable lengths to manufacture the threat, which went into full effect in May. It employed the usual means of rumors, double-agent traffic, simulated radio activity, and dummy displays. To this was added a large-scale amphibious exercise involving 13,000 troops, the storage of 10,000 tons of supplies, bombing raids on southern

France, and the distribution of maps to the invasion forces. An additional measure was the procurement of Red Cross facilities from Spain in an effort to cope with the expected casualties. Although the Germans did not consider the threat to southern France urgent, they nevertheless had ten divisions stationed there to meet the threat should it materialize.[37] Vendetta may not have achieved the exact results "A" Force had hoped for, but it most certainly succeeded in keeping ten divisions pinned down in the south and away from Normandy.

Plan Zeppelin came to an end on July 6. Clarke had successfully exploited the Germans' deep fears about the Balkans and southern France through the medium of deception. As a result, the Germans held a total of twenty-two divisions in the Balkans and an additional ten in southern France to meet imaginary threats.[38] Although it is impossible to determine what the exact outcome may have been if those divisions had been used to reinforce Normandy instead, it is not difficult to imagine that the story of D day as we know it today may have had a drastically different ending. Regardless, what we do know is that Operation Bodyguard, in all its elements, was a resounding success. The Germans were misled as to the time and precise location of the attack, as well as to the existence of other threats.

Operation Bodyguard was inarguably the product of the deception model forged over years of trial and error in the desert and was crafted after the blueprint established at El Alamein. Moreover, the grand deception operation was largely created by, and implemented by, men who had served under Clarke at "A" Force. Furthermore, Clarke's expertise was put to excellent use as he spent considerable time consulting with Bevan of the LCS, Wild of Ops B, and others regarding Bodyguard.[39] The Mediterranean component of Bodyguard, Plan Zeppelin, was itself an "A" Force plan. As a result, Bodyguard cannot be divorced from "A" Force—even if the plan was created in London—especially because it is highly unlikely that Bodyguard would have ever even been attempted had it not been for the years "A" Force spent developing deception into a true weapon of war with proven results.

"A" Force began to shut down in October 1944. Because Germany's military situation was deteriorating, the enemy was no longer capable of efficiently processing the deceptive information being fed to him. Deception had done all it could; the rest was up to the Allied military.

When Clarke arrived in Cairo in December 1940, he was the sole practitioner of strategic deception. There was no precedent or model to follow, so Clarke had to chart his own path. In March/April 1941 he became the head of "A" Force, a deception agency that was unique in that it was the first organization of its kind. "A" Force spent the next couple of years experimenting with deception, learning what the enemy was willing to accept, and perfecting its techniques. Although not every deception succeeded, each attempt provided invaluable experience that was applied to the next deception. By the fall of 1942 the deception machine had matured to the point that it had finally come into its own, and the blueprint established at El Alamein served as the model for successful deception practiced throughout the remainder of the war.

The credit for Britain's wartime deception goes primarily to two men—Archibald Wavell and Dudley Clarke. Wavell was the first not only to acknowledge the need for deception but to recognize its future potential as a strategic and tactical weapon of war. In addition, Wavell had the foresight to bring Clarke to the Middle East for the singular purpose of deceiving the enemy.

In the absence of a parent organization or a specific set of guidelines to follow, Clarke was presented with a daunting challenge. Nevertheless, he rose to the challenge and single-handedly created and nurtured a deception organization that was eventually capable of pulling off the largest deception coups in recorded history. Furthermore, he was able to accomplish all that he did because he had the unique ability to understand the enemy and to think like the enemy. He was creative, meticulous in his work, and able to cultivate exceptional working relationships with the other deception and intelligence organizations.

Another of Clarke's accomplishments was convincing the leadership in London and the Middle East of the usefulness of deception. His success in this area can clearly be seen in the numerous war establishments granted to deceptive entities and in the eventual size of "A" Force itself. Although Clarke began his work alone, "A" Force came to employ forty-one officers, seventy-six non-commissioned officers, and three company-strength units used for carrying out visual deception.[40] "A" Force was truly an impressive organization, and its commander was one of a kind.

Clarke died in 1974 in relative anonymity, as most never knew what he did. In 1953 he requested permission to publish the story of his "eighth assignment," titled *The Secret War*, but the British government denied his request. Clarke accepted the decision with grace, for he was never in the deception business for fame. To the contrary, we get a glimpse of his motivations in the foreword of his unpublished book: "The secret war was waged rather to conserve than to destroy: the stakes were the lives of the front-line troops." He added that as a measure of success "A" Force was "able to count its gains from the number of casualties it could avert."[41] In other words, Clarke's efforts at deception were never about the personal glory, but always about the potential to spare lives and win the war at the least cost to Britain.

There is unfortunately no way to tell how many soldiers survived the war as a result of the deception plans or how many battles were won simply because deception gave the military the decisive advantage before it arrived on the battlefield. One can only imagine. What must be acknowledged, however, is that Dudley Clarke played an instrumental role in facilitating the ultimate victory of the Allies and saving the lives of countless soldiers who never even knew that he existed or that deception was being practiced all around them.

The achievement of surprise on the battlefield was indeed invaluable, and so was Dudley Clarke. If one could measure his worth, it would amount to at least three armies.

NOTES

INTRODUCTION

1. Developments in Tactical Deception, WO 169/24870, "A" Force Permanent Record Files, National Archives, Kew, UK.
2. For a more comprehensive look at deceptions throughout history, see James F. Dunnigan and Albert A. Nofi, *Victory and Deceit: Dirty Tricks at War* (New York: William Morrow, 1995).
3. Ibid.
4. Dudley Clarke Papers, Box 99/2/1, Imperial War Museum, London, UK.
5. John Robert Ferris, "The British Army: Signals and Security in the Desert Campaign, 1940–1942," in *Intelligence and Strategy: Selected Essays* (London: Routledge, 2005).
6. Because Rommel initially enjoyed superior communications and intelligence, he was not quick to believe information that ran counter to that provided by his own intelligence officers. As a result, the efforts of the deceptionists all too often failed to produce the intended results. However, the situation began to change by 1942, after the British cracked the German codes and learned how to best exploit their access to the enemy's private communications. This translated into a much higher rate of success for British deception.
7. Developments in Strategic Deception, WO 169/24871, "A" Force Permanent Record Files, National Archives, Kew, UK.
8. Charles Cruickshank, *Deception in World War II* (Oxford: Oxford University Press, 1979), i.
9. Papers Concerning the Theory and Practice of Deception in General, WO 169/24874, "A" Force Permanent Record Files, National Archives, Kew, UK.
10. Ibid.
11. "A" Force Narrative War Diary, January 1, 1942–December 31, 1942, WO 169/24848, "A" Force Permanent Record Files, National Archives, Kew, UK.
12. Anthony Cave Brown, *Bodyguard of Lies* (New York: Harper & Row, 1975), 4.
13. Martin Young and Robbie Stamp, *Trojan Horses: Deception Operations in the Second World War* (London: Bodley Head, 1989), 239.

14. Thaddeus Holt, *The Deceivers: Allied Military Deception in the Second World War* (New York: Scribner, 2004), 184.

15. Quoted in BERTRAM: Notes on Deception Practised by the Eighth Army Prior to Its Offensive of October 1942, WO 201/2023, National Archives, Kew, UK.

16. Winston S. Churchill, *Memoirs of the Second World War* (Boston: Houghton Mifflin, 1959), 767.

17. Ewen Montagu, *The Man Who Never Was: World War II's Boldest Counterintelligence Operation* (New York: Oxford University Press, 1953).

18. F. W. Winterbotham, *The Ultra Secret* (New York: Harper & Row, 1974).

19. F. H. Hinsley, *British Intelligence in the Second World War: Its Influence on Strategy and Operations*, 5 vols. (London: Her Majesty's Stationery Office, 1979–90).

20. Brown, *Bodyguard of Lies*; Cruickshank, *Deception in World War II*.

21. Young and Stamp, *Trojan Horses*.

22. Michael Howard, *British Intelligence in the Second World War*, vol. 5, *Strategic Deception* (London: Her Majesty's Stationery Office, 1990). Hereafter cited as Howard, *Strategic Deception*.

23. David Mure, *Practise to Deceive* (London: William Kimber, 1977).

24. David Mure, *Master of Deception: Tangled Webs in London and the Middle East* (London: William Kimber, 1980).

25. H. O. Dovey, "The Eighth Assignment, 1941–1942," *Intelligence and National Security* 11, no. 4 (October 1996): 672–95; and "The Eighth Assignment, 1943–1945," *Intelligence and National Security* 12, no. 2 (April 1997): 69–90.

26. Holt, *Deceivers*.

27. Terry Crowdy, *Deceiving Hitler: Double Cross and Deception in World War II* (Oxford, UK: Osprey Publishing, 2008).

28. Nicholas Rankin, *Churchill's Wizards: The British Genius for Deception, 1941–1945* (London: Faber and Faber, 2008).

29. Michael Handel, ed., *Intelligence and Military Operations* (London: Frank Cass, 1990), 71–72.

30. I. S. O. Playfair, *The Mediterranean and Middle East*, 6 vols. (London: Her Majesty's Stationery Office, 1954–88).

CHAPTER 1. THE "MIGHTY" BRITISH EMPIRE DURING THE INTERWAR YEARS

1. Paul M. Kennedy, *The Rise and Fall of British Naval Mastery* (New York: Charles Scribner's Sons, 1976), 259.

2. Britain typically funded its coalition of allies and used its navy to establish an economic blockade against its enemy. It rarely sent an army to fight battles on the Continent.

3. Kennedy, *Rise and Fall*, 260.

4. Ibid. This stands in stark contrast to the prewar national debt of £650 million.

5. There is considerable scholarly debate as to whether this period represents a decline of the British Empire. For opposing views, see Kennedy, *Rise and Fall*, and David Edgerton, *Warfare State: Britain, 1920–1970* (Cambridge, UK: Cambridge University Press, 2006).

6. Kennedy, *Rise and Fall*, 270.

7. David Dilks, introduction to *Retreat from Power: Studies in Britain's Foreign Policy of the Twentieth Century*, ed. David Dilks (London: Macmillan Press, 1981), 1:10–12.

8. David French, *Raising Churchill's Army: The British Army and the War against Germany, 1919–1945* (Oxford: Oxford University Press, 2000), 13.

9. Paul Kennedy, *The Realities behind Diplomacy: Background Influences on British External Policy, 1865–1980* (London: George Allen & Unwin, 1981), 231.

10. Instead of helping the economy, it had the unfortunate consequence of increasing unemployment.

11. French, *Raising Churchill's Army*, 15

12. Williamson Murray, "Armored Warfare: The British, French, and German Experiences," in *Military Innovation in the Interwar Period*, ed. Williamson Murray and Allan R. Millet (New York: Cambridge University Press, 1996), 9.

13. Dilks, introduction to *Retreat from Power*, 15.

14. Murray, "Armored Warfare," 10; and Michael Howard, "British Military Preparations for the Second World War," in Dilks, *Retreat from Power*, 102.

15. Howard, "British Military Preparations," 105.

16. By 1938 the antiaircraft defense system was Britain's paramount focus. See Howard, "British Military Preparations," 106.

17. Dilks, introduction to *Retreat from Power*, 1–3, 12.

18. Kennedy, *Rise and Fall*, 275.

19. Dilks, introduction to *Retreat from Power*, 14.

20. It is ironic that the British were dependent on the League of Nations to maintain the status quo and prevent future aggression, while the member nations of the league were dependent on the British to be the enforcers of the covenant.

21. Dilks, introduction to *Retreat from Power*, 16.

22. Kennedy, *Realities behind Diplomacy*, 279.

23. Howard, "British Military Preparations," 107.

24. Norton Medlicott, "Britain and Germany: The Search for Agreement, 1930–37," in Dilks, *Retreat from Power*, 81.

25. Chiefs of Staff, quoted in Kennedy, *Realities behind Diplomacy*, 273.

26. Ethiopia was more commonly referred to as Abyssinia by the British until after the Second World War.

27. Until the outbreak of war, the Sudanese and Italians enjoyed good relations.

28. Martin Kolinsky, *Britain's War in the Middle East: Strategy and Diplomacy, 1936–42* (New York: St. Martin's Press, 1999), 17.

29. Norton Medlicott, "The Hoare-Laval Pact," in Dilks, *Retreat from Power*, 129.

30. Churchill, *Memoirs*, 79.

31. Kolinsky, *Britain's War*, 18.

32. Howard, "British Military Preparations," 103–4.

33. Medlicott, "Britain and Germany," 88. For more information on Germany's rearmament efforts and economic potential, see Adam Tooze, *The Wages of Destruction: The Making and Breaking of the Nazi Economy* (London: Allen Lane, 2006).

34. The year 1936 also saw the outbreak of the Arab Revolt in Palestine and the Spanish Civil War.

35. Stephen A. Schuker, "France and the Remilitarization of the Rhineland, 1936," *French Historical Studies* 14, no. 3 (Spring 1986): 299–338.

36. Kolinsky, *Britain's War*, 17–18. It was impossible to impose significant sanctions when the league powers were unwilling to go to war, and the world's largest industrial powers, including the United States and Soviet Union, remained neutral and continued to trade with Italy (see Medlicott, "Hoare-Laval Pact," 138).

37. Howard, "British Military Preparations," 110.

38. Kennedy, *Realities behind Diplomacy*, 280, 231.

39. Although Chamberlain has been lambasted for his policy of appeasement, Paul Kennedy provides perspective on why the prime minister pursued that option. For more information, see Kennedy, *Realities behind Diplomacy*, 291–301.

40. Many top German officials opposed Hitler's plan to take Czechoslovakia. They realized that German aggression in Czechoslovakia would likely result in British and French intervention. Because of Germany's own financial weakness, as well as the likelihood of American support for Britain and France in case of war, German leaders recognized that their country would be at a great disadvantage if it entered into war prematurely. For more information see Tooze, *Wages of Destruction*.

41. Dilks, "Appeasement and 'Intelligence,'" in Dilks, *Retreat from Power*, 156–59.

42. Ibid., 159–61.

43. Dilks, introduction to *Retreat from Power*, 18.

44. Kennedy, *Rise and Fall*, 294–95.

45. Tooze, *Wages of Destruction*, 311.

46. Kennedy, *Realities behind Diplomacy*, 230.

47. Howard, "British Military Preparations," 116–17. Howard remarks that the British managed to follow this exact strategy throughout the war.

48. I. S. O. Playfair, *The Mediterranean and Middle East*, vol. 1, *The Early Successes against Italy* (London: Her Majesty's Stationery Office, 1954), 23.

49. Tooze, *Wages of Destruction*, 269.

50. Ibid., 322–25.

51. Playfair, *Mediterranean and Middle East*, 1:116.

52. French, *Raising Churchill's Army*, 157.

53. Churchill, *Memoirs*, 189.

54. Hugh Sebag-Montefiore, *Dunkirk: Fight to the Last Man* (Cambridge, MA: Harvard University Press, 2006), 59.

55. French, *Raising Churchill's Army*, 157.

56. Ibid., 159; and Churchill, *Memoirs*, 189, 195.

57. French, *Raising Churchill's Army*, 159.

58. Sebag-Montefiore, *Dunkirk*, 8.

59. Churchill, *Memoirs*, 249–54.

60. Sebag-Montefiore, *Dunkirk*, 458.

61. French, *Raising Churchill's Army*, 156.

62. Churchill, *Memoirs*, 295, 334.

63. Ibid., 287.

64. Ibid., 270–71.
65. For a broader discussion of the factors that contributed to the Allied victory in the Second World War, see Richard Overy, *Why the Allies Won* (New York: W. W. Norton, 1995).
66. See, for example, Nigel West, *MI5: British Security Service Operations 1909–1945* (London: Bodley Head, 1981). West points out that in 1937 MI5 had only twenty-eight staff members, a pitiful number compared to its 1918 strength of eight hundred. It was also desperately short on funds.
67. Dunnigan and Nofi, *Victory and Deceit*, 140.
68. Ibid., 141.
69. Ibid., 141–42.
70. See discussion in introduction.
71. Ibid., 145–46.
72. Rankin, *Churchill's Wizards*, 113. See also Richard Meinertzhagen, *Diary of a Black Sheep* (Edinburgh: Oliver & Boyd, 1964). Rankin notes that Meinertzhagen's version of events has been challenged by others. In fact, Meinertzhagen may not have masterminded the plan as he claimed in his diary but instead took credit for someone else's idea.
73. Dunnigan and Nofi, *Victory and Deceit*, 147.
74. Ibid.
75. Ibid., 153. This effort is strikingly similar to the tactics the British used in preparation for the second Battle of El Alamein discussed in chapter 7.
76. Ibid.
77. Wavell held Allenby in high esteem and authored a biography on the commander. For more, see Archibald P. Wavell, *Allenby, a Study in Greatness: The Biography of Field-Marshal Viscount Allenby of Megiddo and Felixstowe* (Oxford: Oxford University Press, 1941).
78. Rankin, *Churchill's Wizards*, 50.
79. Handel, *Intelligence and Military Operations*, 24.

CHAPTER 2. ITALY JOINS THE GAME

1. Hinsley, *British Intelligence*, 1:202–5.
2. Michael Glover, *An Improvised War: The Ethiopian Campaign, 1940–1941* (London: Leo Cooper, 1987), 18.
3. In this context, the term "Middle East" does not refer to the geographic region. The Middle East command had its headquarters in Cairo and, initially under the leadership of General Archibald Wavell, was responsible for all British forces in Aden, British Somaliland, Cyprus, Egypt, Iraq, Palestine, the Persian Gulf, the Sudan, and Transjordan in time of war. The Mediterranean theater refers to the body of water, which was under the control of the Royal Navy's Mediterranean Fleet, and all the surrounding countries. Some of the countries bordering the Mediterranean also fell under the command of the Middle East theater. This work largely deals with the land war in North and East Africa, which were part of the Middle East theater.
   The term "British forces" will be used throughout to refer to all forces, including both British and native troops, under British leadership.

4. Harold E. Raugh Jr., *Wavell in the Middle East 1939–1941: A Study in Generalship* (London: Brassey's, 1993), 45.

5. Playfair, *Mediterranean and Middle East*, 1:xxv. After the German invasion of Russia in June 1941, operations in the Mediterranean also served to divert German resources away from Russia. Whether the Mediterranean qualified as a "second front" is debatable, but it did tie down troops and resources that the Germans could have otherwise sent to the eastern front. The British specifically viewed the Mediterranean as offering the opportunity to bring Soviet Russia "immediate and continuing help" throughout the war. For more information, see Michael Howard, *The Mediterranean Strategy in the Second World War* (New York: Frederick A. Praeger, 1968), 35–36, 70.

6. See John Ellis, *Brute Force: Allied Strategy and Tactics in the Second World War* (New York: Viking Press, 1990). See also Kennedy, *Realities behind Diplomacy*, 351–59, for a discussion of the "indirect" approach.

7. Quoted in Douglas Porch, *The Path to Victory: The Mediterranean Theater in World War II* (New York: Farrar, Straus, and Giroux, 2004), 7.

8. Playfair, *Mediterranean and Middle East*, 1:23.

9. "Notes for BGS, Middle East Command," memo, July 31, 1939, WO 201/2379, 1, National Archives, Kew, UK.

10. Kennedy, *Realities behind Diplomacy*, 352.

11. Porch, *Path to Victory*, 7.

12. "Notes for BGS, Middle East Command," 1–2.

13. Denis Mack Smith, *Italy: A Modern History* (Ann Arbor: University of Michigan Press, 1969), 457; and Playfair, *Mediterranean and Middle East*, 1:7.

14. Playfair, *Mediterranean and Middle East*, 1:7–9, 11.

15. Galeazzo Ciano, "August 24, 1939," in *Diary: 1937–1943* (New York: Enigma Books, 2002), 264.

16. Ibid.

17. Porch, *Path to Victory*, 36.

18. Playfair, *Mediterranean and Middle East*, 1:81.

19. Ibid., 25–28.

20. Kolinsky, *Britain's War*, 8.

21. Porch, *Path to Victory*, 43.

22. Playfair, *Mediterranean and Middle East*, 1:3.

23. Ibid., 18, 61.

24. "Notes for BGS, Middle East Command," 1–2.

25. Archibald P. Wavell, Despatch Covering August 1939–November 1940, Sheet 2, CAB 106/472, National Archives, Kew, UK.

26. Kolisnky, *Britain's War*, 102.

27. Playfair, *Mediterranean and Middle East*, 1:83.

28. Wavell, Despatch Covering August 1939–November 1940, Sheet 2.

29. Ibid., Sheet 4.

30. Ibid., Sheet 5–7.

31. Glover, *Improvised War*, 19; and Playfair, *Mediterranean and Middle East*, 1:95–96.

32. Alan Moorehead, *The March to Tunis: The North African War 1940–1943* (New York: Harper & Row, 1965), 17–18.

33. Playfair, *Mediterranean and the Middle East*, 1:190.
34. Churchill, *Memoirs*, 389–90.
35. Quoted in Raugh, *Wavell in the Middle East*, 204.
36. Crowdy, *Deceiving Hitler*, 128.
37. The British also had to contend with growing anti-British sentiment among the Egyptian nationalists. Because Egypt declared neutrality, the British could do little to counter the possibility of a Fifth Column threat. For more information, see Crowdy, *Deceiving Hitler*, 129.
38. Playfair, *Mediterranean and the Middle East*, 1:167.
39. Wavell, Despatch Covering August 1939–November 1940, Sheet 8.
40. Playfair, *Mediterranean and the Middle East*, 1:170, 181; Anthony Mockler, *Haile Selassie's War* (Oxford, UK: Oxford University Press, 1984), 237–39.
41. Mockler, *Haile Selassie's War*, 209.
42. Playfair, *Mediterranean and the Middle East*, 1:171.
43. Mack Smith, *Italy*, 476.
44. Mockler, *Haile Selassie's War*, 273.
45. Ibid., 276.
46. Ibid., 279.
47. Wavell, Despatch Covering August 1939–November 1940, Sheet 16.
48. Ibid., Sheet 15; Mockler, *Haile Selassie's War*, 273–79.
49. Playfair, *Mediterranean and the Middle East*, 1:127.
50. J. E. B. Barton, 101 Mission Reports, Section 5, Chapter "G," June 1940–May 1941, WO 201/278, National Archives, Kew, UK.
51. Ibid. It must be noted that the promise of supplies came before France's defeat and the disastrous loss of equipment at Dunkirk. When it came to actually supplying the rebels, the British found themselves shorthanded.
52. See David Shirreff, *Bare Feet and Bandoliers: Wingate, Sandford, the Patriots and the Part They Played in the Liberation of Ethiopia* (London: Radcliffe Press, 1995).
53. Barton, 101 Mission Reports.
54. Ibid.
55. Wavell, Despatch Covering August 1939–November 1940, Sheet 10.
56. Ibid., Sheet 9.
57. Moorehead, *March to Tunis*, 22–23.
58. Wavell, Despatch Covering August 1939–November 1940, Sheet 11.
59. Ibid., Sheet 12.
60. Playfair, *Mediterranean and the Middle East*, 1:114.
61. Wavell, Despatch Covering August 1939–November 1940, Sheet 13.
62. Ciano, "September 9, 1940," in *Diary*, 381.
63. Ciano, "September 30, 1940," in ibid., 386.
64. Churchill, *Memoirs*, 396.
65. Archibald P. Wavell, Operations in the Western Desert, December 7, 1940–February 7, 1941, WO 106/2133, 3–4, National Archives, Kew, UK.
66. Ibid., 4.
67. Howard, *Strategic Deception*, 31.
68. Ibid., 32; and Playfair, *Mediterranean and the Middle East*, 1:263.

69. Dovey, "Eighth Assignment, 1941–1942," 672–95.
70. French, *Raising Churchill's Army*, 214.
71. "How and Why Italy Lost Ethiopia," *Il Tempo*, August 2, 1944, in Plan "CAMILLA" (British Somaliland), December 1940–January 1941, WO 169/24903, "A" Force Permanent Record Files, National Archives, Kew, UK.
72. Howard, *Strategic Deception*, 31–32.
73. Archibald P. Wavell, *Soldiers and Soldiering* (Oxford, UK: Alden Press, 1953), 134.
74. "A" Force Narrative War Diary, November 13, 1940–December 31, 1941, WO 169/24847, 1, "A" Force Permanent Record Files, National Archives, Kew, UK.
75. Playfair, *Mediterranean and the Middle East*, 1:266.
76. Henrietta Goodden, *Camouflage and Art: Design for Deception in World War 2* (London: Unicorn Press, 2007), 106.
77. Mure, *Master of Deception*, 63.
78. Playfair, *Mediterranean and the Middle East*, 1:266.
79. French, *Raising Churchill's Army*, 214.
80. Wavell, Operations in the Western Desert, 8.
81. Rankin, *Churchill's Wizards*, 315.
82. Erwin Rommel, *The Rommel Papers*, ed. B. H. Liddell Hart (New York: Harcourt, Brace, 1953), 92. The Italian forces were at a constant disadvantage owing to the lack of motorized units.
83. Playfair, *Mediterranean and the Middle East*, 1:274.
84. Howard, *Strategic Deception*, 33.
85. Archibald Wavell, introduction to Dudley Clarke, *Seven Assignments* (London: Jonathan Cape, 1948), 7.
86. "A" Force War Establishment and Organization, November 13, 1940, WO 169/24866, "A" Force Permanent Record Files, National Archives, Kew, UK.

CHAPTER 3. CLARKE'S GRAND DEBUT

1. Holt, *Deceivers*, 9–12.
2. Ibid.; Clarke, *Seven Assignments*.
3. Mure, *Practise to Deceive*, 249.
4. October 5, 1939, Dudley Clarke Papers, Box 99/2/1.
5. Dudley Clarke Papers, Box 99/2/1. The British government refused to allow Clarke to publish his story.
6. Wavell, introduction to Clarke, *Seven Assignments*, 7.
7. Clarke, *Seven Assignments*, 262.
8. Rankin, *Churchill's Wizards*, 314.
9. Crowdy, *Deceiving Hitler*, 142–43. Clarke's purpose in Madrid was to establish channels through which he could pass his deceptions. It is interesting that his release came about at the urging of a German agent in Madrid whom Clarke had been in communication with. This agent apparently believed Clarke was sympathetic to the German cause.
10. Holt, *Deceivers*, 143.
11. Crowdy, *Deceiving Hitler*, 143.
12. Guy Liddell, "11 November 1941," *The Guy Liddell Diaries*, ed. Nigel West (London: Routledge, 2005), 1:192.

13. Quoted in Crowdy, *Deceiving Hitler*, 144.

14. Rankin, *Churchill's Wizards*, 316.

15. Papers Concerning the Theory and Practice of Deception in General, WO 169/24874.

16. Holt, *Deceivers*, 19; and Howard, *Strategic Deception*, 33.

17. "A" Force Narrative War Diary, November 13, 1940–December 31, 1941, WO 169/24847, 6.

18. Probably the greatest example of this was when the British had to withdraw from Greece and Crete following the successful German offensives.

19. "A" Force War Establishment and Organization, WO 169/24866.

20. Hinsley, *British Intelligence*, 1:191.

21. For more information on Egypt's decision to remain neutral and the repercussions for British security in Egypt, see Kolinsky, *Britain's War*.

22. Howard, *Strategic Deception*, 31.

23. Ibid.

24. "Organisation of the Middle East Intelligence Centre," Middle East Security Section, January 1, 1939–December 31, 1939, KV 4/305, National Archives, Kew, UK; and Hinsley, *British Intelligence*, 1:36.

25. Middle East Security Section, KV 4/305.

26. Ibid.

27. Crowdy, *Deceiving Hitler*, 129–30.

28. Holt, *Deceivers*, 19. Holt points out that SIME finally gained official independence in 1942.

29. Ibid., 20.

30. Ibid., 19.

31. Hinsley, *British Intelligence*, 1:197; and Howard, *Strategic Deception*, 31–32.

32. "A" Force Narrative War Diary, November 13, 1940–December 31, 1941, WO 169/24847, 56–57.

33. Howard, *Strategic Deception*, 32.

34. "A" Force Narrative War Diary, November 13, 1940–December 31, 1941, WO 169/24847, 23.

35. Ibid., 22

36. Mure, *Practise to Deceive*, 21.

37. "A" Force Narrative War Diary, November 13, 1940–December 31, 1941, WO 169/24847, 7. See also Plan "ABEAM" (Special Air Service Brigade), January 1941–August 1941, WO 169/24904, "A" Force Permanent Record Files, National Archives, Kew, UK.

38. "A" Force Narrative War Diary, November 13, 1940–December 31, 1941, WO 169/24847, 7.

39. Ibid., 56.

40. Developments in Strategic Deception, WO 169/24871.

41. Ibid.

42. Crowdy, *Deceiving Hitler*, 140. Before Stanley was appointed, Admiral Dudley Pound asked Clarke if he would accept the position of controlling officer. Clarke, who was by that time working under Commander in Chief Claude Auchinleck, responded that "you can't pinch a man's butler when he has only

been lent to you for the night." (Dudley Clarke Papers, quoted in Holt, *Deceivers*, 42.)

43. J. C. Masterman, *The Double-Cross System in the War of 1939 to 1945* (New Haven: Yale University Press, 1972), 107.

44. Ibid., 140–48. The LCS was made up of Bevan; representatives from the Foreign Office, Special Operations Executive (SOE), MI5, MI6, and the Middle East and Indian commands; and four permanent members: Commander James Arbuthnott of the Royal Navy, Major Ronald Wingate of the Army, Squadron Leader Dennis Wheatley of the RAF, and Major Harold Petavel. For more information, see Liaison with LCS, WO 169/24872, National Archives, Kew, UK.

45. Liaison with LCS, WO 169/24872. Before 1942 there were only two controllers: Stanley in London and Clarke in the Middle East. In 1942 Peter Fleming, representing India, became the third controller. A fourth was added at the end of 1943 to cover the countries of northwestern Europe under the control of the Supreme Commander of the Allied Expeditionary Force (AEF). For more information, see "A" Force Narrative War Diary, November 13, 1940–December 31, 1941, WO 169/24847, 77.

46. Developments in Strategic Deception, WO 169/24871.

47. "A" Force Narrative War Diary, November 13, 1940–December 31, 1941, WO 169/24847, 3.

48. Raugh, *Wavell in the Middle East*, 172.

49. Quoted in ibid., 172.

50. Barton, 101 Mission Reports.

51. Ibid.

52. Ibid.

53. In the latter part of 1940, the patriot movement suffered some serious setbacks as the patriots became demoralized and old rivalries flared up. Sandford made a concerted, and ultimately successful, effort to bring the rival chiefs together to fight for the common cause. For more information, see Playfair, *Mediterranean and the Middle East*, 1:402–4.

54. Barton, 101 Mission Reports.

55. Ibid.

56. Ibid.

57. Ibid.

58. Playfair, *Mediterranean and Middle East*, 1:406.

59. Barton, 101 Mission Reports.

60. "A" Force Narrative War Diary, November 13, 1940–December 31, 1941, WO 169/24847, 3.

61. Ibid.

62. Plan "CAMILLA," WO 169/24903.

63. "A" Force Narrative War Diary, November 13, 1940–December 31, 1941, WO 169/24847, 3.

64. Plan "CAMILLA," WO 169/24903.

65. "A" Force Narrative War Diary, November 13, 1940–December 31, 1941, WO 169/24847, 5; Rankin, *Churchill's Wizards*, 316.

66. "A" Force Narrative War Diary, November 13, 1940–December 31, 1941, WO 169/24847, 4.

67. See article in Plan "CAMILLA," WO 169/24903.

68. Plan "CAMILLA," WO 169/24903.

69. Ibid.

70. "A" Force Narrative War Diary, November 13, 1940–December 31, 1941, WO 169/24847, 3.

71. Plan "CAMILLA," WO 169/24903.

72. Ibid.

73. "A" Force Narrative War Diary, November 13, 1940–December 31, 1941, WO 169/24847, 3–4.

74. Papers Concerning the Theory and Practice of Deception in General, WO 169/24874.

75. Developments in Tactical Deception, WO 169/24870.

76. Ibid.

77. Dudley Clarke Papers, Box 99/2/1.

78. Papers Concerning the Theory and Practice of Deception in General, WO 169/24874.

79. Ibid.

80. Glover, *Improvised War*, 15–16.

81. Quoted in Raugh, *Wavell in the Middle East*, 183.

82. Playfair, *Mediterranean and Middle East*, 1:394.

83. Ibid., 431.

84. Howard, *Strategic Deception*, 35; Hinsley, *British Intelligence*, 1:380–81.

85. Hinsley, *British Intelligence*, 1:381.

86. Alan G. Cunningham, Report on Operations, East Africa Force, November 1, 1940–April 5, 1941, CAB 106/469, National Archives, Kew, UK.

87. Glover, *Improvised War*, 103.

88. Playfair, *Mediterranean and Middle East*, 1:431.

89. Glover, *Improvised War*, 105.

90. Quoted in Raugh, *Wavell in the Middle East*, 178.

91. Playfair, *Mediterranean and Middle East*, 1:417–18.

92. Raugh, *Wavell in the Middle East*, 180.

93. Ibid., 177.

94. Quoted in Raugh, *Wavell in the Middle East*, 180.

95. Playfair, *Mediterranean and Middle East*, 439.

96. Mockler, *Haile Selassie's War*, 370–71.

97. Playfair, *Mediterranean and Middle East*, 1:425–26.

98. Barton, Mission 101 Reports.

99. Glover, *Improvised War*, xxi.

100. Hinsley, *British Intelligence*, 1:391.

CHAPTER 4. THE WESTERN DESERT FROM JANUARY TO JULY 1941

1. In June Wavell estimated that the Italians had 215,000 troops in Libya and 200,000 in East Africa. Those numbers increased significantly in the months following the Italian declaration of war. The British had roughly 55,000 in all Africa.

2. Wavell, Operations in the Western Desert, 8.

3. Wavell, Operations in the Western Desert, 9; and Playfair, *Mediterranean and Middle East*, 1:287.

4. Hinsley, *British Intelligence*, 1:379.

5. Playfair, *Mediterranean and Middle East*, 1:287.

6. Wavell, Operations in the Western Desert, 9.

7. Ibid., 11.

8. Playfair, *Mediterranean and Middle East*, 1:293.

9. I. S. O. Playfair, *The Mediterranean and Middle East*, vol. 2, "The Germans Come to the Help of Their Ally" (1941) (London: Her Majesty's Stationery Office, 1954), 1, 114.

10. Playfair, *Mediterranean and Middle East*, 1:343.

11. Wavell, Operations in the Western Desert, 11. The British were also aided by their capture of vehicles and fuel from Bardia and Tobruk.

12. Barrie Pitt, *The Crucible of War: Western Desert 1941* (London: Jonathan Cape, 1980), 192–93.

13. *Rommel Papers*, 95. There is much debate as to whether or not the British offensive could have, or should have, continued on to Tripoli. Many scholars, as well as contemporaries such as Bernard Montgomery and Alan Moorehead, agree that the offensive should have continued and would have resulted in success. (See Bernard Montgomery, foreword to Moorehead, *March to Tunis*). Others, Niall Barr, for example, believe that Wavell's forces had extended themselves too far beyond their supply lines to sustain a further advance, so it was not feasible to try to take Tripoli. (See Niall Barr, *Pendulum of War: The Three Battles of El Alamein* [Woodstock: Overlook Press, 2004], 5–6).

14. Wavell, Operations in the Western Desert, 13.

15. Playfair, *Mediterranean and Middle East*, 1:364.

16. "A" Force Narrative War Diary, November 13, 1940–December 31, 1941, WO 169/24847, 34.

17. Playfair, *Mediterranean and Middle East*, 1:353–54.

18. "A" Force Narrative War Diary, November 13, 1940–December 31, 1941, WO 169/24847, 34.

19. Geoffrey Barkas, *The Camouflage Story (From Aintree to Alamein)* (London: Cassell, 1952), 3, 45–52.

20. Ibid., 43.

21. Ibid.

22. Ibid., 94.

23. In 1941 "A" Force and G(CAM) functioned as two completely separate organizations. As deception efforts increased, greater cooperation between the two agencies became necessary. By mutual agreement, "A" Force assumed responsibility for creating deceptions and determining the overall strategy, specific policies, and scope and timetable. G(CAM) maintained control over the means of physical deception where camouflage was concerned and implemented physical deception in the field. By 1943 G(CAM) was unofficially under the control of "A" Force. For more information, see Co-Operation with the Camouflage Organization, WO 169/24880, and The Production of Special

Devices Required for Deception, WO 169/24883, "A" Force Permanent Record Files, National Archives, Kew, UK.

24. "A" Force Narrative War Diary, November 13, 1940–December 31, 1941, WO 169/24847, 7.

25. Plan "ABEAM," WO 169/24904.

26. "A" Force Narrative War Diary, November 13, 1940–December 31, 1941, WO 169/24847, 7–8.

27. See articles "Presentation of 'ABEAM'" and "Instructions for Lance Corporal Smith and Trooper Gurmin" in Plan "ABEAM," WO 169/24904.

28. Rankin, *Churchill's Wizards*, 327.

29. Hervie Haufler, *The Spies Who Never Were: The True Story of the Nazi Spies Who Were Actually Allied Double Agents* (New York: NAL Caliber, 2006), 113.

30. "A" Force Narrative War Diary, November 13, 1940–December 31, 1941, WO 169/24847, 9.

31. Ibid.

32. Ibid., 8, 10.

33. Ibid., 8. The 8th Army was formed in September 1941 by General Claude Auchinleck in preparation for Operation Crusader.

34. Rankin, *Churchill's Wizards*, 324.

35. Playfair, *Mediterranean and Middle East*, 2:2.

36. Ibid., 2–3.

37. "A" Force Narrative War Diary, November 13, 1940–December 31, 1941, WO 169/24847, 11.

38. Clarke came down with jaundice and was admitted to the hospital on February 12. He remained hospitalized until March 4, so his ability to coordinate deception was limited during that time. Maunsell's SIME continued to spread rumors, and Maunsell stayed in constant contact with Clarke.

39. Playfair, *Mediterranean and Middle East*, 1:366.

40. *Rommel Papers*, 98.

41. Quoted in Raugh, *Wavell in the Middle East*, 138.

42. Hinsley, *British Intelligence*, 1:382–87.

43. Raugh, *Wavell in the Middle East*, 142.

44. Playfair, *Mediterranean and Middle East*, 2:9–11.

45. Archibald P. Wavell, Despatch on Operations in the Middle East, February 7–July 15, 1941, CAB 106/379, 6, National Archives, Kew, UK.

46. Ibid.

47. Rankin, *Churchill's Wizards*, 327–28.

48. Churchill, *Memoirs*, 426.

49. Playfair, *Mediterranean and Middle East*, 2:1–3.

50. Churchill, *Memoirs*, 436.

51. For more information on Rommel, see Desmond Young, *Rommel: The Desert Fox* (New York: Harper & Brothers, 1950).

52. Playfair, *Mediterranean and Middle East*, 2:6.

53. *Rommel Papers*, 109.

54. Ibid., 111.

55. Ibid.
56. Playfair, *Mediterranean and Middle East*, 2:156.
57. Raugh, *Wavell in the Middle East*, 206.
58. "Plan A-R," in Western Desert Plans for 1941, WO 169/24905, "A" Force Permanent Record Files, National Archives, Kew, UK.
59. Ibid.; "A" Force Narrative War Diary, November 13, 1940–December 31, 1941, WO 169/24847, 19–20.
60. "Plan A-R."
61. "A" Force Narrative War Diary, November 13, 1940–December 31, 1941, WO 169/24847, 20.
62. Ibid.
63. "Plan A-R."
64. Camilla was the first.
65. "Plan A-R."
66. "A" Force Narrative War Diary, November 13, 1940–December 31, 1941, WO 169/24847, 20.
67. Ibid., 9.
68. Howard, *Strategic Deception*, 35. Although captured German documents revealed that the Germans did accept the 1st SAS as a genuine unit, Rommel apparently did not consider it to be a threat at that particular time.
69. "A" Force Narrative War Diary, November 13, 1940–December 31, 1941, WO 169/24847, 21.
70. Ibid.
71. For more information on the Byng Boys Scheme and Plan Dolphin, see ibid., 16–18.
72. "A" Force Narrative War Diary, November 13, 1940–December 31, 1941, WO 169/24847, 23.
73. This trip predated Clarke's visit to Madrid when he was arrested while impersonating a female. Both trips had the same purpose of making contacts with enemy agents to set up new channels for passing along Allied deceptions.
74. Papers Concerning the Theory and Practice of Deception in General, WO 169/24874.
75. "A" Force Narrative War Diary, November 13, 1940–December 31, 1941, WO 169/24847, 25.
76. Because the focus of this work is the development of deception in the deserts of Africa, the deceptions pertaining specifically to the Balkans and Syria are not discussed here. For detailed information on those deception efforts, see ibid.
77. "A" Force War Establishment and Organization, WO 169/24866.
78. Playfair, *Mediterranean and Middle East*, 2:83.
79. Ibid., 105.
80. Churchill, *Memoirs*, 442.
81. Raugh, *Wavell in the Middle East*, 228. Clarke met with the king of Greece and learned from him that at least six hundred German parachutists had died as a result of their parachutes failing to open. In response, the conniving Clarke wrote, "It would be interesting to get as much evidence to this effect as we can

for the benefit of the press. It would be an admirable thing for other German parachute units to feel that there was a good chance of their parachutes failing to operate. We might induce them to think that most of the failures were due to the use of Japanese silk." See Dudley Clarke Papers, Box 99/2/2.

82. Playfair, *Mediterranean and Middle East*, 2:104–5, 146–47; "A" Force Narrative War Diary, November 13, 1940–December 31, 1941, WO 169/24847, 28; Churchill, *Memoirs*, 437.

83. Churchill, *Memoirs*, 451.

84. Raugh, *Wavell in the Middle East*, 215.

85. Churchill, *Memoirs*, 449–53. The use of the term "Persia" is in line with British terminology of the day. The Iranians called their country Iran, not Persia, by this time.

86. Wavell, Despatch on Operations in the Middle East, CAB 106/379.

87. Churchill, *Memoirs*, 453.

88. For more information on the Exporter Cover Plan, see "A" Force Narrative War Diary, November 13, 1940–December 31, 1941, WO 169/24847, 29.

89. Churchill, *Memoirs*, 450–54.

90. Ibid., 454.

91. Ibid., 455.

92. The interception of Britain's wireless transmissions was the direct result of lax security on the part of Britain's military services and the American military attaché in Cairo. Those gaps were not identified and fixed until mid-1942.

93. Hinsley, *British Intelligence*, 1:398.

94. Playfair, *Mediterranean and Middle East*, 2:159–62.

95. Raugh, *Wavell in the Middle East*, 227.

96. Ibid., 229.

97. Quoted in ibid., 231.

98. Ibid., 231–32; Churchill, *Memoirs*, 455.

99. "A" Force Narrative War Diary, November 13, 1940–December 31, 1941, WO 169/24847, 30.

100. Ibid. The intelligence gaps were also to blame.

101. Playfair, *Mediterranean and Middle East*, 2:168–69.

102. *Rommel Papers*, 145.

103. Playfair, *Mediterranean and Middle East*, 2:167–70.

104. French, *Raising Churchill's Army*, 218.

105. Hinsley, *British Intelligence*, 1:399.

106. Wavell, Despatch on Operations in the Middle East, CAB 106/379.

107. *Rommel Papers*, 146.

108. French, *Raising Churchill's Army*, 217.

109. Playfair, *Mediterranean and Middle East*, 2:174.

110. The Germans converted antiaircraft guns into antitank weapons that were extremely effective in the desert. The once seemingly invincible Matilda tanks proved highly vulnerable to the Germans' antitank guns.

111. *Rommel Papers*, 146.

112. Churchill, *Memoirs*, 456.

113. Ibid., 457.

114. C. J. E. Auchileck, despatch, July–October 1941, WO 106/2169, National Archives, Kew, UK.
115. Ibid.
116. Dudley Clarke Papers, Box 99/2/1.
117. Holt, *Deceivers*, 34.

CHAPTER 5. CRUISING ALONG DURING THE LAST HALF OF 1941

1. The Germans and Italians settled into a defensive position almost immediately after Operation Battleaxe. Although the Axis powers prevented the British from achieving their goals of retaking Cyrenaica and raising the siege of Tobruk, the campaign was costly for the Axis forces. Also, the Germans invaded Soviet Russia on June 22, 1941, so their attention was increasingly focused on the eastern front instead of the Middle East. Rommel could not expect to receive sizable reinforcements of troops, equipment, or supplies until the war in Russia ended. He was thus unable to mount an offensive and forced to maintain a defensive posture.
2. Churchill, *Memoirs*, 495.
3. Hinsley, *British Intelligence*, 2:280.
4. Churchill, *Memoirs*, 495–96.
5. Major General I. S. O. Playfair agrees with Auchinleck's approach and states that it would have been disastrous to follow Churchill's strategy. He argues that Auchinleck's forces would have been "used up piecemeal" and that the effort would most likely have ended in a stalemate as opposed to a victory of any sort. For more information, see I. S. O. Playfair, *The Mediterranean and the Middle East*, vol. 3, *British Fortunes Reach Their Lowest Ebb* (London: Her Majesty's Stationery Office, 1960).
6. Churchill, *Memoirs*, 496.
7. Ibid.
8. Deception Plan on Defense of Cyprus, WO 169/24925, "A" Force Permanent Record Files, National Archives, Kew, UK.
9. "A" Force Narrative War Diary, November 13, 1940–December 31, 1941, WO 169/24847, 31–32.
10. The Employment of Special Deception Units in the Field, WO 169/24882, "A" Force Permanent Record Files, National Archives, Kew, UK. The 38th and 39th RTRs were formed in April 1941. An additional dummy tank unit, the 37th, was formed in June. The 37th, 38th, and 39th were all static dummy units. These units eventually came to make up the notional 74th Armoured Brigade, later renamed the 24th Armoured Brigade—a mobile dummy unit. All dummy tank units fell under the direct control of Major Jones of "A" Force.
11. "A" Force Narrative War Diary, November 13, 1940–December 31, 1941, WO 169/24847, 33.
12. Ibid., 32–33.
13. Papers Concerning the Theory and Practice of Deception in General, WO 169/24874.
14. Employment of Special Deception Units in the Field, WO 169/24882.

15. Ibid.
16. Ibid.
17. Ibid. The static dummies were very easy to transport. The British modified trucks to carry eight to nine dummy tanks apiece. A squadron of dummies could fit inside three trucks and travel between fifty and sixty miles a day, using minimal resources. Each dummy tank could be erected in approximately fifteen minutes. The static dummies were later replaced by rubber inflatable tanks.
18. Ibid.
19. "A" Force Narrative War Diary, November 13, 1940–December 31, 1941, WO 169/24847, 45.
20. Employment of Special Deception Units in the Field, WO 169/24882
21. "G"(Cam.), WO 169/3976, National Archives, Kew, UK.
22. The sun shields came into greater use in 1942 when the deception planners began attempts to hide entire armored units. They were used extensively in preparation for the El Alamein offensive. For more information on the design of track makers, see Development of "A" Force Special Units, WO 169/24869, "A" Force Permanent Record Files, National Archives, Kew, UK.
23. "A" Force Narrative War Diary, November 13, 1940–December 31, 1941, WO 169/24847, 48.
24. Auchinleck, despatch, WO 106/2169. This was the result of a general reorganization of the forces in the Middle East. The Western Desert Force became part of the new 8th Army. In the north, namely, Syria and Palestine, Auchinleck formed the 9th Army under the leadership of General Maitland Wilson. The 8th Army commander, Cunningham, was the brother of the naval commander in chief, Admiral Andrew Cunningham.
25. For more information, see Cunningham, Report on Operations, CAB 106/469.
26. "A" Force Narrative War Diary, November 13, 1940–December 31, 1941, WO 169/24847, 51.
27. Ibid., 36.
28. Ibid.
29. Papers Concerning the Theory and Practice of Deception in General, WO 169/24874. For more information on the creation of GSI(d) and its responsibilities, see Developments in Tactical Deception, WO 169/24870.
30. "A" Force Narrative War Diary, November 13, 1940–December 31, 1941, WO 169/24847, 36.
31. Howard, *Strategic Deception*, 39.
32. Ibid.
33. Ibid.
34. Ibid.
35. Reports on Miscellaneous Activities, 1941–1942, WO 169/24877, "A" Force Permanent Records Files, National Archives, Kew UK.
36. Papers Concerning the Theory and Practice of Deception in General, WO 169/24874; "A" Force Narrative War Diary, November 13, 1940–December 31, 1941, WO 169/24847, 37.

37. Reports on Miscellaneous Activities, WO 169/24877.
38. "A" Force Narrative War Diary, November 13, 1940–December 31, 1941, WO 169/24847, 37.
39. Ibid., 39.
40. Ibid.; Reports on Miscellaneous Activities, WO 169/24877.
41. "A" Force Narrative War Diary, November 13, 1940–December 31, 1941, WO 169/24847, 38.
42. Churchill, *Memoirs*, 498.
43. Hinsley, *British Intelligence*, 2:280.
44. "A" Force Narrative War Diary, November 13, 1940–December 31, 1941, WO 169/24847, 40.
45. Ibid., 41.
46. Western Desert Plans for 1941, WO 169/24905.
47. "A" Force Narrative War Diary, November 13, 1940–December 31, 1941, WO 169/24847, 41.
48. Western Desert Plans for 1941, WO 169/24905.
49. *Rommel Papers*, 150.
50. Western Desert Plans for 1941, WO 169/24905.
51. *Rommel Papers*, 155–56.
52. An earlier double bluff discussed in this work occurred as part of Camilla, which was planned by Wavell and predated the formation of "A" Force.
53. Western Desert Plans for 1941, WO 169/24905.
54. Ibid.
55. Ibid.
56. "A" Force Narrative War Diary, November 13, 1940–December 31, 1941, WO 169/24847, 62.
57. According to Ken Jones, who was one of Cheese's initial controllers, it was actually MI6 in London that informed SIME of Levi's impending arrival. For more information, see the Dudley Clarke Papers, Box 99/2/1.
58. Case History of Agent Known as CHEESE, WO 169/24893, "A" Force Permanent Record Files, National Archives, Kew, UK.
59. "A" Force Narrative War Diary, November 13, 1940–December 31, 1941, WO 169/24847, 62.
60. At that point, the Germans and Italians shared control of Levi's case.
61. Case History of Agent Known as CHEESE, WO 169/24893. Because Levi was working as a British double agent, he automatically fell under the control of SIME.
62. "A" Force Narrative War Diary, November 13, 1940–December 31, 1941, WO 169/24847, 63.
63. Case History of Agent Known as CHEESE, WO 169/24893.
64. Ibid.
65. "A" Force Narrative War Diary, November 13, 1940–December 31, 1941, WO 169/24847, 68.
66. Ibid.
67. Case History of Agent Known as CHEESE, WO 169/24893. "Levi's" was censored in the original document.

68. Ibid. Oddly enough, the Italians were suspect of the Cheese channel, but the Germans did not appear to doubt Nicossof's loyalty at all.

69. Organisation and Functions of SIME Special Section, KV 4/197, National Archives, Kew, UK. It is logical that SIME would defer to "A" Force for guidance and instruction in running double agents because "A" Force was directly responsible for planning, preparing, and carrying out all deception plans in the region.

70. Case History of Agent Known as CHEESE, WO 169/24893.

71. "A" Force Narrative War Diary, November 13, 1940–December 31, 1941, WO 169/24847, 71.

72. Western Desert Plans for 1941, WO 169/24905.

73. Case History of Agent Known as CHEESE, WO 169/24893. The author of the telegram is not identified.

74. Although the Germans did begin to question the channel as a result of the offensive, SIME was able to reestablish its credibility in a relatively short amount of time. Cheese's case officer, Captain Simpson, never lost hope that Nicossof could be rehabilitated.

75. "A" Force Narrative War Diary, November 13, 1940–December 31, 1941, WO 169/24847, 42.

76. Ibid., 42–43. See also Western Desert Plans for 1941, WO 169/24905.

77. Cruickshank, *Deception in World War II*, 22; "A" Force Narrative War Diary, November 13, 1940–December 31, 1941, WO 169/24847, 73.

78. Barkas, *Camouflage Story*, 143.

79. Ibid.

80. Ibid.

81. "A" Force Narrative War Diary, November 13, 1940–December 31, 1941, WO 169/24847, 73.

82. Ibid.

83. Western Desert Plans for 1941, WO 169/24905.

84. Cruickshank, *Deception in World War II*, 23.

85. Developments in Tactical Deception, WO 169/24870.

86. For specific details as to how the dummy line was constructed, see Barkas, *Camouflage Story*.

87. Cruickshank, *Deception in World War II*, 24.

88. Hinsley, *British Intelligence*, 2:280–81.

89. Ibid., 294–95. Until then, GC&CS was able to read the German Air Force Enigma only. Although it provided valuable information, it did not provide an accurate picture of Germany's forces on the ground.

90. Ibid., 302–4.

91. Pitt, *Crucible of War: Western Desert 1941*, 353.

92. Playfair, *Mediterranean and the Middle East*, 3:15.

93. Fritz Bayerlein, "The Winter Campaign, 1941–2," in *Rommel Papers*, 158.

94. Playfair, *Mediterranean and the Middle East*, 3:17–18.

95. Hinsley, *British Intelligence*, 2:305.

96. Western Desert Plans for 1941, WO 169/24905.

97. Bayerlein, "Winter Campaign, 1941–2," 158. Bayerlein could not address the effects that the strategic deception had on Germany's lack of knowledge because it is unlikely that he was ever aware that the intelligence was the product of a calculated British deception.
98. Hinsley, *British Intelligence*, 2:305.
99. Pitt, *Crucible of War: Western Desert 1941*, 358.
100. Playfair, *Mediterranean and the Middle East*, 3:44.
101. Ibid.
102. The British began the battle with more than 700 tanks and another 200 in reserve. The Germans and Italians combined had 568. See *Rommel Papers*.
103. Playfair, *Mediterranean and the Middle East*, 3:52, 60–61.
104. Ibid., 69–78.
105. *Rommel Papers*, 175.
106. Playfair, *Mediterranean and the Middle East*, 3:79–92.
107. Development of "A" Force Special Units, WO 169/24869.
108. "A" Force Narrative War Diary, November 13, 1940–December 31, 1941, WO 169/24847, 87.
109. The Technical Unit received its war establishment on December 4, initially under the name of "Printing Section (Type X)." Up until that time, Mr. Titterington had worked for the Anglo-Egyptian Censorship Department's Testing Section. For more information, see "A" Force Technical Unit, WO 169/24868, "A" Force Permanent Record Files, National Archives, Kew, UK.
110. Western Desert Plans for 1941, WO 169/24905.
111. Ibid.
112. Ibid.
113. French, *Raising Churchill's Army*, 219–21.
114. *Rommel Papers*, 178.
115. "A" Force Narrative War Diary, November 13, 1940–December 31, 1941, WO 169/24847, 92.
116. Ibid., 93.
117. Ibid., 49–50.
118. Clarke hoped to establish lucrative networks in these neutral lands just as he had in Turkey. Because the British feared that the Germans intended to invade Turkey, Clarke had to look elsewhere to set up alternative channels in case his assets in Turkey were lost. That is what led him to travel to Western Europe at a time when "A" Force was heavily involved in a major deception campaign. It was also during his visit to Madrid in October that he was arrested for impersonating a female.
119. Churchill, *Memoirs*, 505–7.
120. The U.S. declaration of war on December 11 followed Germany's and Italy's declaration of war on the United States earlier that same day.

CHAPTER 6. THE GREAT ALLIED RETREAT

1. Playfair, *Mediterranean and the Middle East*, 3:137.
2. Hinsley, *British Intelligence*, 2:334.
3. Churchill, *Memoirs*, 505–7.

4. Ibid., 507–8.
5. "A" Force Narrative War Diary, January 1, 1942–December 31, 1942, WO 169/24848, 2.
6. Playfair, *Mediterranean and the Middle East*, 3:122–23, 133.
7. Ibid., 142.
8. Hinsley, *British Intelligence*, 2:331. German intelligence sources were able to read the wireless messages sent by the U.S. military attaché in Cairo, which included detailed information on the weakened state of the 8th Army.
9. Playfair, *Mediterranean and Middle East*, 3:137–39.
10. Ibid., 140–42.
11. Ibid., 151.
12. Western Desert Plans for 1942, WO 169/24906, "A" Force Permanent Record Files, National Archives, Kew UK.
13. "A" Force Narrative War Diary, January 1, 1942–December 31, 1942, WO 169/24848, 22.
14. The problems with GSI(d) were many. First, it was never able to effectively implement tactical deception. Second, its responsibilities often overlapped with those of "A" Force, causing considerable confusion. Third, and connected to the second, there was no clear dividing line between strategic and tactical deception, so the separation of responsibilities was not always straightforward. Fourth, there were too many personnel involved in deception within the army's structure. That meant that there was a dangerous lack of security.
15. "A" Force Narrative War Diary, January 1, 1942–December 31, 1942, WO 169/24848, 19–20, 22.
16. Ibid., 26.
17. Dudley Clarke Papers, Box 99/2/1.
18. "A" Force Narrative War Diary, January 1, 1942–December 31, 1942, WO 169/24848, 24.
19. Ibid.
20. "A" Force Narrative War Diary, November 13, 1940–December 31, 1941, WO 169/24847, 93.
21. "A" Force Narrative War Diary, January 1, 1942–December 31, 1942, WO 169/24848, 6.
22. M. R. D. Foot and J. M. Langley, *MI9: The British Secret Service That Fostered Escape and Evasion, 1939–1945, and Its American Counterpart* (London: Bodley Head, 1979), 89. Tony Simonds had served as the head of MI9 in the Middle East since September 21, 1941.
23. "A" Force Narrative War Diary, January 1, 1942–December 31, 1942, WO 169/24848, 28.
24. Ibid., 26, 27.
25. Ibid., 24, 45–49.
26. Western Desert Plans for 1942, WO 169/24906.
27. Playfair, *Mediterranean and Middle East*, 3:244–45.
28. Western Desert Plans for 1942, WO 169/24906.
29. Ibid.
30. Ibid.

31. Ibid.; "A" Force Narrative War Diary, January 1, 1942–December 31, 1942, WO 169/24848, 13.

32. Western Desert Plans for 1942, WO 169/24906; "A" Force Narrative War Diary, January 1, 1942–December 31, 1942, WO 169/24848, 13–14.

33. See Barkas, *Camouflage Story*.

34. Western Desert Plans for 1942, WO 169/24906.

35. "A" Force Narrative War Diary, January 1, 1942–December 31, 1942, WO 169/24848, 11, 12.

36. Western Desert Plans for 1942, WO 169/24906.

37. "A" Force Narrative War Diary, January 1, 1942–December 31, 1942, WO 169/24848, 15.

38. Ibid.

39. Hinsley, *British Intelligence*, 2:340.

40. See *Rommel Papers*.

41. See Plan "CAMILLA," WO 169/24903.

42. "A" Force Narrative War Diary, January 1, 1942–December 31, 1942, WO 169/24848, 16.

43. Ibid., 17.

44. Ibid., 17–18.

45. Playfair, *Mediterranean and the Middle East*, 3:365.

46. "A" Force Narrative War Diary, January 1, 1942–December 31, 1942, WO 169/24848, 35; "CASCADE" Order of Battle Plan, 1942–43, WO 169/24926, "A" Force Permanent Record Files, National Archives, Kew, UK.

47. "CASCADE" Order of Battle Plan, WO 169/24926.

48. Ibid.

49. "A" Force Narrative War Diary, January 1, 1942–December 31, 1942, WO 169/24848, 36.

50. Dudley Clarke Papers, Box 99/2/1.

51. "A" Force Narrative War Diary, January 1, 1942–December 31, 1942, WO 169/24848, 36.

52. Ibid. 36–37.

53. Papers Concerning the Theory and Practice of Deception in General, WO 169/24874.

54. "A" Force Narrative War Diary, January 1, 1942–December 31, 1942, WO 169/24848, 40.

55. Ibid., 39–42.

56. For more information, see "WANTAGE" Order of Battle Plan, February 1944–July 1946, WO 169/24927, "A" Force Permanent Record Files, National Archives, Kew, UK.

57. "A" Force Narrative War Diary, January 1, 1942–December 31, 1942, WO 169/24848, 43.

58. Ibid.

59. Western Desert Plans for 1942, WO 169/24906.

60. "A" Force Narrative War Diary, January 1, 1942–December 31, 1942, WO 169/24848, 50.

61. Ibid., 55.

62. Western Desert Plans for 1942, WO 169/24906. The deception regarding the Grant tanks is known as Plan Crystal. For more information on Crystal, see "A" Force Narrative War Diary, January 1, 1942–December 31, 1942, WO 169/24848, 29–31.

63. *Rommel Papers*, 196, 206.

64. Employment of Special Deception Units, WO 169/24882. The 33rd Armoured Brigade included two of the original dummy RTRs, the 38th and 101st.

65. Western Desert Plans for 1942, WO 169/24906.

66. Ibid.

67. Ibid.

68. "A" Force Narrative War Diary, January 1, 1942–December 31, 1942, WO 169/24848, 59.

69. Ibid., 56.

70. Western Desert Plans for 1942, WO 169/24906.

71. "A" Force Narrative War Diary, January 1, 1942–December 31, 1942, WO 169/24848, 56.

72. Western Desert Plans for 1942, WO 169/24906.

73. One has to wonder if the deception might have had the reverse effect and encouraged Rommel to attack when he did. If he was convinced that the British were truly vulnerable, there is no doubt that he would have exploited the situation immediately. In *The Rommel Papers*, it is clear that Rommel had in fact underestimated the size of the British armored forces opposing him (196).

74. Hinsley, *British Intelligence*, 2:345, 350.

75. Western Desert Plans for 1942, WO 169/24906.

76. "A" Force Narrative War Diary, January 1, 1942–December 31, 1942, WO 169/24848, 51.

77. Jack Greene and Alessandro Massignani, *Rommel's North Africa Campaign: September 1940–November 1942* (Conshohocken, PA: Combined Publishing, 1994), 150.

78. Ibid., 152.

79. Hinsley, *British Intelligence*, 2:341.

80. Ibid., 347–49.

81. It is interesting that Rommel decided to attack in the south, especially since Fabric sought to convey a greater sense of weakness in the south than in the north.

82. *Rommel Papers*, 201–2.

83. Hinsley, *British Intelligence*, 2:361–62, 367.

84. Janusz Piekalkiewicz, *Rommel and the Secret War in North Africa, 1941–1943* (West Chester, PA: Schiffer Military History, 1992), 125–27.

85. *Rommel Papers*, 208.

86. French, *Raising Churchill's Army*, 223.

87. Quoted in *Rommel Papers*, 216. See also Hinsley, *British Intelligence*, 2:370.

88. Playfair, *Mediterranean and the Middle East*, 3:197.

89. Churchill, *Memoirs*, 579.

90. Playfair, *Mediterranean and the Middle East*, 3:253–74.

91. Churchill, *Memoirs*, 583–84.

92. Playfair, *Mediterranean and the Middle East*, 3:275–78.

93. Jon Latimer, *Alamein* (Cambridge, MA: Harvard University Press, 2002), 58.
94. Playfair, *Mediterranean and the Middle East*, 3:285, 296.
95. "A" Force Narrative War Diary, January 1, 1942–December 31, 1942, WO 169/24848, 68.
96. Barkas, *Camouflage Story*, 179–80.
97. "A" Force Narrative War Diary, January 1, 1942–December 31, 1942, WO 169/24848, 68.
98. Playfair, *Mediterranean and the Middle East*, 3:331.
99. Hinsley, *British Intelligence*, 2:392–93. By the end of May the British had broken every Enigma key used in North Africa. Also, in July CBME was granted permission to decrypt messages in the Middle East, so intelligence made it to 8th Army headquarters much faster than before (375).
100. Latimer, *Alamein*, 63.
101. *Rommel Papers*, 245.
102. Western Desert Plans for 1942, WO 169/24906.
103. Barkas, *Camouflage Story*, 181.
104. "A" Force Narrative War Diary, January 1, 1942–December 31, 1942, WO 169/24848, 83.
105. Barkas, *Camouflage Story*, 182.
106. Ibid., 181–83.
107. "A" Force Narrative War Diary, January 1, 1942–December 31, 1942, WO 169/24848, 73.
108. Case History of Agent Known as CHEESE, WO 169/24893.
109. Howard, *Strategic Deception*, 41.
110. Case History of Agent Known as CHEESE, WO 169/24893.
111. Ibid.
112. Western Desert Plans for 1942, WO 169/24906.
113. "A" Force Narrative War Diary, January 1, 1942–December 31, 1942, WO 169/24848, 82.
114. Ibid.
115. Michael J. Lyons, *World War II: A Short History*, 3rd ed. (Upper Saddle River, NJ: Prentice Hall, 1999), 160, 161, 175.
116. Middle East Strategic Plans for 1942, WO 169/24907, "A" Force Permanent Record Files, National Archives, Kew, UK.
117. Churchill, *Memoirs*, 608–9.
118. Ibid., 578–79.
119. Latimer, *Alamein*, 91.
120. Ibid.
121. Playfair, *Mediterranean and the Middle East*, 3:367, 375–76.
122. Churchill, *Memoirs*, 612–13.
123. Bernard Montgomery, *The Memoirs of Field-Marshal Montgomery* (Cleveland, OH: World Publishing Company, 1958), 91–92.
124. General Harold Alexander, Despatch on the Campaign from Alamein to Tunis, August 10, 1942–May 13, 1943, CAB 106/613, National Archives, Kew, UK.
125. Montgomery, *Memoirs*, 92.
126. Ibid., 93.

127. Playfair, *Mediterranean and the Middle East*, 3:369–70.
128. Montgomery, *Memoirs*, 91.
129. Ibid., 93.
130. Playfair, *Mediterranean and the Middle East*, 3:370.
131. Montgomery, *Memoirs*, 93.
132. Churchill, *Memoirs*, 637.
133. Quoted in Playfair, *Mediterranean and the Middle East*, 3:370.

CHAPTER 7. VICTORY IN THE DESERT

1. Haufler, *Spies Who Never Were*, 116.
2. Mure, *Master of Deception*, 120.
3. Howard, *Strategic Deception*, 65; Hinsley, *British Intelligence*, 2:640.
4. This is perhaps ironic given that the British turned to deception in the first place because of their weakness, but the reality of the situation was that deception worked best when the military was strong and the deceptionists had ample time to thoroughly implement their plans.
5. Plan Fabric provides a perfect example of the difficulties encountered in running a deception when the army and "A" Force had different objectives.
6. Alexander, Despatch on the Campaign, CAB 106/613; Montgomery, *Memoirs*, 92.
7. Alexander, Despatch on the Campaign, CAB 106/613.
8. The Axis supply problems were the result not only of distance but also of the tireless effort of the RAF in the Mediterranean. The RAF went to great lengths to locate and destroy Axis supply convoys.
9. *Rommel Papers*, 264.
10. Howard, *Strategic Deception*, 64.
11. Alexander, Despatch on the Campaign, CAB 106/613.
12. Howard, *Strategic Deception*, 64. The dummy landing craft were new additions to Major Jones' collection.
13. "A" Force Narrative War Diary, January 1, 1942–December 31, 1942, WO 169/24848, 79.
14. Western Desert Plans for 1942, WO 169/24906.
15. "A" Force Narrative War Diary, January 1, 1942–December 31, 1942, WO 169/24848, 83–84.
16. David Mure claims that there was a corpse of a British officer in the car, but that particular detail is not corroborated in other sources.
17. Alexander, Despatch on the Campaign, CAB 106/613.
18. Ibid.
19. Playfair, *Mediterranean and the Middle East*, 3:387–88.
20. *Rommel Papers*, 283.
21. Alexander, Despatch on the Campaign, CAB 106/613.
22. Montgomery, *Memoirs*, 99.
23. Ibid., 100.
24. Ibid.
25. *Rommel Papers*, 280.
26. Charles Richardson, *Flashback: A Soldier's Story* (London: William Kimber, 1985), 113.

27. Montgomery, *Memoirs*, 100–101.
28. Ibid., 103–4; Alexander, Despatch on the Campaign, CAB 106/613.
29. French, *Raising Churchill's Army*, 240. French was referring to Operation Crusader and the Battle of Gazala. Although Crusader ultimately ended in victory, it did so at a devastating loss to British armor. It also took much longer than intended, negating Britain's plans to follow up the campaign with a thrust into Tripolitania. Although the British had the numerical advantage, the Germans employed superior tactics.
30. *Rommel Papers*, 297, 300.
31. Montgomery, *Memoirs*, 106.
32. Ibid., 106, 108.
33. "A" Force Narrative War Diary, January 1, 1942–December 31, 1942, WO 169/24848, 111–12.
34. Instructions and Special Orders, February 1942–December 1944, WO 169/24860, "A" Force Permanent Record Files, National Archives, Kew, UK.
35. "A" Force Narrative War Diary, January 1, 1942–December 31, 1942, WO 169/24848, 108.
36. Quite a number of authors, including Anthony Cave Brown, Jon Latimer, David Mure, and Michael Howard, claim that Clarke was the one who created the tactical plan. On the other hand, Richardson said that he devised the plan, and Geoffrey Barkas related his role in determining what could be accomplished in regard to camouflage. It is, therefore, a bit unclear who exactly authored the idea. It is likely the case that Clarke provided the overall strategic objective on which the individual strategic and tactical plans were then based, but it was up to "A" Force to hammer out the details of the strategic implementation and the army to devise the actual physical plan. This would be most consistent with the way Clarke wanted deception campaigns to work. Nonetheless, the constant contact and cooperation between Richardson, Barkas, and Clarke (or Wild) made it clear that all their efforts represented a common strategic aim—to deceive.
37. "A" Force Narrative War Diary, January 1, 1942–December 31, 1942, WO 169/24848, 109.
38. Ibid.
39. Ultra intercepts revealed that Hitler was greatly concerned about the possibility of an invasion of Crete; as a result, Clarke played on the Führer's fears and repeatedly revived the threat to the island throughout the war.
40. This was important because the enemy expected the British to attack during a full moon period as it would help illuminate the minefields that they would be forced to traverse.
41. "A" Force Narrative War Diary, January 1, 1942–December 31, 1942, WO 169/24848, 108.
42. Ibid., 110.
43. See chapter 6. Although Fabric ended prematurely, many of its components were incorporated into Treatment. In that respect, it had served as a perfect trial run for "A" Force.

44. "A" Force Narrative War Diary, January 1, 1942–December 31, 1942, WO 169/24848, 110; Howard, *Strategic Deception*, 66.

45. "A" Force Narrative War Diary, January 1, 1942–December 31, 1942, WO 169/24848, 110.

46. Western Desert Plans for 1942, WO 169/24906.

47. Ibid.

48. Ibid.

49. "A" Force Narrative War Diary, January 1, 1942–December 31, 1942, WO 169/24848, 111.

50. Western Desert Plans for 1942, WO 169/24906.

51. Hitler's first order for the reinforcement of Crete was issued on September 23, most likely in response to Plan Rayon.

52. Howard, *Strategic Deception*, 67.

53. Barkas was elated as this was the first time that his organization was included in the deception plan from the beginning. From his viewpoint, it was the ultimate fulfillment of everything he had worked toward since he had arrived in North Africa.

54. Barkas, *Camouflage Story*, 191.

55. Ibid., 195.

56. Alexander, Despatch on the Campaign, CAB 106/613.

57. Barkas, *Camouflage Story*, 198.

58. Ibid., 197–98; "BERTRAM," WO 201/2023.

59. Barkas, *Camouflage Story*, 198–99.

60. Ibid.; "BERTRAM," WO 201/2033.

61. "BERTRAM," WO 201/2033.

62. Barkas, *Camouflage Story*, 197.

63. Ibid., 200–201.

64. Ibid., 201. The Bertram file and the "A" Force Narrative War Diary both indicate that only 360 guns were hidden according to this method.

65. "BERTRAM," WO 201/2033; Barkas, *Camouflage Story*, 202–3.

66. Wavell can be credited with the original idea to create such a device. The sun shields were produced by "A" Force.

67. "BERTRAM," WO 201/2033.

68. Barkas, *Camouflage Story*, 203.

69. Ibid., 196.

70. Ibid., 204.

71. Ibid.

72. Ibid., 204–5; "BERTRAM," WO 201/2033.

73. Barkas, *Camouflage Story*, 205.

74. The work carried out for Brian provides a wonderful example of the absolute resourcefulness of the deception crews and their ability to make use of products native to the desert environment. To create the illusion of dumps, they used timber, bales of hessian, mesh cloth, sandbags, palm beds, wicker tomato cases, garnished netting, wire coils, and the now infamous reusable petrol tins.

75. "BERTRAM," WO 201/2033.

76. Barkas, *Camouflage Story*, 205–6.
77. Ibid., 206–7.
78. Instructions and Special Orders, WO 169/24860. Sonic deception was not limited to land. "A" Force also had recordings made to simulate the sounds of a seaborne invasion. On October 23 and 24 the enemy could hear the sounds of anchors dropping at and near Baccush.
79. Alexander, Despatch on the Campaign, CAB 106/613.
80. Barkas, *Camouflage Story*, 207.
81. Ibid.
82. The stand-in vehicles were on loan from the 13th Corps and 30th Corps, so they either returned to their units or were used in another deceptive capacity.
83. Barkas, *Camouflage Story*, 207.
84. Instructions and Special Orders, WO 169/24860.
85. The army provided thousands of real vehicles as well.
86. Barkas, *Camouflage Story*, 208.
87. Ibid., 209. The army was responsible for placing the orders with the locals and ensuring that the materials were transported to G(CAM)'s makeshift factories in a timely manner.
88. Barkas, *Camouflage Story*, 208–11.
89. Ibid., 212.
90. Ibid.
91. After the army and G(CAM) had completed their deceptive operations, the enemy should have noticed massive concentrations of thin-skinned vehicles and tanks—both dummy and genuine. It is interesting to note that in *The Rommel Papers*, Rommel repeatedly makes the erroneous claim that Britain's forces were completely motorized; Liddell Hart provides frequent footnotes of correction. However, given the scale of the deception efforts and the sheer numbers of canvas and dummy vehicles employed in the desert throughout the war in Africa, and especially at El Alamein, Rommel's assertion is not at all surprising.
92. Western Desert Plans for 1942, WO 169/24906.
93. Ibid.
94. "A" Force Narrative War Diary, January 1, 1942–December 31, 1942, WO 169/24848, 113–14.
95. Barkas, *Camouflage Story*, 210.
96. Montgomery, *Memoirs*, 113.
97. I. S. O. Playfair and C. J. C. Molony, *The Mediterranean and Middle East*, vol. 4, *The Destruction of the Axis Forces in Africa* (London: Her Majesty's Stationery Office, 1966), 31.
98. Montgomery, *Memoirs*, 113.
99. Hinsley, *British Intelligence*, 2:435.
100. Howard, *Strategic Deception*, 67–68.
101. John Pimlott, ed., *Rommel: In His Own Words* (London: Greenhill Books, 1994), 137.
102. Playfair and Molony, *Mediterranean and the Middle East*, 4:36–37; Montgomery, *Memoirs*, 116.

103. "A" Force Narrative War Diary, January 1, 1942–December 31, 1942, WO 169/24848, 111–12.

104. Montgomery, *Memoirs*, 116.

105. "A" Force Narrative War Diary, January 1, 1942–December 31, 1942, WO 169/24848, 111–12.

106. Montgomery, *Memoirs*, 116–17; Playfair and Molony, *Mediterranean and the Middle East*, 4:78–79.

107. Playfair and Molony, *Mediterranean and the Middle East*, 4:43–44.

108. Hinsley, *British Intelligence*, 2:438.

109. Playfair and Molony, *Mediterranean and the Middle East*, 4:51. It is interesting that the traditional roles were reversed with the enemy now sending his armor out into the open in set-piece attacks, only to be destroyed by the British.

110. Instructions and Special Orders, WO 169/24860.

111. *Rommel Papers*, 303–7. Rommel disapproved of the decision and felt that his forces would have had a better chance of stopping the British if Stumme had acted aggressively from the beginning.

112. Ibid., 308.

113. Montgomery, *Memoirs*, 119–20, 123.

114. "BERTRAM," WO 201/2023.

115. *Rommel Papers*, 317.

116. Quoted in Playfair and Molony, *Mediterranean and the Middle East*, 4:475.

117. Playfair and Molony, *Mediterranean and the Middle East*, 4:72–73.

118. *Rommel Papers*, 321.

119. Playfair and Molony, *Mediterranean and the Middle East*, 4:79.

120. Ibid., 78–79. Combined, the Germans and Italians flew only 3,120 sorties.

121. Playfair and Molony, *Mediterranean and the Middle East*, 4:94–98.

122. Montgomery, *Memoirs*, 132–33.

123. Western Desert Plans for 1942, WO 169/24906.

124. "A" Force Narrative War Diary, January 1, 1942–December 31, 1942, WO 169/24848, 128–29.

125. Western Desert Plans for 1942, WO 169/24906.

126. Montgomery, *Memoirs*, 137–38.

127. Playfair and Molony, *Mediterranean and the Middle East*, 4:238.

128. For more information, see Mark A. Stoler, *Allies and Adversaries: The Joint Chiefs of Staff, the Grand Alliance, and U.S. Strategy in World War II* (Chapel Hill: University of North Carolina Press, 2000).

129. The first conference took place in December after the Japanese bombing of Pearl Harbor.

130. Playfair and Molony, *Mediterranean and the Middle East*, 4:110–12.

131. Ibid., 112.

132. Howard, *Strategic Deception*, 57. Most of the rumors Garbo referenced were to the effect that the British did not yet have the ability to mount a seaborne invasion. See also *GARBO: the Spy Who Saved D-Day* (Kew: Public Record Office, 2000); and West, *MI5*.

133. Howard, *Strategic Deception*, 59.

134. Ibid.

135. Ibid., 59–61.
136. "A" Force Narrative War Diary, January 1, 1942–December 31, 1942, WO 169/24848, 103, 107.
137. Howard, *Strategic Deception*, 59–61.
138. This was done specifically to help support the deception effort for Lightfoot, part of which stated that the British were planning an invasion of Crete in November.
139. "A" Force Narrative War Diary, January 1, 1942–December 31, 1942, WO 169/24848, 105.
140. Middle East Strategic Plans for 1942, WO 169/24907.
141. Western Desert Plans for 1942, WO 169/24906.
142. Howard, *Strategic Deception*, 61.
143. Ibid., 60.
144. Developments in Strategic Deception, WO 169/24871.
145. "A" Force Narrative War Diary, January 1, 1942–December 31, 1942, WO 169/24848, 106.
146. It is interesting to note that the Germans considered the Tripoli-Benghazi area in Rommel's rear as the most likely target, whereas the British discounted it as a threat because they did not think the Germans would view it as plausible.
147. Howard, *Strategic Deception*; "A" Force Narrative War Diary, January 1, 1942–December 31, 1942, WO 169/24848, 106.
148. Developments in Strategic Deception, WO 169/24871.
149. Playfair and Molony, *Mediterranean and the Middle East*, 4:142–51. See also Arthur Funk, "Negotiating the 'Deal with Darlan,'" *Journal of Contemporary History* 8, no. 2 (April 1973): 81–117.
150. Middle East Strategic Plans for 1942, WO 169/24907.
151. Playfair and Molony, *Mediterranean and the Middle East*, 4:164.
152. Howard, *Strategic Deception*, 61.
153. Among others, see Playfair and Molony, *Mediterranean and the Middle East*, 4:151–52; Porch, *Path to Victory*, 366–67; and Lyons, *World War II*, 190.
154. *Rommel Papers*, 345.
155. Porch, *Path to Victory*, 379–81, 395.
156. Montgomery, *Memoirs*, 142–46.
157. *Rommel Papers*, 419.
158. Montgomery, *Memoirs*, 147–49.
159. Porch, *Path to Victory*, 412–13.
160. Ibid., 412.
161. Alexander, Despatch on the Campaign, CAB 106/613.

CONCLUSION

1. Churchill, *Memoirs*, 653.
2. Alexander, Despatch on the Campaign, CAB 106/613.
3. Churchill, *Memoirs*, 687.
4. "A" Force Narrative War Diary, January 1, 1942–December 31, 1942, WO 169/24848, 107.
5. Mure, *Master of Deception*, 129.

6. "A" Force Narrative War Diary, January 1, 1942–December 31, 1942, WO 169/24848, 136.

7. Mure, *Master of Deception*, 143.

8. "A" Force Narrative War Diary, January 1, 1942–December 31, 1942, WO 169/24848, 136–37.

9. Howard, *Strategic Deception*, 83–84.

10. Strategic Plans, January–March 1943, WO 169/24910, "A" Force Permanent Record Files, National Archives, Kew, UK.

11. Strategic Plans, April–July 1943—Plan BARCLAY, WO 169/24911, "A" Force Permanent Record Files, National Archives, Kew, UK.

12. Strategic Plans, April–July 1943—Plan BARCLAY II, WO 169/24912, "A" Force Permanent Record Files, National Archives, Kew, UK. This operation was known as Waterfall.

13. The expansion of the double-agent network began when British intelligence tightened its security and plugged the leaks in its communications system. This led the Germans to send additional agents to Africa in the hopes of collecting information, but many of them ended up in British hands. Similarly, in November 1942 the French Deuxième Bureau provided its double agents for Allied use. Through these means, the double-cross system in the Mediterranean greatly expanded. For more information, see Howard, *Strategic Deception*, 68, 84.

14. Plan BARCLAY, WO 169/24911.

15. "A" Force Narrative War Diary, January 1, 1943–December 31, 1943, WO 169/24849, National Archives, Kew, UK. For more information, see Montagu, *Man Who Never Was*.

16. "A" Force Narrative War Diary, January 1, 1943–December 31, 1943, WO 169/24849.

17. Howard, *Strategic Deception*, 92.

18. "A" Force Narrative War Diary, January 1, 1942–December 31, 1942, WO 169/24848, 138.

19. "A" Force Narrative War Diary, January 1, 1943–December 31, 1943, WO 169/24849. "A" Force was again reorganized at this time to allow it to concentrate solely on assisting the deception effort in Europe from its base in the Middle East. It was, therefore, relieved of its responsibilities in all other theaters. Clarke was promoted to brigadier.

20. Noël Wild, foreword to Mure, *Master of Deception*, 10.

21. Mure, *Master of Deception*, 101.

22. For a comprehensive and authoritative account of the two plans, see Roger Hesketh, *Fortitude: The D-Day Deception Campaign* (Woodstock, NY: Overlook Press, 2000).

23. Howard, *Strategic Deception*, 115–19.

24. Ibid., 108.

25. Young and Stamp, *Trojan Horses*, 27–28. As the authors point out, "R" Force was London's equivalent to Clarke's "A" Force.

26. Howard, *Strategic Deception*, 119–21.

27. GARBO to Madrid, June 9, 1944, KV 2/69, National Archives, Kew, UK.

28. "A" Force Narrative War Diary, January 1944–December 1944, WO 169/24850, 64, "A" Force Permanent Record Files, National Archives, Kew, UK.

29. Cruickshank, *Deception in World War II*, 148–49.

30. Plan ZEPPELIN—Connected Plan TURPITUDE, WO 169/24921, National Archives, Kew, UK.

31. Howard, *Strategic Deception*, 138. See also Plan ZEPPELIN, WO 169/24915 and WO 169/24916, "A" Force Permanent Record Files, National Archives, Kew, UK.

32. Plan ZEPPELIN, WO 169/24916.

33. "A" Force Narrative War Diary, January 1944–December 1944, WO 169/24850, 94.

34. "A" Force Narrative War Diary, January 1, 1942–December 31, 1942, WO 169/24848, 138.

35. Plan ZEPPELIN—Connected Plan VENDETTA, WO 169/24922, "A" Force Permanent Record Files, National Archives, Kew, UK.

36. Approximately two-thirds of the Seventh Army was imaginary. According to the cover story, the Seventh Army was initially supposed to spearhead an attack into the Balkans, but its mission was changed because of genuine political disputes in the region.

37. Howard, *Strategic Deception*, 149, 152.

38. The Allies actually did invade southern France on August 15.

39. Holt, *Deceivers*, 599.

40. Mure, *Master of Deception*, 103.

41. Dudley Clarke Papers, Box 99/2/1.

BIBLIOGRAPHY

UNPUBLISHED DOCUMENTS

National Archives (former PRO), Kew, UK

CAB 106/379, Archibald P. Wavell, Despatch on Operations in the Middle East, February 7–July 15, 1941.

CAB 106/469, Alan G. Cunningham, Report on Operations, East Africa Force, November 1, 1940–April 5, 1941.

CAB 106/472, Archibald P. Wavell, Despatch Covering August 1939–November 1940.

CAB 106/613, Harold Alexander, Despatch on the Campaign from Alamein to Tunis, August 10, 1942–May 13, 1943.

KV 2/69, GARBO to Madrid, June 9, 1944.

KV 4/197, Organisation and Functions of SIME Special Section.

KV 4/305, Middle East Security Section, January 1, 1939–December 31, 1939.

KV 4/306, Middle East Security Section, January 1, 1939–December 31, 1942.

WO 106/2133, Archibald P. Wavell, Operations in the Western Desert, December 7, 1940–February 7, 1941.

WO 106/2169. C. J. E. Auchinleck, Despatch, July–October 1941.

WO 106/2254, Battle of El Alamein: Personal Messages from Army Commander to 8th Army.

WO 169/3976, "G"(Cam.).

WO 201/278, J. E. B. Barton, 101 Mission Reports, Section 5, Chapter "G," June 1940–May 1941.

WO 201/2023, BERTRAM: Notes on Deception Practised by the Eighth Army Prior to Its Offensive of October 1942.

WO 201/2379, "Notes for BGS, Middle East Command," Memo, July 31, 1939.

"A" Force Permanent Record Files (released in 1991), National Archives, Kew, UK

WO 169/24847–51, "A" Force Narrative War Diary, November 1940–July 1945 (also listed under CAB 154/1–5).

WO 169/24860, Instructions and Special Orders, February 1942–December 1944.

WO 169/24866, "A" Force War Establishment and Organization.

WO 169/24868, "A" Force Technical Unit.

WO 169/24869, Development of "A" Force Special Units.

WO 169/24870, Developments in Tactical Deception.

WO 169/24871, Developments in Strategic Deception.

WO 169/24872, Liaison with LCS.

WO 169/24873, Development of Special Inter-Theatre Communications Procedure.

WO 169/24874, Papers Concerning the Theory and Practice of Deception in General.

WO 169/24877, Reports on Miscellaneous Activities, 1941–1942.

WO 169/24878, Reports on Miscellaneous Activities, 1943–1944.

WO 169/24880, Co-Operation with the Camouflage Organization.

WO 169/24882, The Employment of Special Deception Units in the Field.

WO 169/24883, The Production of Special Devices Required for Deception.

WO 169/24884, Implementation by Most Secret Intelligence Methods in General.

WO 169/24891, Middle East Channels in General.

WO 169/24893, Case History of Agent Known as CHEESE.

WO 169/24894, Record of CHEESE Traffic.

WO 169/24903, Plan "CAMILLA" (British Somaliland), December 1940–January 1941.

WO 169/24904, Plan "ABEAM" (Special Air Service Brigade), January 1941–August 1941.

WO 169/24905, Western Desert Plans for 1941.

WO 169/24906, Western Desert Plans for 1942.

WO 169/24907, Middle East Strategic Plans for 1942.

WO 169/24910, Strategic Plans, January–March 1943.

WO 169/24911, Strategic Plans, April–July 1943—Plan BARCLAY.

WO 169/24912, Strategic Plans, April–July 1943—Plan BARCLAY II.

WO 169/24915–23, Plan ZEPPELIN files.

WO 169/24924, Strategic Plans for 1944.

WO 169/24925, Deception Plan on Defense of Cyprus.

WO 169/24926, "CASCADE" Order of Battle Plan, 1942–43.

WO 169/24927, "WANTAGE" Order of Battle Plan, February 1944–July 1946.

Imperial War Museum, London, UK
Dudley Clarke Papers, Boxes 99/2/1–3.

PUBLISHED PRIMARY SOURCES

Barkas, Geoffrey. *The Camouflage Story (From Aintree to Alamein)*. London: Cassell, 1952.

Bayerlein, Fritz. "The Winter Campaign, 1941–2." In *The Rommel Papers*, edited by B. H. Liddell Hart. New York: Harcourt, Brace, 1953.

Churchill, Winston S. *Memoirs of the Second World War*. Boston: Houghton Mifflin, 1959.

Ciano, Galeazzo. *Diary: 1937–1943*. New York: Enigma Books, 2002 (originally published by Doubleday in 1946).

Clarke, Dudley. *Seven Assignments*. London: Jonathan Cape, 1948.

GARBO: The Spy Who Saved D-Day. Kew: Public Record Office, 2000.

Hesketh, Roger. *Fortitude: The D-Day Deception Campaign*. Woodstock, NY: Overlook Press, 2000.

Liddell, Guy. *The Guy Liddell Diaries*. Vol. 1, *1941–1942*. Edited by Nigel West. London: Routledge, 2005.

———. *The Guy Liddell Diaries*. Vol. 2, *1942–1945*. Edited by Nigel West. London: Routledge, 2005.

Maskelyn, Jasper. *Magic—Top Secret*. London: Stanley Paul, 1950.

Masterman, J. C. *The Double-Cross System in the War of 1939 to 1945*. New Haven: Yale University Press, 1972.

Meinertzhagen, Richard. *Diary of a Black Sheep*. Edinburgh: Oliver & Boyd, 1964.

Montagu, Ewen. *The Man Who Never Was: World War II's Boldest Counterintelligence Operation*. New York: Oxford University Press, 1953.

Montgomery, Bernard Law. *El Alamein to the River Sangro*. London: Hutchinson, 1948.

———. Foreword to *The March to Tunis*, by Alan Moorehead. New York: Harper & Row, 1965.

———. *The Memoirs of Field-Marshal Montgomery*. Cleveland, OH: World Publishing Company, 1958.

Moorehead, Alan. *The March to Tunis: The North African War 1940–1943*. New York: Harper & Row, 1965.

Mure, David. *Practise to Deceive*. London: William Kimber, 1977.

Pujol, Juan, and Nigel West. *GARBO: The Personal Story of the Most Successful Double Agent Ever . . .* London: Weidenfeld and Nicolson, 1985.

Richardson, Charles. *Flashback: A Soldier's Story*. London: William Kimber, 1985.

Rommel, Erwin. *The Rommel Papers*. Edited by B. H. Liddell Hart. New York: Harcourt, Brace, 1953.

Wavell, Archibald P. *Allenby, a Study in Greatness: The Biography of Field-Marshal Viscount Allenby of Megiddo and Felixstowe*. Oxford: Oxford University Press, 1941.

———. Introduction to *Seven Assignments*, by Dudley Clarke. London: Jonathan Cape, 1948.

———. *Soldiers and Soldiering*. Oxford, UK: Alden Press, 1953.

Wild, Noël. Foreword to *Master of Deception: Tangled Webs in London and the Middle East*, by David Mure. London: William Kimber, 1980.

Winterbotham, F. W. *The Ultra Secret*. New York: Harper & Row, Publishers, Inc., 1974.

PUBLISHED SECONDARY SOURCES

The Abyssinian Campaign: The Official Story of the Conquest of Italian East Africa. London: His Majesty's Stationery Office, 1942.

Barr, Niall. *Pendulum of War: The Three Battles of El Alamein.* Woodstock: Overlook Press, 2004.

Bierman, John, and Colin Smith. *The Battle of Alamein: Turning Point, World War II.* New York: Viking Press, 2002.

Breuer, William B. *Deceptions of World War II.* New York: John Wiley & Sons, 2001.

Cave Brown, Anthony. *Bodyguard of Lies.* New York: Harper & Row, 1975.

Crowdy, Terry. *Deceiving Hitler: Double Cross and Deception in World War II.* Oxford, UK: Osprey Publishing, 2008.

Cruickshank, Charles. *Deception in World War II.* Oxford: Oxford University Press, 1979.

Dilks, David. "Appeasement and 'Intelligence.'" In *Retreat from Power*, edited by David Dilks, 139–69. London: Macmillan Press, 1981.

Dilks, David, ed. *Retreat from Power: Studies in Britain's Foreign Policy of the Twentieth Century.* Vol. 1, *1906–1939.* London: Macmillan Press, 1981.

Dovey, H. O. "The Eighth Assignment, 1941–1942." *Intelligence and National Security* 11, no. 4 (October 1996): 672–95.

———. "The Eighth Assignment, 1943–1945." *Intelligence and National Security* 12, no. 2 (April 1997): 69–90.

Dunnigan, James F., and Albert A. Nofi. *Victory and Deceit: Dirty Tricks at War.* New York: William Morrow, 1995.

Edgerton, David. *Warfare State: Britain, 1920–1970.* Cambridge, UK: Cambridge University Press, 2006.

Ellis, John. *Brute Force: Allied Strategy and Tactics in the Second World War.* New York: Viking Press, 1990.

Ferris, John Robert. *Intelligence and Strategy: Selected Essays.* London: Routledge, 2005.

Foot, M. R. D., and J. M. Langley. *MI9: The British Secret Service That Fostered Escape and Evasion, 1939–1945, and Its American Counterpart.* London: Bodley Head, 1979.

French, David. *Raising Churchill's Army: The British Army and the War against Germany, 1919–1945.* Oxford: Oxford University Press, 2000.

Funk, Arthur. "Negotiating the 'Deal with Darlan.'" *Journal of Contemporary History* 8, no. 2 (April 1973): 81–117.

Glover, Michael. *An Improvised War: The Ethiopian Campaign, 1940–1941.* London: Leo Cooper, 1987.

Goodden, Henrietta. *Camouflage and Art: Design for Deception in World War 2.* London: Unicorn Press, 2007.

Greene, Jack, and Alessandro Massignani. *Rommel's North Africa Campaign: September 1940–November 1942.* Conshohocken, PA: Combined Publishing, 1994.

Handel, Michael, ed. *Intelligence and Military Operations.* London: Frank Cass, 1990.

Haufler, Hervie. *The Spies Who Never Were: The True Story of the Nazi Spies Who Were Actually Allied Double Agents.* New York: NAL Caliber, 2006.

Hinsley, F. H. *British Intelligence in the Second World War: Its Influence on Strategy and Operations*, Vol. 1. London: Her Majesty's Stationery Office, 1979.

———. *British Intelligence in the Second World War: Its Influence on Strategy and Operations*, Vol. 2. London: Her Majesty's Stationery Office, 1981.

Holt, Thaddeus. *The Deceivers: Allied Military Deception in the Second World War.* New York: Scribner, 2004.

Howard, Michael. *British Intelligence in the Second World War.* Vol. 5, *Strategic Deception.* London: Her Majesty's Stationery Office, 1990.

———. "British Military Preparations for the Second World War." In *Retreat from Power*, edited by David Dilks, 102–17. London: Macmillan Press, 1981.

———. *The Mediterranean Strategy in the Second World War.* New York: Frederick A. Praeger, 1968.

Kennedy, Paul M. *The Realities behind Diplomacy: Background Influences on British External Policy, 1865–1980.* London: George Allen & Unwin, 1981.

———. *The Rise and Fall of British Naval Mastery.* New York: Charles Scribner's Sons, 1976.

Kiesling, Eugenia C. *Arming against Hitler: France and the Limits of Military Planning.* Lawrence: University of Kansas Press, 1996.

Kolinsky, Martin. *Britain's War in the Middle East: Strategy and Diplomacy, 1936–42.* New York: St. Martin's Press, 1999.

Kriebel, Colonel Rainer. *Inside the Afrika Korps: The Crusader Battles, 1941–1942.* London: Greenhill Books, 1999.

Latimer, Jon. *Alamein.* Cambridge, MA: Harvard University Press, 2002.

Lyons, Michael J. *World War II: A Short History.* 3rd ed. Upper Saddle River, NJ: Prentice Hall, 1999.

Mack Smith, Denis. *Italy: A Modern History.* Ann Arbor: University of Michigan Press, 1969.

May, Ernest R. *Strange Victory: Hitler's Conquest of France.* New York: Hill and Wang, 2000.

Medlicott, Norton. "Britain and Germany: The Search for Agreement, 1930–37." In *Retreat from Power*, edited by David Dilks, 78–101. London: Macmillan Press, 1981.

———. "The Hoare-Laval Pact." In Dilks, *Retreat from Power*, 118–69.

Mockler, Anthony. *Haile Selassie's War.* Oxford, UK: Oxford University Press, 1984.

Mure, David. *Master of Deception: Tangled Webs in London and the Middle East.* London: William Kimber, 1980.

Murray, Williamson. "Armored Warfare: The British, French, and German Experiences." In *Military Innovation in the Interwar Period*, edited by Williamson Murray and Allan R. Millet. New York: Cambridge University Press, 1996.

Murray, Williamson, and Allan R. Millet, eds. *Military Innovation in the Interwar Period.* Cambridge: Cambridge University Press, 1996.

Overy, Richard. *Why the Allies Won.* New York: W.W. Norton, 1995.

Piekalkiewicz, Janusz. *Rommel and the Secret War in North Africa, 1941–1943*. West Chester, PA: Schiffer Military History, 1992.

Pimlott, John, ed. *Rommel: In His Own Words*. London: Greenhill Books, 1994.

Pitt, Barrie. *The Crucible of War: Western Desert 1941*. London: Jonathan Cape, 1980.

———. *The Crucible of War: Year of Alamein 1942*. London: Jonathan Cape, 1982.

Playfair, I. S. O. *The Mediterranean and Middle East*. Vol. 1, *The Early Successes against Italy*. London: Her Majesty's Stationery Office, 1954.

———. *The Mediterranean and Middle East*. Vol. 2, *"The Germans Come to the Help of Their Ally" (1941)*. London: Her Majesty's Stationery Office, 1954.

———. *The Mediterranean and Middle East*. Vol. 3, *British Fortunes Reach Their Lowest Ebb*. London: Her Majesty's Stationery Office, 1960.

Playfair, I. S. O., and C. J. C. Molony. *The Mediterranean and Middle East*. Vol. 4, *The Destruction of the Axis Forces in Africa*. London: Her Majesty's Stationery Office, 1966.

Porch, Douglas. *The Path to Victory: The Mediterranean Theater in World War II*. New York: Farrar, Straus, and Giroux, 2004.

Rankin, Nicholas. *Churchill's Wizards: The British Genius for Deception, 1941–1945*. London: Faber and Faber, 2008.

Raugh, Harold E., Jr. *Wavell in the Middle East 1939–1941: A Study in Generalship*. London: Brassey's, 1993.

Reit, Seymour. *Masquerade: The Amazing Camouflage Deceptions of World War II*. New York: Hawthorn Books, 1978.

Schuker, Stephen A. "France and the Remilitarization of the Rhineland, 1936." *French Historical Studies* 14, no. 3 (Spring 1986): 299–338.

Sebag-Montefiore, Hugh. *Dunkirk: Fight to the Last Man*. Cambridge, MA: Harvard University Press, 2006.

Shirreff, David. *Bare Feet and Bandoliers: Wingate, Sandford, the Patriots and the Part They Played in the Liberation of Ethiopia*. London: Radcliffe Press, 1995.

Stoler, Mark A. *Allies and Adversaries: The Joint Chiefs of Staff, the Grand Alliance, and U.S. Strategy in World War II*. Chapel Hill: University of North Carolina Press, 2000.

Sun-Tzu. *The Art of Warfare*, translated by Roger T. Ames. New York: Ballantine Books, 1993.

The Tiger Kills: The Story of the Indian Divisions in the North African Campaign. London: His Majesty's Stationery Office, 1944.

Tooze, Adam. *The Wages of Destruction: The Making and Breaking of the Nazi Economy*. London: Allen Lane, 2006.

West, Nigel. *MI5: British Security Service Operations 1909–1945*. London: Bodley Head, 1981.

Young, Desmond. *Rommel: The Desert Fox*. New York: Harper & Brothers, 1950.

Young, Martin, and Robbie Stamp. *Trojan Horses: Deception Operations in the Second World War*. London: Bodley Head, 1989.

INDEX

ABOUT THE AUTHOR

Whitney **T. Bendeck** has pursued a career in the field of history, focusing on deception, after visiting Normandy in 1998. Holding a PhD in history, she works for the International Affairs Program at Florida State University, where she is an assistant instructor as well as the director of Undergraduate Studies. She lives in Crawfordville, Florida, with her husband and two children.